New diasporas

Global diasporas

Series Editor: Robin Cohen

The assumption that minorities and migrants will demonstrate an exclusive loyalty to the nation-state is now questionable. Scholars of nationalism, international migration and ethnic relations need new conceptual maps and fresh case studies to understand the growth of complex transnational identities. The old idea of "diaspora" may provide this framework. Though often conceived in terms of a catastrophic dispersion, widening the notion of diaspora to include trade, imperial, labour and cultural diaporas can provide a more nuanced understanding of the often positive relationships between migrants' homelands and their places of work and settlement.

This book forms part of an ambitious and interlinked series of volumes trying to capture the new relationships between home and abroad. Historians, political scientists, sociologists and anthropologists from a number of countries have collaborated on this forward-looking project. This is one of two books providing the defining, comparative and synoptic aspects of diasporas, while over fifteen further titles are planned. These will look both at traditionally recognized diasporas and those newer claimants who define their collective experiences and aspirations in terms of a diasporic identity.

This series is associated with the Transnational Communities Programme at the University of Oxford funded by the UK's Economic and Social Research Council.

Already published:
Global diasporas: an introduction. Robin Cohen

Forthcoming books include:
The Sikh diaspora: the search for statehood. Darshan Singh Tatla
The Italian labour diaspora. Donna Gabaccia
The Greek diaspora: from Odyssey to EU. George Stubos
The Japanese diaspora. Michael Weiner, Roger Daniels,
Hiroshi Komai

New diasporas

The mass exodus, dispersal and regrouping of migrant communities

Nicholas Van Hear
University of Oxford

First published in 1998 by UCL Press

UCL Press Limited
1 Gunpowder Square
London EC4A 3DE
UK

The name of University College London (UCL) is a registered
trade mark used by UCL Press with the consent of the owner.

British Library Cataloguing in Publication Data
A catalogue record for this book is available
from the British Library.

ISBNs: 1-85728-837-8
1-85728-838-6

Typeset in Palatino.
Printed by T.J. International Ltd, Padstow, UK.

Far between sundown's finish and midnight's broken toll
We ducked inside the doorway, thunder crashing
As majestic bells of bolt struck shadows in the sounds
Seeming to be the chimes of freedom flashing
Flashing for the warriors whose strength is not to fight
Flashing for the refugees on the unarmed road of flight
And for each and every underdog soldier in the night
And we gazed upon the chimes of freedom flashing.

Bob Dylan, 'Chimes of Freedom' (Words: Bob Dylan/Special Rider Music/Sony/ATV Music Publishing).

* * *

Mr. Venkatesan threw himself into the planning. He didn't trust the man with the cauliflower ears. Routes, circuitous enough to fool border guards, had to be figured out. He could fly to Frankfurt via Malta, for instance, then hole up in a ship's cargo hold for the long, bouncy passage on Canadian seas. Or he could take the more predictable (and therefore, cheaper but with more surveillance) detours through the Gulf Emirates.

The go-between or travel agent took his time. Fake travel documents and work permits had to be printed up. Costs, commissions, bribes had to be calculated. On each visit, the man helped himself to a double peg of Mr. Venkatesan's whiskey.

In early September, three weeks after Mr. Venkatesan had paid in full for a roundabout one-way ticket to Hamburg and for a passport impressive with fake visas, the travel agent stowed him in the damp smelly bottom of a fisherman's dinghy and had him ferried across the Palk Strait to Tuticorin in the palm-green tip of mainland India.

Tuticorin was the town Mr. Venkatesan's ancestors had left to find their fortunes in Ceylon's tea-covered northern hills. The irony struck him with such force that he rocked and tipped the dinghy, and had to be fished out of the sea.

Bharati Mukherjee, 'Buried lives', in *The middleman and other stories*, London: Virago, 1989.

Contents

Tables

Preface

My interest in the subject of this book – forced mass exodus of migrants and the making and unmaking of migrant communities – developed in a roundabout way. It was sparked by the expulsion of Ghanaians and other West African migrants from Nigeria in 1983, shortly after I completed my doctoral research in Ghana. I reported on the expulsion as a journalist. My interest grew when I worked in the mid-1980s for the Geneva-based Independent Commission on International Humanitarian Issues, when it became increasingly clear that here was a category of forced migrants not covered by the "refugee regime", nor subject to much attention by researchers. My interest was rekindled when, during a visit to Ghana in 1987, I interviewed a small number of Ghanaian returnees who had experienced expulsion in the early 1980s.

Later, shortly after I took up a research position at the Refugee Studies Programme at the University of Oxford, the Gulf crisis erupted, generating large scale upheavals among migrant communities in the Middle East. I began research on the consequences of these upheavals, making a number of short research visits to Jordan and Yemen in 1990–92. Organizing a conference in Oxford in 1992 to mark 20 years since the expulsion of the Ugandan Asians provided the opportunity to look at a long-established community of migrant origin that had experienced forced exodus and dispersal. I then began to think about how such crises fit in the broader, global migration order, and in particular the part they play in making and unmaking transnational communities. These are the main themes pursued in this volume.

The bulk of the research on which this book is based was funded by two consecutive awards from the Economic and Social Research Council, whose support is gratefully acknowledged. Earlier research in the Middle East was supported by a fellowship funded by HRH Crown Prince Hassan bin Talal of Jordan. I am also grateful to the University of Oxford and my department, Queen Elizabeth House, for providing supplementary support. The first ESRC award (R000 23 3831) funded much of the fieldwork and primary research I undertook in Yemen and Jordan, two of the countries experiencing large scale migration upheavals in the wake of the Gulf crisis. I interviewed a sample of about 100 returnees in each country in 1993 and consulted a range of government bodies, international agencies and non-governmental organizations. The second award (R000 23 5074) supported the extension of the research on migration crises worldwide, and involved research visits to New York, Washington, Boston, Brussels, Luxembourg, Geneva, Strasbourg, Bangkok, Singapore and Kuala Lumpur.

I incurred many debts to helpful people during my work in Yemen and Jordan, but I should single out Fahd Eryani in Yemen and Ahmad Noubeh in Jordan for their patience and skill in interpretation and translation. Patricia Salti and Yahya el Oteibi in Jordan and David Warburton and Abdul Malik al Maqramy in Yemen also provided invaluable help. Ben Sunkari assisted me with earlier research work in Ghana.

I am grateful to all those who spared the time to talk to me in the course of my travels in the Middle East, Africa, Europe, North America and Asia. Staff of many government, intergovernmental, international, non-governmental and academic bodies generously provided material, gave interviews or helped in other ways.

International and intergovernmental organizations consulted included the UN Development Programme (UNDP), the Office of the UN High Commissioner for Refugees (UNHCR), the UN Relief and Works Agency for Palestine Refugees in the Near East (UNRWA), the UN Economic and Social Commission for

Western Asia (UNESCWA), the UN Economic and Social Commission for Asia and the Pacific (UNESCAP), the UN Children's Fund (UNICEF), the UN Department for Humanitarian Affairs (UNDHA), the UN Compensation Commission, the UN Secretariat, Department for Economic and Social Information and Policy Analysis, the World Bank, the International Migration for Employment branch of the International Labour Organisation (ILO), the International Organisation for Migration (IOM), the International Committee of the Red Cross (ICRC), the International Federation of Red Cross and Red Crescent Societies (IFRCRCS), the European Commission, and the Council of Europe.

A wide range of non-governmental and human rights organizations assisted in various countries. They included Oxfam, the Catholic Institute for International Relations, the Centre for Migration Studies, the Lawyers Committee for Human Rights, the Open Society Institute's Forced Migration Project, the US Committee for Refugees, the Refugee Policy Group, Human Rights Watch, the European Council on Refugees and Exiles, the Jesuit Refugee Service, and the Churches Commission for Migrants in Europe.

Nearer home I have benefited from the help, advice and support of many people, not least the steady stream of lively and stimulating individuals who passed through the Refugee Studies Programme in Oxford. Some need particular thanks, and although it is difficult to single them out, they include Robin Cohen, a long time mentor and general editor of the series of which this book is part; Jeff Crisp, for the mutual exchange of ideas and jokes; and Andrew Shacknove for intellectual and much-needed moral support. Among the many others I wish to thank are Manolo Abella, Belinda Allan, Diana Cammack, John Chernoff, Thana Chrissanthaki, Dereck Cooper, Patrice Curtis, Tom Forrest, Bill Frelick, Dennis Grace, Sarah Graham-Brown, Barbara Harrell-Bond, Jerry Huguet, Charles Keely, Gil Loescher, Reinhardt Lohrman, Chris McDowell, JoAnn McGregor, Kawa Mohammed, Alhaji Mohammed E. Abukari, Shirley Nuss, Bob Paiva, Rosemary Preston, Anthony Richmond, Sharon Stanton Russell, Abbas Shiblak, Frances Stewart, David Turton, Shiraz Vira, Myron Weiner, Piyasiri

Wickramsekera, and Roger Zetter. As well as stimulating ideas, many of these and others helped sustain me in sometimes adverse circumstances. I would also like to thank for their invaluable help Sarah Rhodes, the librarian at Refugee Studies Programme, Peter Hayward, who drew the map, Julia Knight, the administrative staff at QEH and RSP, and not least Caroline Wintersgill at UCL Press for patiently seeing this project through.

Drafts of various parts of the book have benefited from the comment of colleagues at various seminar presentations and lectures I gave in Britain and abroad. As well as presentations in Oxford, at King's College London, the School of Oriental and African Studies and elsewhere in the UK, I gave a paper at the Inter-University Seminar on International Migration at the Massachussetts Institute of Technology; this became the basis of Chapter 2. The opportunity to speak at a conference on refugees in South Asia at the Regional Centre for Strategic Studies in Colombo gave me a South Asian perspective on the issue. I am grateful for comments at these and other presentations. Needless to say, I alone am responsible for the contents of this book.

Some passages of the material on Yemen and Jordan appeared earlier in the *Journal of Refugee Studies* as "The socio-economic impact of the involuntary mass return to Yemen in 1990", **7**(1), 1994, 18–38, and in the *International Migration Review* as "The impact of involuntary mass 'return' to Jordan in the wake of the Gulf crisis", **29**(2), 1995, 352–374; they are used by kind permission of Oxford University Press and the Center for Migration Studies. Other parts were initially developed in discussion papers for the UN Research Institute for Social Development, published as *Consequences of the forced mass repatriation of migrant communities: recent cases from West Africa and the Middle East*, Geneva: UNRISD, 1992 and *Migration, displacement and social integration*, Geneva: UNRISD, 1994.

This book is dedicated with thanks to my partner Lucy, who kept my spirits up when flagging, to my son Jim, who kept me awake at night, and to my daughter Cathy, who kept the adrenaline flowing.

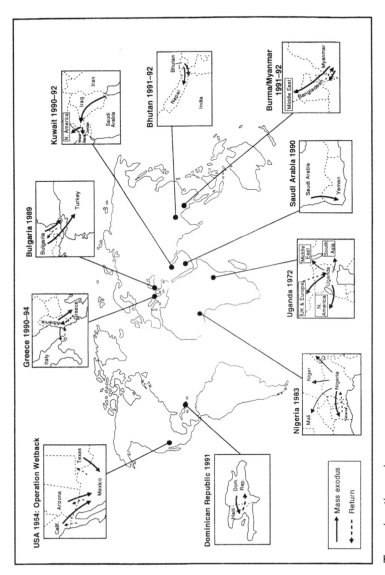

Ten migration crises

ONE

Introduction

Recent profound changes in the world political and economic order have generated large movements of people in almost every region. Contrary to expectations, rather than bringing to an end many of the world's long-standing conflicts, the end of the Cold War has spawned new pressures driving people to move. Resurgent ethnic, religious and nationalist forces have emerged from the often violent disintegration of nation-states and their reconstitution. These new forces and other new features, like the revolution in global communications, have combined with prior social, economic and political pressures to generate new patterns of migration in the post-Cold War era.

As a result, from being a relatively peripheral concern until recently, migration has since the late 1980s moved swiftly up the international agenda to become an issue of heated public debate. International conferences on migration issues have proliferated, and newspapers and magazines carry lengthy features on migrants, refugees and asylum-seekers almost daily. Xenophobia and racism have become prominent once again in countries migrants aspire to reach. The costs and benefits of migration have become matters of lengthy discussion in both the countries of migrants' origin and their countries of destination.

A court case in France reported in 1995 highlighted some of the grimmer features of the changing global migratory order. After trial in Rouen, the Ukrainian captain, chief officer and three crew members of the Bahamas-registered MC *Ruby* were jailed for between 20 years and life for the murder of eight West African stowaways as the vessel steamed from the west coast of Africa towards Europe. The stowaways, Ghanaians and a Cameroonian, were thrown overboard to avoid fines arising from European carrier liability laws, which penalized airlines and shipping companies carrying illegal immigrants. For the captain and crew the penalties would have meant heavy loss of earnings or possibly their jobs. The story only came to light because one of the stowaways, a Ghanaian casual dock worker seeking a better life in Europe, had managed to hide from the crew until the vessel arrived in Le Havre, where he jumped ship (Davies 1995).

This harrowing episode showed the risks which would-be migrants from the developing world were prepared to take in the quest for a better life in the more affluent world. It showed the consequences of measures erected by a key part of that more affluent world – what has become known as "Fortress Europe" – to keep such would-be migrants out. And it showed the desperate lengths to which citizens of the former Soviet Union would go to keep their jobs against the background of social and economic disintegration at home – they were as constrained in their way as the stowaways they killed.

Despite the recent attention it has attracted, migration within and between countries has of course long been a feature of the world stage, a manifestation of wide disparities in socio-economic circumstances, perceived life-chances and human security. But in the post-Cold War period migration has taken on new dimensions and a new character. As various commentators have suggested, four novel features of the current era are adding to pressures generating migration, shaping patterns of movement and increasing anxiety about the issue.

First, technological change has generated a revolution in global communications. One consequence of this is that images of life in the developed world – often heavily distorted images – have spread wider and wider, so that information or mis-information about new opportunities, real or imagined, has become much more accessible to large parts of the world's population. At the same time, long distance travel has become easier and cheaper. These changes have had a particularly significant impact on migration from the "south" or the developing world. Second, loosening of constraints on movement in the countries of the former eastern bloc mean that a huge population – perhaps 450 million people – has been brought into the global pool of potential migrants; this pool is set to enlarge even more if and when the People's Republic of China relaxes its emigration controls. This development is shaping new patterns of east-west migration. Third, the resurgence of ethnic, religious and nationalist aspirations and tensions, in part a consequence of the collapse of the communist bloc, has generated great instability within the current dispensation of nation-states, resulting in the disintegration and reconstitution of many of them and further forced migration. Fourth, there has occurred what has been described as the "rights revolution", seen in the spread of individual rights and entitlements particularly in the more affluent nations; in the migration arena this has been manifested in the growth of ethnic, migrant and refugee lobby groups located mainly in countries receiving migrants and often facilitating their movement (Castles and Miller 1993; Martin and Taylor 1996; Weiner 1995; Zolberg 1989).

These features generating or facilitating migration – which are dimensions of what is summed up by the nebulous term "globalization" – are combining with longer established pressures to change world patterns of migration. But while the cumulative effect of long standing pressures and the new features generating migrants is substantial, there are counter-vailing pressures constraining migration, particularly as many of the countries and regions that have accommodated migrants in the past are now proving unable or unwilling to admit more newcomers, as the distressing story of the stowaways shows. Among the main reasons for this is the fact that economies are less absorptive of labour because of technological and other change. Negative perceptions of the political, social and security impacts of immigration also increasingly hold sway. A potent cocktail of increased pressure to migrate set against hardening barriers to immigration is thus developing; more and more potential migrants are emerging but there appear to be fewer places for them to go.

Another far-reaching consequence of the growth of migration

in the last quarter of this century has been the formation of new diasporas – people with multiple allegiances to place. The emergence of these new transnational populations has attracted increasing interest and commentary in recent years. Glick Schiller et al (1992) consider the emergence or consolidation of what they and others call "transnationalism" – the formation of social, political and economic relationships among migrants that span several societies. They note "a new kind of migrating population is emerging, composed of those whose networks, activities and patterns of life encompass both their host and home societies" (1992: 1). Weiner (1986) writes of "incipient diaspora" among the guest workers of western Europe and the Middle East, and explores what he calls the "illusion of impermanence" surrounding such populations:

> Despite the intention of governments and the expectations of nationals, a large proportion of foreign workers remains indefinitely in the host country, living in a state of legal and political ambiguity, economic insecurity and as social outsiders, if not outcasts. The children who have come with them, or have been born within the host country, are in an even more ambiguous position; though more at home in their host country than in the land of their parents, they too are expected to return "home" (Weiner 1986: 47).

Exploring differences among "classical", "new" and "incipient" diaspora, Sheffer (1993) similarly remarks on the enduring character of what were thought temporary sojourners. Wolfrum (1993) points to the emergence of "new minorities" as a result of migration, and the consequences of this for international law on the protection of minorities and aliens. In the West European context, Hammar (1990: 13) has drawn attention to "a new status group ... not regular and plain foreign citizens any more, but also not naturalized citizens of the receiving country". He styled such alien residents "denizens", using the term to describe the substantial foreign populations of western Europe – often former guest workers and their descendants – who have stayed on for considerable lengths of time and who have

4

developed substantive or partial membership in their host societies, but who do not possess formal citizenship (Hammar 1990). The emergence of such populations holds profound implications for the state. Baubock (1991: 41) sees multiple membership in different societies deriving from migration as a decisive contribution to what he calls the "slow emergence of interstate societies". In a development of Hammar's argument, Cohen (1989: 162) conceives of denizens as "a group ... that can be seen as transcending the limits of the nation-state".

Although the phenomena of transnationalism and diaspora have been the subject of considerable interest, definition or characterization have been less common. Of those commentators that have addressed this, some favour an inclusive and extensive catch-all, while others prefer a more prescriptive definition. Thus Khachig Tölölyan, the editor of *Diaspora: A Journal of Transnational Studies*, sees his journal as embracing the "semantic domain" that includes the terms immigrant, expatriate, refugee, guest-worker, exile community, overseas community and ethnic community – "the vocabulary of transnationalism" (Tölölyan 1991: 4–5). For William Safran, writing in the same issue of the same journal, the term diaspora should be limited to populations who satisfy more precise criteria. He suggests these should include dispersal from an original centre to two or more peripheral regions; retention of collective memory of the homeland; partial alienation from the host society; aspiration to return to an ancestral homeland; commitment to the maintenance or restoration of that homeland; and derivation of collective consciousness and solidarity from a relationship with the homeland (Safran 1991: 83). Others, like Chaliand and Rageau (1995), suggest that catastrophic origins involving forced migration are a prime feature of diaspora: "A diaspora is defined as *the collective forced dispersion of a religious and/or ethnic group* [their emphasis], precipitated by a disaster, often of a political nature" (xiv). Cohen (1995: 6) notes that the catastrophic connotations of diaspora deriving from the Jewish experience obscure the less malign or at least neutral Greek origins of the term, which derives from words for "dispersion" and "to sow or scatter". Used to describe Greek colonization of Asia Minor and the

Mediterranean, the Greek diaspora was established through trade, conquest, free migration and settlement. To the features of diasporas suggested by other commentators, Cohen adds the flowering of the community in exile, often eclipsing the achievements of those who stayed in the homeland (Cohen 1995). For Marienstras (1989) durability is a necessary condition of a diaspora: "its reality is proved in time and tested by time" (1989: 125).

In this book a fairly loose perspective is taken, so that *diaspora* are populations which satisfy three minimal criteria drawn from the above characterizations. First, the population is dispersed from a homeland to two or more other territories. Second, the presence abroad is enduring, although exile is not necessarily permanent, but may include movement between homeland and new host. And third, there is some kind of exchange – social, economic, political or cultural – between or among the spatially separated populations comprising the diaspora. I use another, broader term in the text – *transnational community*. This is a more inclusive notion, which embraces diaspora, but also populations that are contiguous rather than scattered and may straddle just one border.

But is the formation of transnational communities and diaspora now the inevitable concomitant of migration? As I show later on, this is not necessarily the case, for if diaspora formation has accelerated in recent times, so too has the unmaking of diasporas, seen in the *regrouping* or *in-gathering* of migrant communities or dispersed ethnic groups. Like the formation of diaspora, these regroupings may involve voluntary or involuntary movements of people back to their place of origin – however notional or putative this place of origin may be.

In this book I consider populations that are dispersed or regrouped both through force and choice, examining both what are conventionally known as "economic migrants" as well as those forced to move. I attempt to chart the place of migration by force and choice in the formation and unmaking of transnational communities and diasporas. The study takes forced mass exodus of migrant communities as the point of entry for its investigation. By *mass exodus* I mean large scale movement of people out of a given territory, almost always under duress. I use the term *migrant community* to refer to both populations of recent migrants and longer settled populations of migrant origin. The latter may be sufficiently well established to be described in other contexts as ethnic or minority communities, but because it is the migratory dimension of their identity that is of interest in this book, I retain the term migrant community to characterize them.

Some of the most notable forced population movements of recent times have been of such migrant communities – recent migrants or people with migratory backgrounds. Those who have already moved to better their lives or to escape persecution or conflict are prominent in the much noticed growth of forced migration worldwide; so are the descendants of such migrants. Since they often straddle the blurred division between "economic" and "forced" migrants that informs scholarly and policy debate, investigation of such population movements obliges consideration of both the economic and forced migration discourses, which have hitherto, with a few exceptions, made just polite acknowledgement of each other. Investigation of such population movements therefore challenges synthesis of approaches to migration, an attempt at which I make in this book.

I investigate 10 episodes of mass exodus of migrant communities drawn from six regions. Among the better known episodes examined is the mass expulsion of some two million Ghanaians and other West African migrants from Nigeria in the early 1980s. This was just the largest among numerous similar forced migrations in Africa in recent decades, including the earlier mass expulsion of Asians from Uganda in 1972, which is also considered. Turning to the Middle East and more recent history, the Gulf crisis and its aftermath in 1990–92 saw the involuntary mass exodus of two million migrant workers and longer established communities of migrant origin; I examine here the exodus of Palestinians from Kuwait and of Yemenis from Saudi Arabia. Mass exoduses that are perhaps less well-known are drawn from four other regions of the world. Muslims obliged to leave Burma (now known as Myanmar) for Bangladesh and ethnic Nepalis forced to leave Bhutan for Nepal, both in 1991–92, are among the populations of migrant origin or background in south and southeast Asia to have experienced mass expulsion recently. Upheavals since 1989–90 in eastern and southern Europe have spawned similar episodes, including the exodus of ethnic Turks from Bulgaria in 1989 and of Albanians from Greece in 1990–94, which are examined below. The expulsion of Mexican migrants from the southern US in 1954 and of people of Haitian origin from the Dominican Republic in 1991 are the examples I draw from Central America and the Caribbean.

The criteria for the selection of these cases are broadly as follows. The episodes considered involve large movements of people, both absolutely and relative to the populations accommodating or receiving them. They are for the most part sudden, unanticipated and disorderly movements involving considerable degrees of force and which profoundly upset the prior migration order. I have not dealt with deportations of individuals, except where in aggregate they amount to significant episodes of population movement. The migrant communities involved range from short-term, temporary migrants to long established communities of migrant origin, and often include mixtures of both. Most of these cases have taken place in the last quarter of this century; and most have occurred since the end of the Cold War, which is already coming to be seen as a turning point in the world's migratory order. This quarter century has seen globalization gather momentum as the communications, information and rights revolutions referred to above have taken off. It has also been the period when the disintegration and reconstitution of nation-states associated with the legacy of decolonization and the dissolution of the communist bloc have reached a new intensity. Most of the episodes are drawn from developing countries, reflecting the fact that most migration is among such territories; but cases are also drawn from industrialized states and from the former communist bloc to show that forced mass exodus is not a monopoly of the developing world. The global span of the episodes selected illustrates the ubiquity of these forms of forced migration. That most are drawn from the last quarter of this century also demonstrates the recent volatility of the world migration order. The 10 episodes are thus intended to provide a fairly representative sample of the kinds of migration crises that have occurred in recent times – in terms of the character of the migrant communities involved, in terms of the nature of the migration upheaval, and in terms of the global spread of such crises. Some cases draw on field and other primary research by the author, while others rely principally on a range of published and unpublished secondary sources.

I attempt to place these mass exoduses of migrant communities into historical and comparative perspective. How then do these episodes of migrant mass exodus figure in the wider, unfolding migratory dispensation: are they merely ephemeral events, of no lasting significance, or do they signal significant changes in migration patterns? What is the impact of such episodes on the migrant communities involved? These questions are addressed by exploring what I term *migration orders*, and in particular the way such orders change. The book focuses on acute manifestations of such change, which I call *migration crises*; the episodes mentioned above are examples. I attempt to uncover the dynamics of migration and of migrant communities by looking at such moments of crisis. Since the focus is on change in established migration orders, the forms of migration investigated are on the whole secondary or tertiary movements. I look less at the establishment of migration orders than at upheavals in such orders already in being; equally, the focus is less the establishment of migrant communities than the dynamics of changes in migration orders as they are manifested in the making, remaking or unmaking of transnational communities and diasporas.

Before outlining the plan of this book, it might be useful to recapitulate the concepts that have been introduced in this chapter and to indicate where in the text they are explored further. The terms *diaspora* and *transnational community*, defined above, are explored further in Chapters 2, 6 and 7. The terms *migration order* and *migration crisis* are explored more fully in Chapter 2. As I indicated above, the term *migrant community* embraces established populations of migrant origin as well as recent migrants, and its use becomes clear as the book progresses through the episodes of migration crisis reviewed. At the outset though, it has to be acknowledged that *community* is a problematic term. In this book it is used to suggest a social collectivity with a significant dimension in common – here a migratory background. A migrant or transnational community is thus something more than a migrant or transnational population, a mere aggregation of migrants. The term *mass exodus* was introduced earlier; the related terms *forced migration* and *mass expulsion* have already been used but not yet defined. *Forced migration* refers to individuals or communities compelled, obliged or induced to move when otherwise they would choose to stay put; the force involved may be direct, overt and focused or indirect, covert and diffuse. *Mass expulsion* usually refers to a form of mass exodus or forced migration instigated by the state or its surrogates, but can also be instigated by other parties, such as opposition organizations or warlords. The definition of mass expulsion has exercised human rights lawyers in recent years (Coles 1983; Henckaerts 1995). One authority holds that

> mass expulsion results from the use of coercion, including a variety of political, economic and social measures which directly, or even more so indirectly, force people to leave or flee their homelands for fear of life, liberty and security ... "expulsion" ... may be defined as an act, or a failure to act, by a State with the intended effect of forcing the departure of persons against their will from its territory for reasons of race, nationality, membership in a particular social group or political opinion (International Law Association 1986).

This definition has the advantage of drawing attention to the often indirect nature of expulsions, evident in the episodes considered in this book. But it also assumes the state as the agent of expulsion, which is not always the case. The chilling term *ethnic cleansing* entered the lexicon of forced migration in the 1990s, as a result of events in the former Yugoslavia, the former Soviet Union and central Africa. A form of mass expulsion, it has been carried out not just by the state or its surrogates, but by opposition or rebel groups, warlords or others aspiring to power or to control over people or territory. Dimensions of force and choice in migration are explored more fully in the latter part of Chapter 2.

10

The book is laid out as follows.

In the next chapter I elaborate the concept migration order to describe perhaps more dynamically what others have called migration systems or migration patterns. I suggest how migration orders might be characterized and then explore how they can change. Such changes may take gradual or cumulative forms, or they may be more acute or catastrophic; the latter I term migration crises. I suggest that such moments may be revealing of the dynamics of migration orders and ultimately key events in the consolidation, perpetuation, proliferation or diminution of transnational communities. By way of illustration, I examine recent transitions in four migration orders. In the second part of Chapter 2 I consider the place of force, choice and agency in the shaping of migration orders. I suggest a simple framework which combines components of migration – such as outward, onward and return movement – with degrees of choice and force. Migrants' experience of combinations of movement by choice and force results in complex migratory biographies: diasporas accumulate among the most complex migration histories. At the end of the chapter, I return to the question of how migration orders change and look at the agents of such transition.

I give accounts of the historical background and basic features of the 10 episodes introduced above in Chapters 3 and 4. In each case, the background to the presence of the migrant community is explored by outlining the history of the migration order, bringing out the place of movement by force and choice. I examine the motivations for and the circumstances of each episode of mass exodus. Comparative dimensions are drawn out by highlighting features of each migrant community that became matters of contention – their size relative to the host community; their socio-economic composition; and their membership status in the society accommodating them. Finally, I consider the moment of upheaval in each migration order, the precipitation of migration crisis.

In Chapters 5 and 6 I offer further comparative analysis of these episodes, utilizing the frameworks outlined in Chapter 2. Chapter 5 considers the consequences of migration crises. I look first at the effects of crises on the migrant communities themselves, examine demographic and socio-economic effects on the territories receiving uprooted migrant communities, and then turn to the effects of mass departures on the territories such communities leave. I indicate some problems of assessing these effects, particularly over time.

In Chapter 6 I look at how the 10 migration crises have contributed to the formation, consolidation or undoing of diasporas or transnational communities. After refining the framework introduced in Chapter 2 the better to embrace diasporas and transnational communities, the chapter shows how the 10 episodes of migration crisis could over time have three outcomes: diaspora communities might be enhanced and reinvigorated; they might be unmade or diminished; or transnational communities might be reaffirmed. As I show in this chapter, the episodes investigated featured several of these outcomes over time.

After recapitulating the arguments of the book, the final chapter reflects on the nature and content of transnationalism, drawing on some of the lessons suggested by the episodes investigated. Some comments and caveats about the debates on transnationalism and globalization are then offered. I comment on the relations between migrants and hosts, and between transnational populations and those who stay put, before returning to the place of migrant networks in shaping migration orders and transnational communities. I conclude the chapter and the book by offering some comments on the significance of migration for the coherence of society.

TWO

Migration crises and the making of diasporas

In the opening chapter I suggested that one of my concerns is to locate particular episodes of migrant mass exodus in the broader migratory dispensation: are such episodes merely passing events, or do they represent significant changes in migration patterns? These questions lead to a further set of issues. What is the relationship between changes in migration and other changes in the political economy? Under what circumstances are changes in the political economy accompanied by changes in migration; why do some changes in the political economy lead to changes in migration, but not others? Why do changes in migration take an acute form in some cases but not in others? Finally, and not least, how do these changes shape – and how are they shaped by – the migrant communities they embrace?

The groundwork for pursuing these questions is laid out in this chapter. In the first part I sketch the character of migration orders and look at how changes in such orders come about: I distinguish between cumulative change and acute change – or migration crisis. To illustrate these ideas, I outline recent changes in the migration orders of four regions, before offering some refinement of the notions of migration order, transition and crisis. The focus of the chapter then shifts from migration orders and migration crises broadly conceived to the migrants and other people who shape these orders and crises; I explore the place of force, choice and agency in moulding them. I propose a simple framework for considering diverse kinds of movement and permutations of force and choice, and how these shape the making and unmaking of diasporas. This framework provides ways of considering how migrants and their households might make decisions about migration or have movement thrust upon them. Relations between migrants, hosts and the community at home are also discussed within a framework of force and choice. The final section returns to the theme of how migration orders change, looking at the agents of such transitions.

Explaining migration crises

Understanding migration orders

While change in patterns of migration should not be seen as movement from one condition of stasis or equilibrium to another, at a given time the logic or workings of a given migration order or dispensation should be discernible, can be identified and may be delineated. What then might a migration order comprise? Moving from the particular to the general, it would include the features outlined below, which are addressed by various theories of or approaches to migration. The brief outline that follows draws on a very useful exposition of economic theories of migration by Massey et al. (1993), modified and supplemented here by other approaches to migration – notably forced migration – not included in their review.

• *Individual decision-making and motivation.* Migration orders are shaped by the decisions and actions of large numbers of individuals. Some such decisions are cost-benefit judgements made in economic terms, and have been addressed in neo-classical economic perspectives on migration (for example, Harris and Todaro 1970). But other considerations may be just as potent in driving individuals to move. These include social and cultural motivations, such as enhancing status, and above all concerns about safety and security (Cordell et al. 1996; Eades 1987a; Kunz 1973; Shacknove 1985).

• *Household decision-making and strategies.* A growing body of literature suggests that, as much or more so than individuals, the household may be the key locus of decision-making as far as migration is concerned. What has been termed the "new economics of migration" (Stark 1991b) has considered household strategies of minimizing or spreading risk in determining who moves and who stays put. Here again, a baldly economic approach may obscure other important motivations involving strategies of household safety and security, survival and coping that inform decision-making about migration (Hugo 1994; Massey 1990).

• *Disparities between places of origin and destination* have long been seen as key determinants of migration. Economic disparities include the relative weights of economic push and pull factors, including differentials in wages, employment or income generating opportunities and inequalities in standards of living addressed by neo-classical economic theory (Harris and Todaro 1970; Todaro 1989). Drawing on the Marxist tradition, theories of development and underdevelopment, and of labour reserves, among others, have also addressed such disparities (Amin 1974; Cordell et al. 1996; Wolpe 1972). Disparities in the political arena embrace relative human security as determined by the human rights and security environment, a focus of the human rights discourse, and of the refugee studies, political science and international relations literatures (Weiner 1993b; Zolberg et al. 1989). Combining the economic and political arenas, it might be argued that it is disparities in human security broadly conceived that provide the impetus for migration.

• *The state of development of migrant networks and institutions* has recently been recognized as an arena profoundly shaping migration, addressed by theories of chain migration, networks, cultural capital and "cumulative causation" (Boyd 1989; Fawcett 1989; Lim 1987; Massey 1990). Networks comprise relationships that link former, current and potential migrants and those whose do not migrate, in countries of origin and destination, through kinship, friendship, neighbourhood, ethnicity and other types of community or affinity. It is perhaps here that the communications and rights revolutions referred to in the introduction are most salient. Migrant networks shade into migrant trafficking organizations and the activities of advocacy and lobbying groups agitating for and against migration both among established migrant communities and among host populations.

• *The migration regime.* Taking its cue from the political science and international relations literatures (Loescher 1993; Widgren 1990), what can be termed the migration regime encompasses the national and international body of law, regulations, institutions and policy dealing with movement of people. States' rules governing the departure of citizens and the entry of newcomers, their policies for the integration or assimilation of immigrants, and the efforts of international organizations to manage and give order to migration come under the rubric of the migration regime.

• Finally, migration orders are shaped by the *macro-political economy.* By this is meant the distribution of power and resources globally and regionally, reflected in the structure and distribution of production and consumption; in patterns of trade and financial flows; in the development of transport and communications; in the distribution of military might; and in population, environment and other elements of global imbalance. Encompassing the forgoing components, this arena is, like them, shaped by historical ties – colonial, imperial, and of trade, for example – between places of origin and destination. This arena is also somewhat different from the others in that migration is part of the overall political economy, shaping it as well as being shaped by it. Approaches placing primacy in this arena see migration as a consequence of the incorporation of peripheral societies into global capitalism, of the penetration of the market economy worldwide, of the structure of industrial societies, and of unfolding "globalization" (Castles and Kosack 1973; Petras 1981; Piore 1979; Portes and Walton 1981; Sassen 1991).

Most commentators would agree that migration is shaped by these elements or features these levels, although they would ascribe different weights to them. As Massey et al. point out, the different approaches are not inherently incompatible: 'It is quite possible, for example, that individuals act to maximize income while families minimize risk, and that the context within which both decisions are made is shaped by structural forces operating at the national and international levels' (1993: 433). However, it remains a fundamental weakness of migration studies that it is never, or only inadequately shown how these various levels cohere – how, for example, conditions or changes at the level of the macro-political economy play out at the individual or household level, or, vice versa, how decisions made by individuals and households are manifested in aggregate at the macro-level. There have been many calls for an integrated approach:

> ... any discussion of international migration trends and prospects must deal simultaneously at the levels of global trends, national, community and household conditions, and individual behaviors. Unlike the movement of commodities or manufactures, which are driven by market participants who mobilize large volumes, the movement of people involves not only markets and governments but the decisions of millions of families and individuals. In this respect, international migration trends are rather like aggregate fertility rates, which although heavily influenced by societal and governmental forces, ultimately are determined by the rather intimate decisions of individuals (Russell and Teitelbaum 1992: 5).

But the question remains: how precisely to "deal simultaneously" with these various levels – from individual decision-making to the macro-political economy?

One integrative approach developed in recent years is the systems perspective on migration (Fawcett 1989; Kritz, Lim & Zlotnik 1992; Lim 1987; Zlotnik 1992). A recent definition suggests a migration system "is a network of countries linked by migration flows or relationships" (Bilsborrow & Zlotnik 1995: 63). This rather general observation is refined by reference to five premises: migration creates a "unified space" between places of migrants' origin and their destination; it is usually but one of a number of historical, economic, cultural, political and other linkages; it changes over time through mechanisms of feedback; states play a crucial role both through explicit policies and more indirect interventions; and networks are among the mechanisms that translate macro-level forces into the migration decisions of individuals. In principle, the systems approach has the advantage of inclusivity, coherently linking the spatial and temporal dimensions of migration, its stages and components. The approach attempts to give weight to both macro-level and micro-level relations between places linked by migration. But the shortcomings of this approach are that it lacks specificity (see Boutang & Papademetriou 1994); the notion of a "system" is inadequately defined; and the approach has yet to be convincingly applied. The systems approach is also somewhat uncomfortably mechanistic and functionalist, suggestive of equilibrium, and not amenable to encompassing the ruptures of forced migration. Indeed, the systems approach is largely a model of economic migration, not intended to embrace forced movement.

Here a different integrative approach is suggested, drawing on the literature on forced migration to recast the various approaches to migration outlined above. In respect of an integrated approach, the literature on forced migration is in some ways perhaps more suggestive than that on economic migration. The following synthesizes and refines the approaches of authors who have tried to develop models of forced migratory movements, some for the purposes of early warning (notably Clark 1989), and others as part of more general theoretical investigation (notably Richmond 1994). Their approaches are modified substantially here, and an attempt is made to incorporate in addition approaches to so-called economic or voluntary migration.

If the features outlined on pages 14–16 can be seen as components of migration orders, their dynamics might be located in four *domains*. In the first domain are located what are variously described as root causes, or as structural, background, underlying factors which predispose a population to migrate. These derive mainly from the macro-political economy as defined above, and in particular from the disparities between places of migrant origin and destination. Among the dimensions featuring in this domain are the state of supply and demand for labour and the structure of employment in countries of destination; the state of social order and security in countries of origin; and trends of nation-building, disintegration and reconstitution in regions of migrants' origin. Economic disparities between territories sending and receiving migrants include differences in earnings, livelihoods and living standards. What might be called political disparities include the relative prevalence of conflict, persecution and other dimensions of human rights and human security. Environmental disparities between sending and receiving territories might be added; these include the relative state of the land, water supply, forest and other resources. Some of these components are measurable, such as differentials in income per capita, in per capita expenditure on health and education, in the number of health workers per capita, the relative level of school enrolments and so on. As I suggested above, the economic, political and environmental arenas might be grouped under the rubric human security, disparities in which heavily predispose people to migrate.

The second domain includes what might be termed proximate causes, or factors that bear more immediately on migration. These derive from the working out of the structural features outlined above, and include manifestations such as a downturn in the economic or business cycle, a turn for the worse in the security or human rights environment generated by repression or a power struggle, the construction of a large scale development project that promises to involve displacement, or marked degeneration in the ecological sphere. There is obviously overlap with some of the elements of the previous, structural domain. Again some of these features are to some extent measurable – the economic arena probably more so than the others. This domain includes particular manifestations of the economic, political and environmental disparities – or collectively, of human security – identified above.

In a third domain are found what might be termed precipitating factors, or those actually triggering departure. This may be the arena in which individual and household decisions to move or stay put are made. The precipitating factors may be in the economic sphere, such as general economic collapse, hyperinflation, a leap in unemployment, factory closure, a collapse of farm prices, the imposition of punitive taxation, or the collapse of health, education or other welfare services. Or they may be located in the political sphere, and include persecution, disputed citizenship, the escalation of conflict, massacre, the outbreak of war or invasion. Both arenas are again in some sense dimensions of human security, broadly conceived. As Richmond observes, "Generally, the precipitating event is one that disrupts the normal functioning of the system and thus destroys the capacity of a population to survive under the prevailing conditions" (1994: 65). Unlike the previous two domains, often these precipitating factors are not so much measurable as observable, identifiable events. It is here perhaps that migration crises are manifested. However the precipitating events may not necessarily be phenomena affecting a population collectively; the death of a productive household member or the addition of dependants above a certain threshold may also precipitate a decision to migrate. Indeed, in the case of so-called economic migration there may no particular triggering factor or event – the proximate factors of themselves may be sufficient to stimulate the decision to migrate.

The fourth domain includes what might be termed intervening factors, or those that enable, facilitate, constrain, accelerate or consolidate migration. As Richmond points out, not all predisposing factors and precipitating events generate migration; "some additional enabling circumstances are needed" (Richmond 1994: 66). Facilitating factors include the presence and quality of transport, communications, information and the resources needed for the journey and transit period; constraining factors include the absence of such infrastructure and the lack of information and resources needed to move. Constraining factors may also include, on a more positive note, attachment to a place, for just as there are "push" factors and "pull" factors, there are also "staying put" factors (Hammar

1995; and see pages 41–46). Also located in this domain is what was termed above the "migration regime", which embraces the efforts of national and international organizations to manage migration. Migrant networks encompassing source, transit and destination countries, and the burgeoning trafficking industry likewise feature here. These components are again much less subject to measurement than some of the structural or proximate factors. In this domain of enablement and constraint, the volumes, forms and directions of migration are determined or shaped. If the decision to move is determined by precipitating factors, the decisions how and when to leave, which household members should go, and where to make for are determined in this intervening domain.

The domains outlined above shape the conditions, circumstances or environment within which migrants make choices or have decisions thrust upon them. In aggregate, they constitute a given migration order, the dynamics of which may encompass several countries of origin, transit and destination. The first three domains outlined above can perhaps be seen as embracing the factors *initiating* or *generating* migratory flows, and the fourth as shaping the nature and forms of movement, or the *continuation* or sustaining of migratory flows. As Massey et al. observe, "the conditions that initiate international movement may be quite different from those that perpetuate it across time and space" (1993: 448). Indeed the conditions that initiate movement may well diminish in importance or disappear altogether. This prompts consideration of how migration orders change; looking at migration at its moments of transition illuminates the connections between the levels and components of migration orders outlined above, for it is at such moments that the dynamics of migration are thrown into relief.

Cumulative and acute changes in migration orders

Put simply, changes in the features which make up the domains outlined above, singly or in combination, may trigger a shift in the migration order. Such change might be manifested in terms of the volume, types, composition, sources, routes or destinations of migration. Some changes are more profound and significant than others: the more far-reaching I term *migration transitions*, in which there is fundamental change in a given migration order.

"Feedback" or what has been termed "cumulative causation" are among the mechanisms through which migration orders change: "Causation is cumulative in that each act of migration alters the social context within which subsequent migration decisions are made, typically in ways that make subsequent movement more likely" (Massey et al. 1993: 451). Thus emigration may weaken the home economy or the social cohesiveness of the community of origin, leading to further socio-economic disintegration and further out-migration. The establishment of enclaves of migrants in countries of destination may make it easier and cheaper for subsequent cohorts of migrants to join them, which can itself be a force accelerating migration. The development of migrant networks with a broad reach, considered further below, can be an important determinant of change in migration orders, for "network connections constitute a form of social capital that people can draw upon" to migrate (Massey et al. 1993: 450). There is a threshold or point of critical mass beyond which the costs and risks of migration are lowered, making it a more and more attractive proposition.

Changes through feedback are typically gradual, but may nonetheless be profound, in which case they might be termed *cumulative transitions*; here there is no particular point or moment at which transition can be observed to occur. One prominent example of a cumulative transition has occurred in many parts of the affluent world in recent times. The structure of the economy and employment has changed in many such countries, so that migrant labour is no longer needed, or at least not in the mixes of labour power or skills hitherto. Such a shift is likely to be manifested in changes in the migration regime, and specifically in the rules governing entry of migrants into such countries. It is also likely to be manifested in the political arena, where competition for employment and other resources may well make host societies less welcoming. For many European countries, a date could be put on such a transformation, the early to mid-1970s.

Cumulative changes may take other forms, and are not only determined at the destination end of the migration order.

Economic and political disparities do not only widen, they may also narrow between countries of origin and countries of destination. Such is the case in East and Southeast Asia where the new cohorts of newly-industrializing countries have changed from being territories of emigration to those of immigration, as is shown later in this chapter. In southern Europe a similar process has been under way. It has also been the case in West Africa, where, pendulum-like, Ghana and Nigeria have successively been countries of immigration for each others nationals as their economic fortunes have waxed and waned.

Change may then occur without crisis, and the precipitating domain may be absent or inactive. However, upheavals in the structural or proximate domains may mean changes in the migration order take crisis form, and are marked by some precipitating event. Such acute forms of migration transition I term *migration crises*, involving sudden, massive, disorderly population movements. These may be pivotal episodes or critical moments which signal a juncture between one migration order and the next.

"Crisis" is a much-used term in the context of migration, no less than in other arenas. For example, Myron Weiner (1995) has titled a recent book *The global migration crisis*, referring to what he and others see as a diffuse phenomenon widely felt and experienced throughout the world. In this book the term is used rather more specifically, to denote particular moments in the history or development of a given migration order. Indeed it might be suggested that there is currently less a global migration crisis than a series of migration crises around the globe.

Acute migration transitions then may be generated by changes in the structural and proximate domains similar to those bringing about cumulative changes, but are typically marked or manifested by particular catastrophic events – collapse of the economy, war, invasion, collapse of state institutions, disintegration of the nation-state, persecution of a minority, or a combination of these and other developments. Such crises may initiate a new migration order, set in motion by a movement of refugees for example, or transform or modify migration orders already in being, as in the episodes investigated in this book.

However, not all such upheavals mark ruptures in migration orders. Migration crises may also be acute manifestations or the culmination of long term, cumulative change: they may represent the accentuation of such cumulative change; or they may mark just a temporary upset in a migration order. Some of these outcomes feature in episodes discussed later. In the next section I illustrate the notions of migration order, transition and crisis by recounting briefly recent changes to four key migration orders.

Recent transitions in four migration orders
The former Soviet Union and East-Central Europe: from circumscription to flux and from stasis to transit. As is well known, the break-up of the Soviet Union since 1991 has been accompanied by massive and complex population movement and displacement. Totalling perhaps 9 million people, these movements are the largest in the region since the Second World War (UNHCR 1996a). The roots of many of these movements lie in forced and voluntary migrations in the 70 years of the Soviet era, when the social and ethnic make-up of this vast territory was reshaped. Some of these movements were akin to labour migration in the west, as people sought better opportunities. Some movements involved state-directed settlement of quasi-colonized territories by military, industrial, administrative, managerial and other personnel. Other movements were more coercive, and included deportations of political opponents, wealthier peasants and ethnic minorities of doubted loyalty – among them eight 'peoples' or 'nations' deported by Stalin (see p.26). Some of the movements were centrally planned and directed; others were driven by the social, economic or personal motivations of individuals (Bremmer & Taras 1993; Brubaker 1996; Conquest 1960; Messina 1996).

The recent transformation of the Soviet migration order has been profound – although perhaps less so than had been anticipated. There have been significant exoduses of certain ethnic groups, notably of Jews, Germans and Greeks to regroup with their co-ethnics in Israel, Germany and Greece. But a much-heralded mass exodus of former Soviet citizens to the West has failed to materialize; the mass exodus to the West has in a sense been an acute non-event. Lack of familiarity with foreign travel, of already established migration networks, of information, and not least of convertible currency partly explain this non-movement. In addition, disparities in living standards between East and West have not been as great as those between North and South, and the prospects for improvements have been better despite widespread economic disruption and insecurity in the post-Soviet era (Coleman 1992).

Rather than massive outward or westward migration, the major movements or potential movements have been within or among the successor states of the former Soviet Union. The social and ethnic fabric woven by movement during the Soviet era unravelled as the USSR disintegrated in armed conflict, ethnic tension, a deteriorating economy, the collapse of social cohesion, and accelerating degradation of the environment.

Much of the current movement in the former Soviet Union involves people with migratory backgrounds, including those who have experienced forced movement. When the USSR broke up in 1991, millions of people found themselves outside their territories of origin; they became foreigners overnight. Among the most numerous – some 34 million – were people drawn from the three main Slav nationalities long settled outside their republics: 25 million Russians, nearly 7 million Ukrainians and over 2 million Belorussians were in this position. As bearers of the nationality of the dominant power and agents of quasi-colonization, the Russians in particular had led relatively privileged lives as they spread out in search of opportunities in what became known as the "near abroad" between 1930 and 1970. They formed significant proportions of most of the 14 non-Russian successor states. Only in Armenia was their share less than 5 per cent; in Kyrgystan and Ukraine they accounted for more than 20 per cent, and in Estonia, Latvia and Kazakhstan for more than 30 per cent of the population (*Forced Migration Monitor* January 1995). Repatriations have been under way since the 1970s, but with the break-up of the USSR, these movements accelerated in response to deteriorating economic conditions, ethnic tensions and conflict, and in anticipation of discriminatory measures against expatriates in the successor states. Between 3 and 4 million Russians, Ukrainians and Belorussians are thought to have returned, by force and by choice, to their respective republics since 1991, mainly from the Central Asian states and the Caucasus; they have also come under pressure in the restored Baltic states (Brubaker 1996; Hyman 1993; Messina 1996; UNHCR 1996a). More movement of this kind has been anticipated, although its scale may not be as great as has been feared; there has been and will be great variation according to the rootedness of the Slav populations, the skills they may offer, and the attitudes of the successor states towards them (Brubaker 1996).

Another kind of return movement has been that of people belonging to nationalities deported by Stalin in the 1940s to Central Asia. While some of these groups were allowed to return to their places of origin after Stalin's death in 1953, three continued to be denied the option of repatriation – the Crimean Tatars, the Volga Germans and the Meskhetian Turks, whose historic homeland is in Georgia. Since 1991, however, several hundred thousand Tatars have left Central Asia and the Russian Federation for Crimea in Ukraine, and several hundred thousand Volga Germans have emigrated to Germany under an agreement with the German government. However the Meskhetians, many thousands of whom were displaced by communal conflict in Central Asia to Azerbaijan, have been unable to return to Georgia (Forced Migration Projects 1996; Kreindler 1986; UNHCR 1996a, 1996b).

The unravelling of the legacy of migration in the Soviet era has been manifested then in large scale "unmixing" and forced migration, often under violent conditions, of minorities who do not fit the new dispensation of successor states, particularly in the Caucasus, in the central Asian republics and in the Baltic states. In addition, the post-Soviet states have, largely by default, opened to a large number of transit migrants from the Middle East, Africa and Asia hoping to gain entry one way or another into Western Europe or North America. At the end of 1994, the Russian Federal Migration Service claimed there were 500,000 foreigners from 46 countries in the Russian Federation, although some thought this figure inflated (US

Committee for Refugees 1995). While the intention may have been to use Russia, Ukraine, Belorus or the Baltic states as staging posts to the West, by default they may become enduring destinations for many of these "third country" migrants and asylum seekers.

In aggregate these changes amount to a substantial trans-formation of the post-Soviet migration order, some of which has taken acute or crisis forms. Similar changes have occurred in the migration order of East-Central Europe, which loosened from the Soviet orbit, has moved from stasis to transit as the Czech and Slovak Republics, Hungary and Poland have accom-modated migrants from their less stable and less developed neighbours further east, together with migrants from the developing world seeking new migration routes; Romania and Bulgaria also host such migrants in transit (International Organisation for Migration 1994). Subsequently, these states have implicitly been cast as buffer states to head off migration towards Western Europe: Europe's "protective curtain" (Marie 1994: 16) is being created by a panoply of measures that add up to a significant transformation of the European migration regime. Those particularly affecting countries of East-Central Europe include the development of the "safe country" concept and the related strategy of readmission agreements, often lubricated by financial assistance. Under the safe third country idea, it is argued that asylum seekers may be denied access to refugee status procedures in a West European state on the grounds that they could have applied for asylum in the safe countries or countries through which they have already passed in the east. Readmission agreements are a logical extension of the notion of safe third countries, formalizing the idea that asylum-seekers or other migrants can be returned to such countries, and have been extensively developed between western and eastern European states; the Schengen group concluded a readmission agreement with Poland in 1991, and Germany negotiated such agreements bilaterally with Romania, Poland and the Czech Republic in 1992-94. Each of the latter agreements involved payments or aid, partly to assist with the accommodation and processing of returnees and improvements in border control (Suhrke 1997). As a result of these migration containment strategies, some East-Central European countries are moving from countries of transit to those of destination for would-be migrants to the West.

To summarize, in the former Soviet Union and East-Central Europe, change primarily in the macro-political economy – notably nation-state disintegration and reconstitution and the area of social order and security – has underlaid the transition in the migration order from circumscription to flux and from stasis to transit. Burgeoning migrant networks and trafficking – associated with an explosion of criminal activity – have been both part of the transition and a consequence of it. The migration regime in the region is weakly and unevenly developed. Anxiety in Western Europe about migration resulting from this changed order in the East has stimulated far-reaching changes in the emergent pan-European migration regime – seen not least in the very proliferation of international bodies taking up the migration issue and in a battery of measures introduced to contain movement. Nonetheless, the changes in the migration order in this region, though profound, have not so far been as acute as many anticipated – in particular a feared large scale exodus from the former USSR to the West has not occurred. Acute migration transition has taken place within rather than outside the entity that was the USSR.

The Balkans: the resurgence of population transfer. Europe's particularly acute migration transitions have been seen on its south-eastern flank, the Balkans, manifested notably in the Yugoslavia wars, but also involving Bulgaria and Turkey, and Albania, Greece and Italy (explored in greater detail in Chapter 4). As in the former Soviet Union, it is notable that several of the populations involved in upheaval already had strong migration backgrounds – that is, they were migrants or were communities of migrant origin.

The mass exodus of more than 300,000 ethnic Turks from Bulgaria in 1989 presaged events soon to follow in the region and with the crumbling of its isolationist regime, Albania experienced rapid transformation from closure and immobility to an explosion of out-migration from the end of 1990, seen most dramatically in the mass exoduses by boat to Italy in 1991. But by far the greatest volume of forced movement in Europe in recent times has been associated with the disintegration of Yugoslavia, where the conflicts which erupted in 1991 have given rise to the largest movements of refugees and displaced people in Europe since the Second World War. Almost 4 million people have been forced to leave their homes since the start of the conflict as one republic after another seceded from the Socialist Federal Republic of Yugoslavia (UNHR 1997). Many were displaced within their own republics; others were forced to move to a republic different from the one they lived in before the conflict; still others – between 1.4 million and 1.8 million – became refugees, mainly in Europe. With the conflict over, but tensions still high in many places, there is the prospect of a problematic large scale return of refugees and displaced people to their former places of residence.

The upheaval that culminated in the conflict and displacement from mid-1991 has roots in Yugoslavia's long history of migration. Movement resulting from the rise and fall of the Austro-Hungarian and Ottoman empires, economic migration before the Second World War, internal migration among Yugoslavia's component republics, and, from the mid-1960s, labour migration largely to Germany have contributed to population redistribution that has had a bearing on the conflict (Meznaric 1985; Meznaric & Caci-Kumpes 1993; Zimmerman 1993). As Zimmerman (1993: 78) observed as the Yugoslav conflict gathered momentum, "the contemporary dispute among parts of formerly communist Yugoslavia must ... be seen in the context of migration to Europe of Yugoslav *gastarbeiter* [guest-workers] as well as against the background of Austro-Hungary's search for security against the Ottoman Empire". International migration stimulated further internal migration and population redistribution, as, for example, unskilled workers and peasants from Bosnia moved to replace absent guest-workers from Croatia and Slovenia from the 1960s (Meznaric and Caci-Kumpes 1993). The resulting distribution of very mixed communities was seized upon by nationalists fomenting the violence and ethnic cleansing that erupted in the 1990s.

When the conflict and mass displacement came, refugee

arrivals overlaid the prior presence of such migrants: thus in the early 1990s there were thought to be some 200,000 Bosnian guest-workers in Slovenia, in addition to some 69,000 registered Bosnian refugees (Argent 1992). The distribution of refugees from the ethnic cleansing also partly followed prior migration routes outside former Yugoslavia. It is no accident that the largest number of refugees from former Yugoslavia, outside that country's successor states, made for Germany, the destination of the bulk of Yugoslav labour migrants before the crisis. One estimate put the total number of Yugoslav guest-workers (probably including their dependants) in Germany in 1989 at 600,000, mostly Croatians or ethnic Croats from Bosnia-Herzegovina, but also Muslims, Serbs and ethnic Albanians (Zimmerman 1993). Refugees from former Yugoslavia in Germany at the end of 1995 were estimated at 320,000 (US Committee for Refugees 1996). The interconnections between the guest-worker and refugee populations in Germany and elsewhere have yet to be elucidated, but the prior existence of migration streams and networks appear to have had a strong bearing on the direction of subsequent refugee flows.

What was Yugoslavia has then experienced a stark, painful and acute transformation from a migration order featuring substantial internal (or inter-republic) movement and inter-national labour migration, to the forced migration within and outside the former Yugoslavia entity of "ethnically cleansed" expellees and those fleeing conflict. The victims of ethnic cleansing were often the legacy of these prior migrations. As will be shown below, the migration crises experienced by Bulgaria and Turkey and by Albania, Greece and Italy respectively accentuated a long-established migration order (the emigration of ethnic Turks from Bulgaria) and disrupted and reversed a very recently established pattern of out-migration (of Albanians to Greece). South-eastern Europe has then experienced several disruptive, disorderly mass exoduses, largely resulting from the disintegration of communist regimes, and in the case of Yugoslavia dissolution of the nation-state itself. The political and security domain has been uppermost in shaping these migration crises, but the economic arena has increasingly been brought into play. In longer term perspective, these movements and the region's new migration order have wider resonances of the post-Ottoman population transfers earlier in this century.

East and Southeast Asia: full employment and the migration transition. This region embraces a number of inter-regional and intra-regional migration orders, many of which have undergone substantial transformations in recent years. This section looks just at migration within the region, where "Capital and labour are swirling round ... in currents of ever increasing complexity" (International Labour Office 1992: 48). Important cumulative transitions have occurred within the region, as countries brooking no or only minimal immigration have begun to admit migrants on an increasing scale, or as countries that were sources of migrants have become countries of immigration. This migration transition or turning point – which could be defined as the moment when a country opens up to immigration, or when the number of immigrants exceeds the number of emigrants – has been explained in economic terms, a consequence of the dynamic growth of the Asian newly-industrializing countries (Abella 1994). While there are differences over the relative weights of economic, demographic and social variables in this process, it is argued that reaching full employment marks the turning point at which a migration transition is undergone or is likely.

Very broadly, employers in newly-industrializing countries reaching full employment and thereafter faced by labour shortages and rising wage costs have had four options, similar to those faced earlier by western industrial nations. They could attempt greater utilization of local sources of labour, by encouraging greater labour force participation by women, for example. They could economize on labour by investing in labour-saving technology, or by squeezing more out of their labour force. They could relocate their enterprises to countries with cheaper labour, sometimes involving a move just across the border – such as that between Hong Kong and Guandong in China or between Singapore and Johore in Malaysia. Or they could import labour legally or utilize illegal migrants to supplement the local labour force or free it up (Lim & Abella 1994).

Japan reached full employment in the early 1960s, Taiwan in the late 1960s, Hong Kong and Singapore by the early 1970s, Korea and Malaysia by the late 1980s, and Thailand in the early 1990s (Lim & Abella 1994). In different measures and sometimes modified by political and social considerations, each resorted to these strategies to overcome labour shortages, so that the timing and unwinding of the migration transition was not necessarily contemporary with the attainment of full employment. There were significant differences between the more ethnically homogeneous countries of the northeast (Japan, Korea and Taiwan) and the more multi-ethnic southeast (Malaysia and Singapore); the former utilized other strategies and began importing labour well after full employment was reached, while the latter embraced the import of labour well before. Elsewhere, special circumstances obtained; by virtue of its geographical position, Hong Kong, with its giant migrant-producing neighbour, benefited from the stimulus of cheap migrant labour earlier than the others.

Indeed, there are so many exceptions to the theory than cases conforming to it that its validity might be called into question – prompting consideration of other political and cultural factors. Thus Japan's long reluctance to admit foreigners delayed and made tentative its resort to migrant labour, while Singapore's embrace of strictly controlled migrant entry is shaped by an explicitly articulated intent to avoid following Europe's pattern of migrant settlement (Nagayama 1992; Pang 1992). An economic explanation nonetheless provides at least a partial account of the migration transition that has gathered momentum in the region in the last decade.

These transitions in the migration order have been cumulative. Malaysia now perhaps has the greatest potential for a migration crisis in the region. It has a configuration of conditions that have presaged migration crises elsewhere. First, it has a large absolute and proportionate migrant population, the largest in the region at perhaps more than a million out of a population of 18 million; the main source countries are Indonesia, followed by the Philippines, and to a lesser extent Bangladesh and Thailand. Second, perhaps half of the migrants – particularly the Indonesians – are in Malaysia illegally, despite periodic amnesties and registration exercises. Third, Malaysia has a history of ethnic conflict, notably the disturbances in the late 1960s among the Malay, Chinese and Indian resident communities, and precedents of expulsion, although ethnic tensions have been held in check by economic prosperity. Fourth, Malaysia has a relatively *laissez-faire* migration regime, which is a result partly of policy indecision and neglect; partly of the demands of employers for labour overriding the expression of social and security concerns associated with migration; and partly of difficulties in policing the federation's long land and sea borders (Pillai 1992).

The symptoms of a significant shift in the migration regime have been present for some time, seen in periodic campaigns since the early 1990s to arrest and deport illegals. Such an operation in 1992–93 saw the detention of nearly 63,600 illegals and the deportation of nearly 25,000. Nearly 5,000 were held in the first quarter of 1994. A swoop on 1,200 Filipina domestic workers at a church in Kuala Lumpur late in March 1994 provoked great controversy and threatened to sour relations with the Philippines – most of those arrested turned out to have valid documents (Asian Regional Programme on International Labour Migration 1993, 1994).

The controversy surrounding this episode may have deterred the authorities from acting precipitately again. There were also other, largely political considerations that constrained such actions, among them the desire to maintain neighbourly relations with Indonesia, from where most of the migrants come. Immigration of Indonesians and also of Muslims from the Philippines has been welcomed for nation-building and electoral reasons, as has an increase in those regarded as co-ethnics and co-religionists, which helps to eclipse the influence of other ethnic groups, notably the Chinese, in parts of the country. Last, but possibly most important, Malaysia's economic dynamism has militated against the likelihood of an acute upheaval in the migration order, although this might rapidly change if an economic downturn is coupled with disruptive internal or external political developments (similar to the circumstances encountered by Nigeria in the early 1980s, as is shown below). Threats to Malaysia's one million strong immigrant population have nevertheless continued, with further arrests, deportations and attempts to crack down on migrant smugglers. Early in 1997 the government declared it was preparing to arrest and deport illegal immigrants who failed to make use of an amnesty that expired at the end of 1996 (*AP–Dow Jones News Service*, 2 January 1997). The currency crisis that hit Malaysia and other Asian economies in mid-1997 may presage further stringent moves against the country's migrant population.

China should perhaps be considered to embrace a migration order of its own, apparently on the verge of profound trans-formation. In the People's Republic the *hukou* system of registration, established in the 1950s and which regulated internal, mainly rural to urban migration by tying entitlements to residence, has been loosening with the instigation of market-based reforms: this has resulted in a "tidal wave" of internal movement – of an estimated "floating population" of 80 million in the 1990s, some 50 million are rural-to-urban migrants, perhaps the largest flow of migrant workers in history (Roberts 1997: 250–52). Some 20–30 million people from the countryside have been living illicitly in cities, many responding to the uneven economic boom, concentrated in the southeast. Massive internal movement may well be helping to generate increased emigration from China. Indeed, concern has recently grown about increasing numbers of emigrants, among them a new wave of boat people making for North America often by extremely circuitous routes, together with increasing numbers crossing illegally into Hong Kong and other destinations in Asia. These movements increasingly involve highly organized criminal syndicates and complex routings taking in Taiwan, Thailand, Hong Kong, Central America and the Caribbean, and Russia and Eastern Europe (Hood 1994). In 1993–96, the US authorities detected more than 40 vessels carrying illegal would-be immigrants, mainly Chinese, bound for the US; many more are thought to have escaped detection and landed successfully in the US, Mexico or Central America. The most well-known case was the *Golden Venture* which ran aground off New York in 1993, carrying more than 280 Chinese, ten of whom drowned while trying to swim ashore (*Washington Post* 9 October 96). As well as reflecting the fates of trafficked migrants more widely, the *Golden Venture* episode was among the incidents that heightened anxiety about migration and immigrants among the US population at large and prompted more restrictive controls on immigration in the US. In the foreseeable future, China may relax its exit controls, which may lead to a great increase in emigration or simply make official out-movements already under way. In many ways, this internal and external movement is not a novel transformation, but a reversion to historical patterns of internal and external migration, in the long tradition of the Chinese diaspora (Wang 1991).

In East and Southeast Asia then, the transformation of the migration order within the region has been primarily economically motivated, deriving from the macro-economic arena, notably the structure of employment and trade. But while economic disparities have predominated in determining the migration transition, it has been modified or shaped by political and cultural factors. The regional migration regime is generally well developed, and repressively so. With some exceptions, political conditions – notably the relative weakness of migrant organizations and advocates *vis-à-vis* the state – and relatively well-developed administrative capacity have allowed borders to be policed and migration kept within bounds acceptable to the state – at considerable cost in human rights. Nonetheless, the elaboration of migrant networks and institutions, and not least the burgeoning migrant trafficking business, have shaped the transition and states' responses to it, and continue to do so. Transition has so far been cumulative rather than acute, but there is the potential for migration crises in parts of the region, notably Malaysia. Emigration from China and Hong Kong could also unleash unpredictable changes in the migration orders of the region and beyond.

The Middle East: the Gulf crisis and migration upheaval. The involuntary mass departure of 2 million migrants and members of migrant communities in the course and aftermath of the Gulf crisis (considered in greater detail in Chapter 3) was an acute transformation of lasting significance for the region and its sources of labour. It brought to a head cumulative changes under way in Gulf economies for some time – notably the end of the construction boom and the rise of the service sector – which were redefining demand for migrant labour, both quantitatively and qualitatively. The Gulf crisis also concentrated attention on social, demographic and security concerns that had been worrying Gulf rulers for some time – notably that there was too great a dependency on foreign labour, a view also increasingly articulated by educated young nationals entering the labour market.

The Gulf crisis marked a fundamental shift in the migration order. But this shift was not so much in the tightly controlled, temporary and contract migration from South and Southeast Asia, which although painfully disrupted, subsequently revived. It was rather among the Arab sources of labour – principally Egypt, Jordan, Yemen and the Palestinians – that the fundamental, enduring transformation occurred, bringing to an end the old migration order. As Findlay has remarked of the displacement of Yemenis:

> The contingent historical events of 1990 that permitted Saudi Arabia and other Arab oil states to terminate the employment of most Yemeni migrants was an entirely consistent extension of the migration forces that had been progressively operating to increase restrictions on the movement of Arab migrants from neighbouring countries, and, where possible, to replace them with Asian labour (Findlay 1994: 212–13).

The old migration order that disappeared was relatively free movement and residence for Arabs (albeit discretionary and subject to arbitrary change for some populations, notably Palestinians), diminishing the contribution of Arab migrants to the labour forces of Gulf states, and enhancing the role of migrants from South and Southeast Asia (Van Hear 1993).

As I show in Chapter 3, one of the features of many of the Arab migrants forced to move was their long settlement in their host country. This was particularly the case for the Palestinians obliged to leave Kuwait, many of whom had been settled since the upheavals of 1948 and 1967. It was also true of many of the Yemenis who were forced to leave Saudi Arabia, and many of the Egyptians obliged to leave Iraq, although for the latter the disruption was perhaps less enduring, since many of them were redeployed in Saudi Arabia and Libya. These populations were perhaps "denizens" in the sense referred to in Chapter 1 (Hammar 1990). The migration order that was changed by the Gulf crisis was this pattern of Arab denizenship, which was selectively removed, rather than the pattern of temporary contract migration from Asia, which was correspondingly enhanced.

In the Middle East then, cumulative changes in the demand for labour and the structure of employment – in the macro-economic arena again – provided the basis for a transition that was brought about acutely by the contingency of the Gulf crisis in the macro-political arena, during which labour-importing states seized the opportunity to achieve the rationalization of the labour market they had already been hesitantly reaching for. The rationalization – the replacement of Arab denizens by Asian migrant workers – had political and security as well as economic motivations. Very broadly, until the crisis, two migration regimes operated: a relatively *laissez-faire* regime (though discretionary and subject to arbitrary change) for Arab workers and residents, and relatively strong administrative control and management of migration from Asia. Migrant organization and networks were well developed among Arab workers and residents – and less though still significantly so (despite circumscription) among Asian migrant workers. The role of a largely legal and overt labour recruiting and supply system for Asian workers was important in the transition, which was also shaped by the willingness of Asian workers to continue to be recruited, despite the experience of many of their com-patriots during the Gulf crisis. In so far as this transformation was a sudden and large upheaval, while at the same time bringing to a head a longer term change, it can be seen as an acute manifestation of a cumulative process.

Refining the notions of migration order, transition and crisis
Change in the four migration orders reviewed has taken both acute and cumulative forms. Very broadly, some changes were driven by economic factors, precipitated for example by shifts

in demand for labour or in employment structure, in turn prompted by the working of the business cycle or by longer term economic restructuring. Other changes were generated by political restructuring, notably the disintegration and reconstitution of nation-states in recent years. Commonly, there was a combination of both. Acute transitions or migration crises tend to occur under a combination of conditions; often strong economic change creates the conditions for transition, but it is contingent political factors that actually precipitate migration crises.

In an attempt to refine the notions of migration order, transition and crisis used in this chapter, three common-sense observations may be made. First, some changes to migration orders are more profound than others. Those of greater magnitude warrant the description migration transition. Second, while some of the changes have taken acute or crisis forms and others have been cumulative and gradual, there is no necessary correlation between the depth of a change and its manifestation – profound changes do not necessarily manifest themselves as migration crises. Third, consideration of migration transition should take account of "migration antecedents", often overlooked, that often have a bearing on subsequent migration orders.

Two forms of change featured in the migration orders outlined above appear profound enough to warrant the term transition. The first of these, and ostensibly the simplest, might broadly be described as transition from *immobility to mobility*. The transitions under way in the former communist bloc might be characterized in this way. But this is only a crude characterization of what has occurred in this region; a better description might be transition from regulated mobility to increasingly disorderly movement, beyond the capacity of weakened states to manage.

Taking account of the antecedents gives rise to a still more complex picture. Thus state-directed relocations for political and economic reasons, implemented with varying degrees of force and often on the basis of ethnicity, were components of the Soviet migration order. In the post-Soviet era this order has been unravelling in the form of exodus of Russians and others from the near abroad and the ethnic unmixing that has taken violent forms in the Caucasus and Central Asia. However, much of this unmixing was already well under way before the break-up of the Soviet Union, so some of the current movements can be seen as accentuation of those already under way. Similarly, the forced movements accompanying the wars in former Yugoslavia should be seen in the context of the prior migration order, which included substantial internal or inter-republic migration coupled with well-established migration of guest-workers to other parts of Europe. Taking account of the antecedents helps puts in perspective migrations resulting from the disintegration and reconstitution of states that otherwise might be seen as episodic, single events.

A variant on the transition from immobility to mobility is the shift from closure or minimal immigration to substantial inward movement, as has occurred in Japan. Again, taking account of migration history suggests a different picture over time, for Japan was a country of emigration before the era of closure. Closure or immobility can thus be seen as itself a transient condition. This pattern is related to a second change, or set of changes, appearing to warrant the term *migration transition* – the shift from being a territory predominantly of emigration to becoming one principally of immigration. Some east Asian countries, some southern European countries (notably Spain, Italy and Greece), and some former eastern bloc countries have undergone or are undergoing such a transition. Largely associated with economic change, the pattern is commonly a three-stage one: first, emigration of unskilled labour takes place from an underdeveloped economy; second, as industrialization proceeds and the domestic labour market tightens, emigration of skilled labour is coupled with immigration of unskilled labour; and finally, immigration of foreign labour predominates, with some continuing emigration of highly skilled workers. Alternatively, the second stage may be a different kind of transition, in which the territory is treated by migrants as a country of transit, but by default it subsequently becomes a country of destination; this has been the case in the former eastern bloc.

The second observation made above referred to the relation

between crisis and cumulative transitions and the depth of change. In the case of the East and Southeast Asian newly-industrializing countries sketched above, the transition associated largely with economic change was essentially cumulative; the changes from being countries of emigration to those of immigration or from closure to immigration were profound, but were not accompanied by sudden, disorderly movements. While transition may occur without upheaval, migration crisis is more likely when transformation is under way; among the recent wave of Asian tiger economies, Malaysia appears the most likely candidate for this. In southern Europe migration transition has been signalled by crisis: Italy's rejection of Albanian arrivals by boat and the expulsion of Albanians by Greece confirmed their transition from countries of emigration to those of immigration. The configuration of circumstances that particularly seems to precipitate migration crises is profound cumulative change in the economic arena, coupled with contingent upheaval in the political domain. This configuration features in several of the examples sketched above, and is further illustrated in the migration upheavals outlined in later chapters.

Force, choice and agency in migration orders

The discussion of migration orders, transition and crisis has so far been pitched at a rather general level. But the point should never be lost that migration orders and the changes and upheavals in them are shaped by human agency. While such upheavals may shape migrant communities – contributing to the making and unmaking of diasporas – migrants are also among the agents of such change. I now turn attention to the place of human agency and the related questions of force and choice in shaping migration orders and changes in them.

Moving out, coming in, going back, moving on, staying put
Consideration of contemporary migration reveals a bewildering variety of forms and types of movement. The term *migrant* encompasses diverse types of transient people – among them

permanent emigrants and settlers, temporary contract workers, professional, business or trader migrants, students, refugees and asylum-seekers, and cross border commuters. Moreover, people often shift between these categories: they may enter as students, tourists or visitors, for example, but then illegally overstay, ask for asylum or seek permanent settlement, and eventually become naturalized as citizens. How can one make sense of this diversity? In the following I attempt to establish a framework for thinking about diverse types of movement, and about how they can contribute to the making or unmaking of transnational communities or diasporas. I disaggregate migration into its components and locate these in a framework that takes account of the choice and compulsion confronted by migrants. Looking at migration within a framework of choices and constraints allows an approach that reconciles the discourses on economic and forced migration.

A simple disaggregation of migratory movements might come up with five essential components. All migrations involve some kind of *outward* movement, from a place of origin or residence to some other place. This movement necessarily involves some kind of *inward* movement as a concomitant – people leaving a place must arrive at some other place, even if only temporarily. Subsequently there might be a *return* to the place of origin or previous residence; this likewise involves *inward* movement as a concomitant. Alternatively, following an *outward* movement, there might be *onward* movement to some other place; this must also involve *inward* movement. In addition to these four essential components of movement, account must be taken of another component – non-movement, or *staying put* – for almost all migrations involve leaving behind a portion of the community or population. A subsidiary or intermediary component, *transit*, might be added to the five essentials.

Each of these components involves degrees of choice and coercion, and are conventionally portrayed as voluntary or involuntary movements. The permutations of voluntary and involuntary migration and two of the components identified above, outward and return migration, could be represented in a simple matrix. Some of the types of migration that might be placed in the four cells of this matrix might be presented as in Table 2.1.

Table 2.1: Force and choice in outward and return migration

	voluntary migration	involuntary migration
outward movement	labour migrants professional migrants traders tourists students	refugees internally displaced people development displacement forcible relocation disaster displacement
return movement	returning migrants and refugees voluntary repatriates voluntary returnees	deported or expelled migrants refugees subject to *refoulement* forced repatriates forced returnees

The categories "voluntary" and "involuntary" are not wholly satisfactory and may be misleading, particularly if conceived as discrete. It has become received wisdom that few migrants are wholly voluntary or wholly involuntary. Almost all migration involves some kind of compulsion; at the same time almost all migration involves choices. Economic migrants make choices, but they do so within constraints. For example, what is the balance of force and choice for the supposed "voluntary", economic migrant who "chooses" to seek work in her country's capital or abroad, but whose child would otherwise die if she does not earn money to pay for medical treatment? Forced migrants likewise make choices, within a narrower range of possibilities. But even in the most dire circumstances, there is still some choice, since some may choose to stay and suffer starvation or violence rather than leave their homes. Some migrants nevertheless have more choices than others. Moreover, many if not most migration streams involve migrants with varying degrees of choice and who experience varying degrees of compulsion. These nuances mean that the matrix presented above needs refinement.

These issues of force and compulsion are better presented as lying along an axis ranging from "choice" or "more options" at one end to "little choice" or "few options" at the other. A convincing paradigm along these lines has been suggested by Richmond (1993, 1994), who recognizes

> a continuum at one end of which individuals and collectivities are proactive and at the other reactive. Under certain conditions, the decision to move may be made after due consideration of all relevant information, rationally calculated to maximise net advantage, including both material and symbolic rewards. At the other extreme, the decision to move may be made in a state of panic during a crisis that leaves few alternatives but escape from intolerable threats (Richmond 1994: 55).

Richmond sees "proactive migrants" as those who face choices as to "whether to move at all, when to move, whether to go a long or a short distance, and whether to cross an international border in the process" (Richmond 1994: 59). By reactive migration Richmond means, as the term suggests, movement dictated by events, with minimal choice or planning by the people involved, whose degree of choice is severely constrained. He notes that the line between the two categories is blurred:

> Between the two extremes of proactive and reactive migrants are a large proportion of people crossing state boundaries who combine characteristics, responding to economic, social and political pressures over which they have little control, but exercising a limited degree of choice of the selection of destinations and the timing of their movements (Richmond 1994: 61).

With the dimensions of force and choice conceived as a continuum, the matrix introduced in Table 2.1 can be developed by adding the three other categories – "inward movement", which covers both arrivals in a new society and returnees to the place of origin or last residence; "onward movement" to cover third country resettlement, dispersal and diaspora formation; and "staying put" to cover those who do not or cannot migrate.

At first sight, it might seem odd to include those who stay put in consideration of migration. But comprehensiveness

Table 2.2: Force and choice in five components of migration

	voluntary migration more choice more options	less choice fewer options	involuntary migration little choice few options
	proactive migrants		reactive migrants
outward	tourists visitors students professional transients business travellers	economic/labour migrants rural–urban migrants anticipatory refugees people induced to move	refugees expellees internally displaced people development displacement disaster displacement
inward	primary migrant newcomers family reunion/formation	visitors, students or tourists who seek asylum	asylum seekers refuge seekers
return	returning migrants and refugees voluntary repatriates voluntary returnees repatriates long-settled abroad	returning migrants and refugees mixture of compulsion, inducement and choice	deported or expelled migrants refugees subject to *refoulement* forced returnees repatriates long-settled abroad
onward	resettlement dispersal by strategy	third country resettlement of refugees	scattering forced dispersal
staying put	stayers by choice household dispersal strategy	people confined to safe havens safe countries, safe areas	stayers of necessity containment

demands that those who stay put be included, since they are an essential element in a migration order. Those who stay may service or support migrants abroad, especially in the period immediately after departure, or they may be serviced or supported by the migrant members of their communities, particularly after such members become established abroad.

Like outward and return movements, each of these other components of migration can involve greater or lesser degrees of choice and force. The intermediate category *transit* may also be refined in terms of choice and force, yielding at least two more categories at the "less choice" end of the spectrum. The first may be termed *stranding*, which can be seen as obligatory immobility while in transit, and the other may be termed *orbit*, which can be seen as obligatory and perpetual onward movement while in transit (see page 59). Both of these are usually the result of no territory being willing to accommodate the transients.

Leaving aside forms of transit, the simple matrix in Table 2.1 can be refined then by recasting the "voluntary"/"involuntary" division as a continuum embracing more choice, less choice and little choice, and by adding the categories "inward", "onward" and "staying put". The resulting framework is presented in Table 2.2; some examples of migration are placed in the matrix.

In the *outward* cells, tourists, visitors, students, business travellers, and what have been termed "professional transients" (Appleyard 1991) fit fairly comfortably at the end of the axis encompassing more choice. Refugees, expellees, people displaced in their own countries through conflict or persecution, and people displaced by disasters or ill-conceived development projects largely fall at the other end of the continuum. However, many economic or labour migrants, rural–urban migrants, anticipatory refugees, and others induced to move fall in between these two clusters, since there is usually an element of compulsion involved, while there are still some choices available. Refining Richmond's framework, some of these are perhaps proactive forced migrants, as compared with reactive migrants at the "little choice" end of the continuum.

In the *inward* cells, incoming primary migrants and

household members entering under family reunion programmes are among those who can be located at the end of the axis embracing more choice. Asylum seekers sit at the other end of the scale, while people who enter as visitors, students, tourists or in other ways before claiming asylum perhaps fall into an intermediate area indicating some choice.

The *return* cells include return by choice of economic migrants and voluntary return or repatriation of refugees, displaced people or other forced migrants. At the other end of the axis are located forced return or repatriation of economic migrants, and forced repatriation (known as *refoulement*) of refugees or other forced migrants. Again there is a middle ground of returnees part compelled to move, and part opting to return. Some of these returnees by force and choice may have been long-settled abroad. As will become clear from subsequent chapters, the application of force and choice varies as much in repatriation as in outward movement.

The *onward* cells include households that choose strategically to disperse their members in different parts of the world as a means of insurance or spreading risk. Since they may exercise some choice, refugees or other forced migrants settled in a third country might be located at an intermediate position on the scale, while at the other end of the continuum lie people forcibly scattered or dispersed after prior migration.

Finally, the *staying put* cells include those who opt to stay behind, and those household members who remain at home as part of a household insurance strategy which involves the migration of other members; in this case those who stay put are the counterparts of those who move outward. Those obliged to remain through lack of resources, through physical inability to travel, through the closure of borders, or through other inhibitions to movement fall at the other end of the axis. Examples include those staying put because of national or international policies of containment as well as pastoralists who are forcibly sedentarized. The strategy of fostering safe havens or so-called safe countries can graduate towards this end of the continuum, but may still offer some element of choice.

Disaggregating movement in this way may help to resolve the problematic dichotomy between economic or voluntary migration and forced or involuntary migration that dogs both theory and practice. Separation of movement into outward and inward components can reveal differences in motivation. Thus while *outward* movement may be forced, precipitated by persecution, conflict, war or some other life-threatening circumstance, *inward* movement, including the choice or determination of the destination, may be shaped by economic, livelihood or life-chance considerations. At some point then, forced migration may transmute into economic or livelihood migration. In a way this is a recasting of the old push–pull model of migration, this time explicitly incorporating the dimensions of force and choice.

Diasporas in the making and diasporas unmade
The *making* of transnational communities and diasporas can involve some or all of these component movements in varying combinations of force and choice. As I intimated in Chapter 1, diaspora formation can occur by accretion as a result of steady, gradual, routine migration, which may be a matter of choice or strategy on the part of households and communities (McDowell 1996; Stark 1991; Tinker 1977). Or dispersal may involve coercion, resulting from catastrophe, expulsion or other forcible movement induced by conflict or persecution. Dispersal may well also result from a combination of compulsion and choice; diasporas may be formed as a result of a combination of cumulative processes and crises. Of the classical diasporas, that of the Greeks might be seen as forming cumulatively, through colonization and conquest (although not without trauma and upheaval for the conquered), while the Jews, Africans and Armenians suffered collective trauma or catastrophe in the formation of their diasporas, in some ways analogous to the migration crises described in this book. Subsequent movements by choice or force may lead to further dispersal and add to, reinforce or consolidate diaspora communities already existing – this is again the case with several of the episodes examined in this book. Moreover, forced migrants may opportunistically make the best of a migration crisis; they are not simply victims, but are active within the circumstances in which they find themselves.

Diaspora formation is not necessarily one-way. As well as the formation or reinforcement of diasporas, the reverse process may occur: the *unmaking* of diasporas or what might be termed, somewhat inelegantly, "de-diasporization". The latter movements, which again some of the cases examined in this book illustrate, may be seen as the *regrouping* or *in-gathering* of dispersed people. As several commentators have observed, Europe has recently witnessed this trend towards the so-called "return" or in-gathering of some scattered ethnic populations. I have already referred to the "return" of ethnic Germans to Germany from the former USSR, Poland, and elsewhere, and that of ethnic Greeks, known as Pontics, to Greece from various parts of the former USSR (Brubaker 1996; Chesnais 1992, 1993; Voutira 1991). The "return" of ethnic Germans contributed to much of the newly united Germany's immigration bulge following the revolutions in the eastern bloc in 1989–90. The "return" of Pontic Greeks has been rather smaller in scale.

The term "return" is somewhat of a misnomer as a description of these and other cases, for many of these populations have not known their "homeland" for generations. It would also be a mistake to see these movements as wholly new phenomena. In a stimulating essay on the "unmixing of peoples" in the "aftermaths of empire", Brubaker (1996) has traced the in-gathering of ethnic Turks and Hungarians as the Ottoman and Austro-Hungarian empires intermittently contracted. This in-gathering continued in the twentieth century, finding new impetus in regroupings of Germans and Russians. In the case of the former, he argues, this process appears to be reaching its logical conclusion, as "the once-vast German diaspora of Eastern Europe and Russia is today undergoing a rapid, and probably final, dissolution" (Brubaker 1996: 166).

Predicated on profound changes in the world political economy – principally the collapse of the eastern bloc – substantial changes in the migration regime have precipitated or accelerated these regroupings. Changes in the migration regime of the territories of origin – principally the loosening of rules constraining exit from eastern bloc countries – have facilitated the emigration of these populations. Their in-gathering has been made possible by the existence of co-ethnics and territories ready to accept them, namely Germany, Greece and Israel, the

Table 2.3: Diasporas made and unmade

	voluntary movement more choice	less choice	forced movement little choice
scattering/dispersal	labour diasporas trading diasporas	imperial or colonial auxiliaries	indentured labour refugees
in-gathering/regrouping	post-Soviet ethnic groups repatriates by choice	colonial settlers and their descendants after decolonization	expelled migrant workers, trader diasporas, colonial auxiliaries and their descendants

migration regimes of each of which includes the "right of return" of co-ethnics. Diasporas in Europe and beyond of Armenians, Jews and Roma – and other dispersed populations such as ethnic Hungarians and Poles – are other candidates for such regrouping or in-gathering.

In-gathering or regrouping may be only partial – as is the case with several of the transnational communities examined below – so that the impact on the wider diaspora may vary. As with other movements outlined above, regroupings may involve choice or force, or a combination of both; like their formation, the contraction of diasporas by return or regrouping may occur cumulatively or through crisis. The permutations of force and choice in dispersal or diasporization and regrouping, repatriation or de-diaporization may be represented as in Table 2.3, which is a refinement of the "onward" and "return" parts of Table 2.2. Some examples of scattering and regrouping by force and choice are offered in the table. The focus of this book is diasporization and regrouping induced by migration crises: it is concerned with forced migrations or those towards the end of the axis encompassing people with little or no choice but to move.

Once, twice, many times migrants:
accumulating migratory cultural capital
Reality is of course much more complex than is suggested by the analytical categories outward, inward, return, onward and staying put, and by the force-choice axis. Individual migrants and migrant communities may experience several of these forms of movement, sometimes over a short period of time. Outward movement might involve compulsion or choice, as may subsequent movements back or onwards. An individual or migrant community may experience a range of compulsion and choice over time. Individual migrants therefore develop complex migration biographies; many are twice, three times or many times migrants. Likewise many migrant communities accumulate complex migration histories, involving combinations of outward, inward, onward, and return migration, sometimes forced, sometimes involving varying degrees of choice. Moreover, one type of migration can – and often does –

transmute into another, sometimes as a matter of strategy, sometimes by chance or circumstance. An individual's migratory biography or a community's collective migration history is likely then to include quite a number of different kinds of movement. This leads to the accumulation of what might be called (modifying Massey et al. 1993) "migratory cultural capital" – knowledge of how to go about migration, how to deal with brokers, traffickers, border officials and bureaucrats, how to develop and maintain contacts in receiving countries, and how to find accommodation, secure social security entitlements or gain employment. Diasporas comprise individuals and communities with often complex migration histories. Embracing individuals and communities that may have migrated several times, they include people who carry the historical baggage of migration, sojourners who have accumulated substantial migratory cultural capital.

All of the populations considered in this book have migratory backgrounds, some long-standing and complex. Indeed it is often the uncertain status deriving from their migratory background that renders them liable to expulsion or other forms of forced movement. In the following I indicate some of the kinds of migrant population that have been liable to experience migration crises in the latter part of this century, in the course of which they have regrouped or experienced further dia- sporization. Their migration histories feature a range of force and choice.

Movements associated with decolonization have formed one prominent category. Post-colonial regroupings and in- gatherings have included British, French, Dutch and Portuguese colonialists and settlers; arguably the Russians in the successor states outside the Russian Federation since the end of the Cold War fall into this category. The degree of compulsion involved in these regroupings has varied, but a number of former colonizing or colonial populations were either expelled or induced to leave as decolonization proceeded. Prominent examples include the Portuguese obliged to leave African territories, the French from Algeria and Indo-China, and the Dutch from Southeast Asia. According to one estimate, Portugal received about 800,000 *retornados* between 1974 and 1979; this was a substantial addition to Portugal's current population of about 10 million (Rocha-Trindade 1995). Another commentator offers an estimate of between 5.7 and 8.5 million repatriates associated with European decolonization; of these up to perhaps 6 million were of European origin (of whom more than 2 million were French and up to 1.2 million were Portuguese) and up to 2.5 million were non-European populations of various kinds (Miège 1993).

The non-European peoples included those associated with the "imperial" diasporas, but in a position subordinate to them. One such type were those imported by colonial powers to fulfil administrative and sometimes military roles; some of the South Asians overseas held such positions as "imperial auxiliaries", and were often compromised when decolonization took place (Tinker 1990). Rather different in socio-economic status, but still a legacy of imperialism, were the indentured and other labourers imported by colonial powers to work on railways, plantations and mines – Indians and Chinese again feature among these types of population (Tinker 1977; Wang 1991). Both of these types of population – and their descendants with these colonial roots – have experienced migration crises.

A related type of population are the trader diasporas, sometimes termed "middleman minorities" (Bonacich 1973) or "pariah capitalists" (Hamilton 1978). Apart from some of the Jewish diaspora, prominent examples include Chinese traders in Southeast Asia and elsewhere, Indians in Asia, East Africa, the Caribbean and Oceania, Lebanese in West Africa and the Caribbean, and Greeks in central Africa, each of whom established trading niches under the wing of colonial rule (Cohen 1995). Many of these populations too experienced expulsion in the post-colonial era. In a similar position to the auxiliary, trading and business diasporas have been non- or post-imperial administrators and professionals, such as some of the Palestinian population in Kuwait considered below, who have been subject to repeated forced movement.

As later chapters will show, labour migrants are another major category subject to expulsion or mass exodus. What have been termed "incipient diasporas" (Sheffer 1993; Weiner 1986) have resulted from the labour migration to the industrialized world that accelerated after the Second World War and subsequently to industrializing countries in East and Southeast Asia, the oil-rich Middle East, and among countries of varying affluence in Africa and Latin America. In many of these regions labour migrants have experienced expulsion or other kinds of migration crisis: several such episodes are investigated below.

Many refugee populations and internally displaced people have experienced such crises several times over. Those who have fled persecution or conflict have often found themselves subject to pressure to leave their places of refuge. Such insecurity can be inherited by their descendants if exile is protracted, and if the refugees in nurturing a hope to return to the homeland are loathe to integrate into their host community: "the lack of integration within the country in which the children were born coupled with the inability to reap the usual benefits forthcoming to citizens and full-fledged members of society could, and has, inspired upheaval and flight" (Batchelor 1995: 98). To cite just one example that has had terrible contemporary resonance, refugees from Rwanda and their descendants were among the community known as the Banyarwanda expelled from Uganda in the early 1980s (Clay 1984; US Committee for Refugees 1983, 1991a). As well as refugees, this expelled population included economic migrants seeking a better life as well as those long-settled in Uganda. This is illustrative of a point that will be returned to often below – that those subject to mass exodus are often of very mixed migratory origin, and it is this very fact that makes them vulnerable to expulsion.

Since the end of the Cold War, movements analogous to post-colonial regroupings among western powers have emerged or accelerated in the former eastern bloc. I have already made reference to Russians and Russian-speakers obliged to leave some non-Russian successor states. Many of these had positions akin to colonial settlers: while some had security and military roles, others in technical fields, administrative tasks and ordinary labouring were perhaps more akin to the imperial auxiliaries mentioned above (Brubaker 1996). Reference has also already been made to ethnic Germans and Greeks who have returned to their ancient "homelands" with perhaps less compulsion than in other post-Soviet regroupings. Other deported peoples – particularly the Crimean Tatars and the

Meskhetian Turks – have attempted to return to their historic homelands with greater difficulty and less success (UNHCR 1996a). Mention should also be made of post-Cold War in-gatherings of labourers imported from client countries to the communist bloc. Vietnamese, Mozambicans and Angolans are among the contract migrant workers to be repatriated with little choice from Germany and former east bloc and client states. Early in 1995, Germany and Vietnam reached agreement over the repatriation by the year 2000 of some 40,000 Vietnamese former guest-workers in East Germany, whose claims for asylum had been rejected since German reunification (US Committee for Refugees 1995).

Colonial settlers, imperial auxiliaries, indentured labourers, trader diasporas, labour migrants, refugee communities, forced migrants in the former eastern bloc – all of these and their descendants have experienced uprootings in recent times. These diverse kinds of dispersal and regrouping involving varying degrees of force prompt consideration of the communities that accommodate such migrants.

Force, choice and the host and home communities

The framework I have presented so far essentially encompasses the migrants' perspective. But migrants are not the only people to operate within a framework of choice and constraint; among the others needing to be considered are the host communities that receive migrants and those who stay at home. Full treatment of such relations would require a foray into the literature on ethnic relations which is beyond the scope of this book; this section is confined to dimensions of force and choice as they affect migrant, host and home communities. Relations between migrants and these parties have already been mentioned in passing; I have made reference to those who stay put and to the inward movements that must accompany outward, return or onward movements. The framework embracing force and choice is applicable to the people who stay behind and to the people that accommodate migrants, as well as to migrants themselves. It is an obvious point, but one worth reaffirming, that any consideration of diaspora formation needs to take account of these categories other than migrants.

Newcomers' relations with the host community essentially revolve around issues of integration or its absence; in the case of returning migrants, the issue is reintegration, considered below. Problems of terminology are immediately encountered here. The term "host" community is problematic, not least because it suggests a welcome that is not always present. Alternatives, such as the "native" or "indigenous" community, are still less satisfactory: first, they are also used to describe aboriginal populations, and second, these terms implicitly exclude former migrants who once settled form an integral part of the population. Perhaps the best formulations are "prior" or "established" communities (Bach 1993).

The term "integration" is also not without problems. A more nuanced perspective is needed. The social psychologist, John Berry, has proposed a useful framework for considering the encounter between minority groups (including migrants) and a larger society (Berry 1992). He sees four possible outcomes from this encounter, which he terms "acculturation", determined by a minority's relations with other groups on one hand and maintenance of cultural identity on the other. Submersion within the dominant society he calls "assimilation". Maintenance of identity, but with minimal relations with the larger society, he terms "separation" – or "segregation", where it is imposed. "Marginalization" occurs where a group loses its own identity, but does not become part of the larger society. Finally, Berry reserves the term "integration" for participation in the larger society while maintaining self-identity. While suggested primarily for the investigation of psycho-social dimensions of the encounter between minorities and the larger society, this framework is suggestive for relations between migrants and prior or established communities. Berry's model may be refined for the purposes of this discussion by adding the dimensions of force and choice. Integration implies a greater degree of choice on the part of newcomers than assimilation, marginalization or segregation; however, separation may be a choice by newcomers, at least in part.

Newcomers' choices are more constrained than the range of options for the established community, but the latter are by no means free to choose who they accommodate. Many of the populations and communities accommodating refugees, displaced people or other migrants in their territory or space may have little choice but to do so; in a sense they are "forced accommodators" of migrants. They may not have been consulted in the decision to admit newcomers, but nevertheless have to accommodate the consequences – the burdens as well as the benefits – that newcomers may bring. It is therefore not only in-coming migrants that are obliged to adapt.

Migrants' relations with the home community depend on whether the migrant population is resident abroad or returning home. While migrants are abroad, relations with home may be actively maintained, they may be dormant or latent, or they may be severed. Active maintenance of relations with the home community may include transactions or exchanges ranging from visits, remittances, letters and messages at the personal or family level, to support for ruling regimes or opposition movements at home in the political arena. Relations with the home community, or with those who stayed behind, may be rather different on return. The reception of returnees by those who stayed behind can vary as much as reception in a new society, particularly when the period abroad has been long. It is an obvious fact, but it bears noting that both the returnees and the home community will have changed during the absence of the migrants. The circumstances of the return, not least the degree of choice or force involved, obviously bear on reception and ultimately reintegration – or otherwise. A modified version of Berry's model may again be useful for thinking about the range of outcomes that could result, which might include reintegration, reassimilation, marginalization or separation. For returnees, the identity maintained or lost will be that of the expatriate – evidence of maintaining an expatriate identity after return might include dwelling on the experience abroad, keeping up relations with people still abroad, sending children abroad for education or experience, and communicating with or encouraging visits by those met abroad. For those who stayed behind, among the reactions to returnees may be welcome, toleration, grudging acceptance, rejection, antagonism or conflict. While the capacity of the extended family to absorb newcomers or returnees has proved surprisingly large, it has its limits, and is not without costs. For both established communities receiving newcomers and home communities receiving returnees, much depends on class and on resources available. Much also depends on timing. Reception by the established community depends on how quickly newcomers are to be accommodated; arrival of migrants, refugees or returnees in large, sudden influxes may offer few options for the community accommodating them.

There is a further nexus of relations to be considered – those with other migrants. Reception and integration involves not only relations with established populations; it also involves relations with other recently arrived migrants, who may be co-ethnics. These relations, usually assumed to be positive, are not necessarily so. Like those with the host and home communities, relations with the transnational community of other migrants may be actively maintained, dormant, latent or avoided. Active relations involve transactions and exchanges which may span a number of territories in which transnational or diaspora communities are located. Coupled with exchanges with host and home communities, these form the basis of migrant networks, which are among the important agents shaping migration orders. It is to these and other agents, and their influence on migration orders, that the final section of this chapter turns.

Agency in the transformation of migration orders

In the first part of this chapter I outlined the conditions and forces determining the environment within which changes in migration orders occur. I later reaffirmed that it is human agency that actually shapes these changes, and the dimensions of force and choice they may involve. The two main parties determining outcomes are states on one hand and migrants and their networks on the other. International or transnational organizations take a subsidiary, intermediary or supplementary role.

States vary in their capacity, or indeed their desire to manage migration in response to changes in the political economy. Apart from variation in administrative capacity, not least among the reasons for this are the different interests within the state or influencing it. Treasuries, security agencies, employers, labour organizations, advocacy groups and other lobbies pursue diverse positions regarding migration. Nonetheless, some transitions may be quite substantially managed or administered by states which receive migrants. As has been particularly evident recently, through combinations of incentives and deterrents, states may open doors to particular kinds of migrants and close the doors to others. At different times, according to political and economic conditions, states may encourage immigration, curtail or limit it, encourage repatriations or deport illegal immigrants.

Commonly such measures are cumulative in their impact, but there are circumstances in which state intervention results in acute changes or migration crises. Thus migration crises may be purposive – states may expel or deliberately engineer the departure of unwanted migrants. Mass expulsion is in a sense an extreme form of managed transition, although paradoxically it tends to be used by states whose migration regime has been *laissez faire* or one of neglect, and whose administrative capacity is poor. Alternatively, migration crises may be used opportunistically – mass exodus precipitated by circumstance (such as war) may be seized upon by the state since it offers the opportunity to implement a desired policy, such as getting rid of an unwanted population. Some of the migration upheavals examined in later chapters can be seen in this way.

However, even among states with well-developed administrative capacity and, for them, favourable political conditions (such as non-existent opposition or weak migrant advocacy bodies), policies to transform migration often do not work, succeed only partially or have unintended consequences. They do so largely because of the activities of migrants themselves in response to and in spite of state policies. States may be more powerful than migrants in determining outcomes, but transitions in migration orders are also made by the strategies and decision-making of migrant individuals and households, and through the development and working out of their networks.

As is well known, migrants develop new patterns, means and routes of migration as states close successive gates of entry. As Lim (1987), Massey et al (1993) and others have observed, migration often continues in different forms even though the economic rationale for import of labour may no longer exist. By generating its own momentum, migration is perpetuated after the reasons for its instigation may have ceased. As was noted earlier in this chapter, "cumulative causation", or what used to be termed "chain migration" from villages and districts neighbouring those of earlier migrants, continues to develop and perpetuate movement. After primary economic migration is halted, a common pattern has been for family reunion, family formation, or dependent migration to gather momentum. Meanwhile, primary migrants seek entry by different means, as witness the explosion in asylum claims and in illegal entry in Europe and North America; entry through asylum procedures was in the early 1990s said to be "the single most important component of immigration to Europe" (Coleman 1992: 4). New migrant strategies have spawned new state strategies to combat them, and vice versa, in a cat and mouse game of move and counter-move; thus the migrant strategy labelled "asylum shopping" had its counterpart in the practice of asylum-seekers being placed "in orbit". While some asylum-seekers shopped among West European countries for admission by submitting successive, or sometimes simultaneous, asylum claims, others found themselves shuttled from one airport transit lounge to another as they sought and were refused entry into a state prepared to look at their asylum claim (Byrne and Shacknove 1996: 207–12; UNHCR 1997). As the asylum route has been curtailed, marriages arranged with EU nationals have come into favour among those seeking entry into the European Union.

The networks that sustain migration, often against or despite the wishes of states, have become important transnational entities. One quantitative expression of their importance is the current scale of remittances – estimated at between $70 and $75 billion a year in the early 1990s, representing a large proportion of world financial flows, second in value only to oil among aggregate international trade and financial transactions (Russell & Teitelbaum 1992). As well as means of distributing funds, migrant networks are means of disseminating knowledge about routes and means of travel, about means of entry, about ways of finding accommodation, welfare and work, and about how to adapt to new environments; they are the vehicle for the transmission of migratory cultural capital referred to above. Drawing their resilience from the organic development of personal, family, kin, friendship, community and ethnic ties, the networks are strongest when they embrace links with the established populations of the countries of destination. Even when migration transformations take the form of crises, and where disruption of migrants' lives is acute, their networks enhance migrants' capacity to adapt to new circumstances.

Besides their own networks, and often interlocking with them, transnational networks of traffickers have played an important, if ambivalent role in sustaining migration as migration orders change. Trafficking is now a multi-million dollar business, involving the movement of possibly millions of people, and intricate systems of recruitment, transit and distribution as migrants are transported by plane, ship and truck from China, South Asia, Africa, the Middle East and Central America to Western Europe, North America, Japan, and other thriving East Asian countries (*International Herald Tribune* 28 June 1996). As a monetary measure of its scale, one observer has ventured that trafficking generated between $5 and $7 billion worldwide in 1993, equivalent to world trade in some commodities (Widgren 1995). Two clusters of developments account for this burgeoning. First, the trafficking industry has been greatly stimulated by the array of restrictive measures erected against migrants by the world's richer countries. As legitimate entry has increasingly been closed off, tighter state control of migration has thus had the perverse effect of driving migration flows underground and making them more difficult to regulate. Second, the transformation of the CIS region and eastern Europe into an arena for trafficking has been very significant in the proliferation and enlargement of the industry. The countries that have succeeded the Soviet Union act as holding stations for perhaps several hundred thousand migrants at any time. Many are bound for Western Europe, but the region is also transit territory for those en route to North America. The lack of agreement among CIS governments over the management of frontiers, lax border control, cheap flights from Asia and Africa to CIS territories, and opportunity once in the CIS region to prepare for further migration have made it more easily accessible than others and therefore attractive to those in the trafficking business (International Organisation for Migration 1997).

While some trafficking is controlled or managed from source to destination by transnational trafficking organizations, much is via chains of traffickers who may have little or no knowledge of earlier or later links in the chain (International Organisation for Migration 1997). The traffickers range in decreasing "migrant-friendliness" from relatives and acquaintances in the networks noted above, through casual smugglers and border guides, to sophisticated, transnational, criminal syndicates. Ambiguously exploitative while at the same time facilitative, traffickers supplement the role of migrants' networks in finding new niches as former ones disappear. They are also often the link between different migration orders, facilitating switches in destinations should conditions become unfavourable. Like migrants' networks, traffickers are agents of diasporization.

These intermediaries are rather more powerful and more far-reaching in their impact than their "official" counterparts in the international migration regime, on which the hopes of managing migration are somewhat unrealistically pinned. While that regime, loosely defined, has greatly elaborated in recent years – itself an indicator of profound change in the world migration order – the prospect of international management of migration in an orderly and principled way to diminish the likelihood of migration crises still seems remote. The principal agents shaping migration orders, and acute or cumulative changes in them, remain states and migrants themselves, with traffickers playing an increasingly important supplementary role, and the international organizations a rather less influential one.

Conclusion

In the first part of this chapter I outlined ideas about migration orders, transition and crisis that inform consideration of the migration upheavals I explore later in this book. In the second part I proposed a simple framework for considering the diverse forms of migration that have emerged in the latter part of this century, and the varying degrees of choice and compulsion such movement has involved. Individual migrants, migrant households and migrant communities experience these dynamics in complex ways, and the notions of migration biography and the accumulation of "migratory cultural capital" were introduced to account for this experience. Diaspora populations tend to have among the most complex migration histories, and to have accumulated the most substantial "migratory cultural capital". Part of that experience may be their very unmaking as previously scattered populations regroup, sometimes by choice and sometimes by force. The following chapters show how migration crises may result in the making, consolidation, or unmaking of transnational communities by investigating episodes in which people of migrant origin have been forcibly uprooted from the places they have made home.

THREE

Migration crises in Africa, the Middle East and Asia

In this and the following chapter, I examine ten migration crises drawn from six parts of the world. In this chapter, the cases drawn from Africa feature two well-known episodes of mass expulsion – that of the Ugandan Asians, a long established minority of migrant origin, and that of the Ghanaians in Nigeria, a migrant population of more recent origin. The cases drawn from the Middle East are a consequence of the Gulf crisis of 1990-91, and each features a mixture of long-established and more recent migrants. The cases taken from Asia present two contemporaneous episodes involving disputed citizenship; again they feature both long-established populations and more recent arrivals. For each case I outline the background to the presence of the migrant community and give an account of the circumstances of their mass exodus. I then reflect on the place of the mass exodus in the migration order and draw out some features for comparison with other cases – notably the migratory antecedents, and the issues of demography, socio-economic status and membership that bear on each migration upheaval.

Africa: expulsion of long-settled and recent migrants

The expulsion of Asians from Uganda

The expulsion of Asians from Uganda in the early 1970s was in many ways a seminal case. In August 1972 President Idi Amin decreed that non-citizens of Uganda's long-established Asian community should leave the country within 90 days. The population of South Asian descent in Uganda in the early 1970s was thought to number just over 74,000. About half held British passports; about one-third were classed as Ugandan citizens, but the status of about half of these had not been formally determined at the time of the expulsion; the remainder were citizens of India, Pakistan and Kenya. As a result of subsequent government directives, many of those with a claim to Ugandan citizenship were effectively rendered stateless in the wake of the expulsion order and left with the non-nationals in a chaotic mass exodus that dispersed Ugandan Asians to Britain, other parts of Europe and North America.

The South Asian presence in Uganda. The South Asian presence on the East African coast was long-standing, but, like Arab and Turkish contemporaries, early Asian inhabitants stayed near the coast to engage in Indian Ocean trade. Movement of South Asians into the interior – what is now Uganda, Kenya and Tanzania – was under way from the middle of the nineteenth century, but until about the second decade of this century this was a movement of individual entrepreneurs. Identifiable South Asian communities did not emerge until later, as the Asian population grew by natural increase and continued immigration, encouraged by the British colonial administration. The South Asian presence in East Africa was thus long-established and diverse in origin, including among its forebears pre-colonial traders and merchants, petty traders who pushed into East Africa's interior before the First World War, indentured labourers and artisans imported to build the railways, recruits into the colonial military and civil service, and cotton ginners and brokers who later diversified into other areas of commerce (Tinker 1977; Twaddle 1990). Newcomers utilized networks of family and friends to find work or opportunity.

Partly in response to African nationalist activity, Asian immigration was restricted during and after the Second World War. South Asian movement and economic activity in rural areas was also controlled and settlement became increasingly concentrated in larger urban centres (Twaddle 1990).

"Africanization" or "indigenization" thus had its roots in colonial strategies to contain African nationalist aspirations; after independence this reappeared in a different guise as African merchants increasingly came to oppose Asian traders (Mamdani 1993). Despite the restrictions on immigration, Uganda's Asian population increased twenty-fold between 1921 and 1969 (Tinker 1977; Twaddle 1990). Even so, it was still very much a minority. Based on the returns of a census in 1969, the community stood at about 74,000 and accounted for less than one per cent of the population of Uganda of just over ten million in 1971 – a rather smaller proportion than in neighbouring territories with a South Asian presence (Tinker 1977; Tribe 1975; UN 1979).

Talking about the South Asian "community" in this context is perhaps mistaken and "communities" is a better term, for the Asian minority was widely differentiated. In terms of ethnic or regional origin and of religious and social background the Asian population included, among others, Gujaratis, Punjabis, Goans and Sikhs, Hindus and Muslims. As already indicated, the Asians were also very diverse in terms of claims to citizenship. Nearly 36,600 held British passports (mostly giving them the anomalous status of British protected persons), nearly 9,000 were Indian citizens, 250 were Pakistani citizens, and some 1,750 were citizens of Kenya. The remaining 26,650 were classed as Ugandan citizens, but this total included 12,000 whose applications for citizenship were still being processed at the time of the expulsion (Tinker 1977). This diversity of citizenship was partly a result of the very mixed origins of the Asian population. It was also partly matter of strategy by Asian households concerned to secure economic rights (notably through trade licences that were restricted to Ugandan citizens), and anxious about changes to UK and East African immigration and nationality law in the later 1960s. In turn, multifarious citizenship and ambivalence about nationality was taken by the government and many Ugandans as a signal of lack of commitment to the country, and contributed to the atmosphere that precipitated the crisis of 1972.

The Asian population was also socio-economically diverse. Government surveys of the labour force in the late 1960s reveal the place of the Asian population in the economy. Along with Europeans, some Asians held senior management and professional positions, but they were particularly important in junior management, in technical positions and as artisans: they were doctors, accountants and school teachers, electricians and engine operators, and secretaries and book-keepers. Asians were heavily concentrated in manufacturing and commerce, mainly in the private sector, but with a strong showing in the public education and health sectors (Tribe 1975). Tribe concludes from the available data,

> that the Asian position in the high level manpower stock in the economy was very significant, that on average the level of income of the Asian community fell between that of Europeans and Africans, that they held a very privileged income position in relation to the African population, and that they owned most of the wholesale trading firms as well as a large segment of the retail trade sector, industry and other commerce (Tribe 1975: 157).

The pattern of Asian control of trade was partly attributable to the history of periodic antagonism towards them. There had been a tendency when threatened for them to withdraw from the more visible retail trade to the less prominent wholesale sector. Nonetheless Asians had long been prominent in cotton ginning – in 1925 100 of the colony's 125 ginneries were Asian-owned – and were thus centrally involved in the production of one of Uganda's main export crops. Another key sector, the sugar industry, was dominated by firms controlled by the Madhvani and Mehta families. Asians were also prominent in the construction industry as contractors and in the ownership of real estate (Tribe 1975).

While the Asian population comprised not just wealthy business families like the Madhvanis and the Mehtas, but a salariat in professional, technical, managerial and administrative positions, as well as small shopkeepers and artisans (Tinker 1977), it was the wealthy who presented the abiding image of the East African Asian. Mamdani (1993) puts this most forcefully, differentiating between on the one hand those in public or private salaried employment, such as teachers and professionals, as well as petty traders and small proprietors, and on the other the owners of large scale industrial, commercial and residential property. It was the latter minority that was seen as the archetype, and for whose activities the less well-off Asians were made to pay. African resentment, directed principally at Asian predominance in some sectors of trade and commerce, was generalized towards the Asian population as a whole, which was also accused of social exclusivity.

The mass expulsion of 1972. Idi Amin came to power early in 1971 after overthrowing the regime of Milton Obote with the support of the armed forces. Ironically, Asians were among the elements of Uganda's population that supported the coup, largely because of Obote's moves to curtail their economic activity and citizenship rights (Twaddle 1975). Uganda's political economy was already in a precarious state in the last years of the Obote regime. Nationalization and other dimensions of a "move to the left" had yielded neither political nor economic rewards. Heavy expenditure on capital projects of dubious value and on the military were making their mark on a poorly performing economy. These trends worsened after the Amin takeover. Government finance veered out of control as the demands of army and other groups had to be satisfied, and the deficit in the balance of payments mounted alarmingly. At the street level economic deterioration was seen in widespread food shortages in the towns and sharp and inexorable rises in food prices. As food prices escalated, dissatisfaction among urban groups and in the army grew acute (Tribe 1975; Twaddle 1975).

Harassment of a traditional scapegoat, resented particularly by sections of the urban African population, must have appeared a way out for the new regime whose support lay in an uneasy coalition of the increasingly rapacious army, African merchants, farmers and some in the public sector. There were precedents to be drawn upon from earlier periods of stress, such as the trade boycott of Asian-owned shops in the late 1950s. Resentment against the Asians had endured after independence, despite measures of Africanization.

Efforts in the later years of the Obote regime to transfer

control of trade to Africans through licensing and other state control had had only limited results. Many Asian traders continued to trade through Africans as fronts, and members of some Asian households took Ugandan nationality as a means of securing trade licences to get around indigenization measures. The result was that by 1972 the Asian community still dominated the commercial sector, increasing the frustration felt by aspirant African business people. At the same time the government measures increased the Asians' insecurity and drove them to courses of action which invited further African hostility (Tribe 1975). Legislative changes in both the UK and East Africa – seen in the British Commonwealth Immigration Acts of 1962 and 1968, the Ugandan Immigration Act of 1969, and measures in neighbouring Kenya – made the Asian community still more nervous. Businessmen reduced the amount of capital tied up in Uganda by reducing stocks and drawing on credit from banks to finance their concerns rather than on their own funds (Tribe 1975). Driven by a spiral of mistrust, perceptions of divided loyalty and a failure to integrate had some foundation.

Towards the end of 1971, Amin assembled representatives of the Asian community and castigated them for failing to integrate and for their dubious economic practices (Henckaerts 1995; Tribe 1975; Twaddle 1975): "It is particularly painful in that about 70 years have elapsed since the first Asians came to Uganda, but despite that length of time the Asian community has continued to live in a world of its own… " (speech of President Amin to a meeting of leaders of the Asian community in Uganda, 6 December 1971, reproduced in Henckaerts 1995: 210–15). After berating the Asians for not intermarrying with black Ugandans, and for abuses over exchange controls, import and export scams, taxation and other malpractices, Amin articulated the grievances of African traders:

It is well known that you are generally importers, wholesalers and retailers at the same time. Many of you have taken advantage of this position to frustrate aspiring African businessmen in every possible way. Again, many of you practice discrimination against African traders, in that you supply your fellow Asians with goods at lower prices than those at which you supply your African traders (ibid.).

He then took up the issue of diverse citizenship, even within households, and the lack of loyalty to the nation-state it implied:

> For example, whereas a head of the family may be a British passport holder, his wife may turn out to be an Indian or Pakistani citizen, whilst their children might be citizens of either Kenya, Uganda, Tanzania. Sometimes two brothers are registered as different citizens. This clearly shows that many of you have no confidence at all in Uganda or any of the other countries, for that matter. I will not hesitate to say that you are gambling with one of the matters which any government takes most seriously, and that is citizenship (ibid.).

Less than a year after this speech, as the need became all the pressing to divert popular attention from mounting economic problems, Amin decreed the expulsion of Asians in August 1972. The expulsion had the added benefit of providing loot with which Amin could reward and appease supporters in the army, who were the chief beneficiaries of the auctioning of Asian assets (Twaddle 1975).

The expulsion order was initially aimed at those Asians who were not citizens of Uganda, and various exemptions (particularly of professionals) meant that it was traders and artisans who were targeted. But later Amin ordered that all Asians should leave, regardless of their citizenship claims. Confusingly, this order was later rescinded, but by then a general exodus was under way (Mamdani 1973; Read 1975).

Whether it was the intention or not, the outpouring of often contradictory decrees compounded the insecurity among Asians fostered by official and popular harassment and intimidation. As Mamdani (1973: 20) recalled, "Every day saw the announcement of another formality to be undergone, a new form to be filled in, one more law to be observed." Asians with a claim to citizenship were required to verify their claims, but when they did so many found their documents declared invalid.

Households found some members declared stateless, while others were deemed Ugandans – but the latter would then be deprived of citizenship.

The Asian exodus was small-scale at first, many hoping that more exemptions would be made or that the deadline would be extended. Many of those leaving early on were robbed on the way to the airport by rank and file soldiers, who realized, rightly, that it would be the higher ranking officers and officials who would be the beneficiaries in the officially sanctioned carve-up of Asian assets later on. Realizing perhaps that this looting was deterring departure, the government gave airport buses armed police escorts. As the deadline drew nearer, the exodus gathered momentum, encouraged by daily reminders of the deadline on radio and television (Mamdani 1973).

Each family was limited to taking just £50 worth of assets out of the country. This led to ingenious ways of transferring assets before departure. Some secured Kenyan number plates for their cars so that they could be driven out of the country; others bought air tickets to go around the world 10 or 20 times in the hope of getting refunds once outside Uganda. These ruses, which helped to reinforce prejudice against them, were rapidly clamped down upon by the government (Mamdani 1973).

A series of retrospective decrees laid a dubious legal basis for the expropriation and disposal of Asian property and other assets following their departure. Departing Asians were required to declare their assets and liabilities and to nominate an agent to oversee their property until it was disposed of to a Ugandan citizen, with the approval of what became the Departed Asians' Property Custodian Board. Otherwise property was vested in the state, and administered by the Custodian Board, which could allocate assets to Ugandan citizens, but was also supposedly responsible for compensating their erstwhile Asian owners (Read 1975).

Upwards of 50,000 Asians left Uganda between the announcement of the expulsion in August and the November deadline, leaving just a small Asian population behind. There is a noticeable discrepancy between the total Ugandan Asian population recorded in the late 1960s (74,000), the numbers reported to have left Uganda after the expulsion order in 1972 (about 50,000), and the numbers remaining (a few thousand). The 20,000 or so people unaccounted for presumably left during the preceding regime of Milton Obote, as a result of that regime's anti-Asian measures and antipathy towards Asians growing in the region generally (Tandon 1984; Tinker 1977; Twaddle 1975).

The majority of the British passport holders in the 1972 exodus, about 28,600, were granted entry into the UK. An unknown number, perhaps of the order of 10,000, made for India and Pakistan. Many of those made stateless or with undetermined nationality were resettled in Europe and North America. After reception in camps in various parts of Europe, some 6,000 people in this position were resettled in Belgium, the Netherlands, Denmark, Norway, Sweden, Austria and Switzerland. Canada accommodated around 6,000 people, including some British passport holders, and the US about 1,500. Of all the episodes examined in this book, the mass expulsion of Ugandan Asians resulted in the most widespread dispersal.

Expulsion and the migration order. Looked at in long term and wider perspective, the expulsion was perhaps not the aberration it has been commonly portrayed (Mamdani 1993). As the above account has shown, prior to the Second World War, South Asian immigration was largely free and self-initiated, with the notable exception of indentured labourers, most of whom did not stay after the completion of the railways. The migration order established during the colonial period changed during and after the Second World War, when new South Asian immigration diminished as African nationalism gathered momentum. The regional context for the expulsion of Asians from Uganda was growing pressure against the Asian population as African nationalism was cast as indigenization or Africanization in Kenya, Tanzania and Uganda (Tinker 1977). Indigenization was embraced by a rising class of Africans who sought more commanding positions in the state and economy – some of which positions were held by Asians. Anticipatory or proactive movement of Asians from the region was under way well before Amin's decree: their exodus from Uganda was part of a wider tide against the East African Asian minority population, which

71

included a less disorderly exodus from Kenya – and indeed from Uganda during the preceding regime of Milton Obote. In some ways, then, Amin's expulsion can be seen as a culmination of long-term and wider trends, taking the acute form of the upheaval that it did because of particularly severe strains in Uganda's political economy and the personality of Amin.

Among the proximate factors leading to the mass exodus were the government's imperative to divert popular attention from the hardship wrought by severe economic difficulties. Monopoly of sectors of commerce against the interests of Africans, and wrecking the economy by exporting capital were among the charges levelled against the Asian population. These charges held some truth. Indeed, the behaviour of many East African Asians generated a self-fulfilling prophecy (Tinker 1977), for as they saw pressure rising inexorably against them, those that could did move their capital to safe havens, helping to invite the accusations of capital flight levelled at the Asian population at large. This generalization of blame from particular sections of the population to the whole of it is a feature of other expulsions considered here. Economic misdemeanours were coupled with accusations of failure to integrate, which again had some foundation in social exclusiveness and in the very ambivalent attitude of Asians to citizenship.

The mass expulsion of Ghanaians from Nigeria

Little more than a decade after the expulsion from Uganda, a much larger population of more recent migrants suffered expulsion in West Africa. In the 1970s, Nigeria's booming economy, underwritten by large revenues from oil, attracted large numbers of migrants from other West African countries. The majority in this largely undocumented and unregulated migration were Ghanaians who left their country as it lurched towards economic collapse; others came from Mali, Niger and Chad, seeking escape from drought, famine and poverty in the Sahel. In the early 1980s, economic contraction in the wake of a slump in world oil prices focused attention on the migrants' presence, which, as in Uganda, provided the Nigerian government with a scapegoat to divert popular attention from the country's worsening circumstances. Early in 1983, the government announced that all illegal immigrants should quit Nigeria. Estimates vary, but up to two million people are thought to have been forced to leave, of whom about half were Ghanaians. Against the background of further economic decline, another expulsion was carried out in 1985 involving perhaps 250,000 people, largely those who had escaped expulsion in 1983 or who had returned since.

Ghanaian migration to Nigeria. In long term perspective, the mass expulsion of the early 1980s marks one of many shifts in the long history of migration in West Africa. From about the turn of the century, the development of cocoa farms and gold mines in the south of the Gold Coast (as it was known then) attracted migrants from what became a labour reserve in the Northern Territories of the British colony and from what was French Upper Volta (Van Hear 1982). As the Gold Coast prospered relatively to other West African colonies, migrant labourers and traders arrived from further afield, including Nigeria. Migrants continued to arrive after independence in 1957, attracted by Ghana's continuing relative affluence. Although principally a country of immigration during this period, there was substantial emigration of Ghanaian traders, fishermen and others to other parts of West Africa, including Nigeria, Liberia and Sierra Leone.

A turnaround occurred from the late 1960s as economic decline took hold in Ghana. Ironically and prophetically this was marked by the expulsion of migrants, including many Nigerians, from Ghana in 1969. Shortly after election to power in that year, Dr K. A. Busia introduced the Aliens' Compliance Order which directed all migrants to regularize their presence in the country within two weeks or leave. The order was made against the background of persistent economic and social malaise, seen in a balance of payments deficit, growing unemployment, the prevalence of smuggling and widespread crime. Aliens were held to have exacerbated all this through their remittances, by holding jobs that Ghanaians could do and by their participation in smuggling and other misdemeanours. Foreigners mainly from Nigeria, Togo, Upper Volta and Niger were rounded up and bussed to the border, often without being able to gather together belongings or to contact relatives. Official action was compounded by intimidation, harassment and extortion by both officials and ordinary citizens (Adomako-Sarfoh 1974; Peil 1971; Van Hear 1982).

Estimates of the numbers leaving between the Compliance Order and mid-1970 vary between 155,000 and 213,000. The action was initially welcomed by the Ghanaian population at large, but very soon it became apparent that the mass departure was wreaking economic damage. Farmers in particular suffered from acute shortages of labour and petitioned the government to exempt farm workers from the order. The government obliged by exempting farm and mine workers in January 1970, but by then many had already left. Despite the recruitment of Ghanaians, there was still a substantial shortfall in farm labour supply, upon which both Ghanaian and foreign farm workers were subsequently able to capitalize. Trade was the other major sector to feel the effects of the mass departure. This was most visible in the abandonment of market stalls in the main towns. Ghanaian traders rapidly stepped into the void created, but were also not slow to take advantage of the disruption, with the result that prices increased rapidly. As enforcement of the Compliance Order was relaxed from mid-1970, foreigners began to drift back. Judging by Ghana's subsequent performance – austerity measures continued and a large devaluation precipitated a coup in January 1972 – few economic benefits were derived from this episode. The enduring effect was to sour relations with neighbours and to upset the tacit understanding among them which derived from a long tradition of accommodating strangers and migrants. This was a rupture that was later to rebound on Ghana (Adomako-Sarfoh 1974; Brydon 1985; Peil 1971; Van Hear 1982).

As economic decline continued in the 1970s, Ghana increasingly became a country of emigration, primarily to Nigeria, but also to Côte d'Ivoire. Emigration of Ghanaians on a large scale was well under way by the mid-1970s (Peil 1995; Swindell 1990; Van Hear 1992). Two million men and women, mainly from southern Ghana, may have gone abroad between 1974 and 1981 (Rimmer 1993). Many of those leaving were highly educated and skilled.

The exodus was precipitated by loss of faith in Ghana's future as successive military and civilian regimes mismanaged the economy and society. Corruption and inflation reached intolerable proportions as Ghana's assets were squandered. Real wages declined sharply, so that popular corruption, known as *kalabule*, was for many the only means of survival. Emigration was the other means. The brief interregnum of Flight Lieutenant Jerry Rawlings in 1979 did not stop the rot, but did incur the ire of Nigeria which disrupted credit for the supply of oil. When Rawlings returned to power in December 1981, after a short period of civilian rule, Ghana was close to its economic and social nadir.

Nigeria meanwhile was enjoying economic prosperity deriving from its large oil earnings as oil prices increased sharply in the first half of the 1970s. There followed a period of unprecedented public and private sector expansion seen in huge capital spending by the government and a consumer boom. Large scale immigration from Nigeria's neighbours, particularly from declining Ghana, was another very visible outcome of the boom.

Migration was given official sanction by a protocol of the ECOWAS treaty which in 1975 established the 16-member Economic Community of West African States. One of the objectives of the regional organization was to facilitate freedom of movement, residence and employment within the community (Brown 1989; Okolo 1984; Onwuka 1982). The 1979 Protocol to the treaty covering freedom of movement of persons, residence and establishment, ratified in 1980, paved the way for realizing this objective by allowing citizens of member states to enter other member states without visas and to stay for up to 90 days. Working was technically not allowed, but many migrants found employment and overstayed the 90-day period. During the boom this was tolerated by the Nigerian authorities.

Most of the Ghanaian migrants were unskilled or semi-skilled workers employed in construction, in the ports, in transport as drivers, in food distribution and in the service sector. Many others were petty traders. The migrant population also included others who were unemployed, casual street vendors, hustlers, prostitutes and criminals. But there was also a significant minority of professionals, administrative and managerial staff, and technicians – among them business people, university lecturers, engineers, surveyors, medical doctors and pharmacists, teachers, laboratory technicians, nurses and other skilled workers (Yeboah 1987).

Few migrant Ghanaians wished to settle permanently in Nigeria and spells in Nigeria were usually short, although they might be repeated. Contemporary press reports and studies based on small samples of migrants in Nigeria (Brydon 1985; Yeboah 1987) suggest that men in their twenties and thirties predominated among the Ghanaian migrant population; their families, if they had them, were left in Ghana. There were significant numbers of women migrants nevertheless. While some had children with them, this was essentially a migration of single men and women rather than of households.

The mass expulsion of 1983. Towards the end of the 1970s the basis for Nigeria's boom dissipated as a world glut of oil developed, the revolution in Iran giving only temporary respite to world oil market. As the military gave way to civilian rule with the election of Shehu Shagari as president in 1979, Nigerian spending continued to outstrip revenue until austerity budgets were introduced in 1981 and 1982 as oil prices slumped further. The austerity measures led to large scale lay-offs of workers and widespread unemployment. Economic deterioration generated increasing social distress and political strain, making Shagari's re-election prospects in 1983 look bleak. A populist diversion was needed. The government began to claim that immigrants were taking jobs to the disadvantage of Nigerians, and to blame them for heavy involvement in crime.

In mid-January 1983 the government announced that all aliens without the necessary papers should leave Nigeria by the end of that month. In the confused mass exodus that followed, most left in a period of about two weeks, under conditions of great distress. Many were harassed and abused and lost assets and belongings or had to sell them cheap. An extension of the deadline for leaving to mid-February for skilled workers, and exemptions from the decree for teachers and other professionals, did little to alleviate the chaos and suffering as up to 2 million foreigners tried to depart. For Ghanaians attempting to leave by land through Benin and Togo, the journey was made all the more difficult by intermittent border closures. Others trying to leave by sea encountered hazardous and sometimes fatal voyages. There was considerable, though unquantified loss of life during the chaotic departure (Adepoju 1984; Brydon 1985; Gravil 1985; Swindell 1990; Van Hear 1983).

Estimates of the numbers leaving in 1983 vary considerably. A common estimate is a total of 2 million, but some sources cite this as the total illegal alien population in Nigeria at the time of the expulsion rather than the number that left. Nigerian press sources suggested that by mid-February, 700,000 Ghanaians, 180,000 people from Niger, 150,000 Chadians, 120,000 Cameroonians, 5,000 Togolese and 5,000 Beninois had left (Gravil 1985). Brydon (1985) cites estimates of between 900,000 and 1.2 million Ghanaian arrivals in their homeland according to a UN General Assembly report.

That many avoided expulsion or returned to Nigeria quite soon after is evident from further expulsions in subsequent years. The military regime which took over late in 1983 continued the policy against aliens instigated by its civilian predecessor. Round-ups and deportation of illegal migrants continued on a small scale in 1984. Continuing economic deterioration was again the background to the expulsions. Stringent austerity measures affecting both the public and private sectors led to more plant closures, redundancies and unemployment. Action against foreigners once again provided a diversion from the disruption wrought by the dire economic situation.

In mid-April 1985 the government again announced that migrants without valid papers should regularize their status or leave the country within 25 days (Adepoju 1986; Van Hear 1985). The Ministry of Internal Affairs estimated that about 700,000 migrants were affected by the new order: again about half of these were Ghanaians and the remainder from drought-affected countries of the Sahel. In the event between 200,000 and 250,000 migrants were expelled, including 100,000 Ghanaians and some 50,000 from Niger. This means that either the number of illegals estimated by the government was an exaggeration or several hundred thousand managed to avoid apprehension. While illicit migration to Nigeria continued, the expulsions of 1983–85 marked another turning point in the migration history of this part of West Africa. As will be shown below, in Chapter 6, diasporization accelerated as Ghanaian migrants began to seek other destinations in preference to Nigeria, whose economic star continued to wane in the later 1980s.

Expulsion and the migration order. The mass expulsions of 1983–85 profoundly disrupted the migration order of West Africa, and marked a subsequent turnaround in that order. While there were long-established migrations between Ghana, Nigeria and other parts of West Africa, substantial Ghanaian labour migration to Nigeria was of relatively recent origin, dating from the mid-1970s as economic and political conditions deteriorated in Ghana and as economic opportunities, fired by oil earnings, concomitantly rose in Nigeria. The decline of Ghana's economy and the inability of many Ghanaians to make ends meet was the driving force behind the emigration. Nigeria's migration regime was lax, allowing easy entry for migrants seeking to take advantage of the country's boom. The mass expulsions of 1983 and 1985 had precedents in the expulsion of Nigerians and others from Ghana in 1969; these upheavals in the migration order reflect pendulum-like shifts in the relative fortunes of Ghana and Nigeria as poles of attraction for migrants.

Like the Ugandan Asians and others investigated in this book, the Ghanaian migrants were diverse in socio-economic status; indeed their diversity is obscured by the application of the term "migrant worker" to describe them. While most of the Ghanaians were unskilled or semi-skilled workers, they also included petty traders, who might be more appropriately termed "migrant entrepreneurs". There was a significant minority of professionals, particularly teachers, but also administrative staff, managers and technicians. As the Nigerian economy declined, the immigrant labour force increasingly became the butt of Nigerian workers' resentment, fanned by a government anxious to divert blame for the country's ills. More widely, immigrants were blamed for a rise in crime as economic deterioration fed social disintegration.

The migrants were large in absolute numbers, but relatively small in proportion to the host population: the 2 million West African migrants, of whom Ghanaians accounted for about half, added just over 2 per cent to the current Nigerian population estimated at 93.6 million (World Bank 1985). This proportion does not rise significantly even if the subsequent substantial downward revision of Nigeria's population estimate is taken into account (World Bank 1993). Other than worries about the impact of immigrants on the labour market, demographic concerns were not significant in bringing about the migration crisis of 1983, unlike some of the other cases considered below.

Disputed nationality or citizenship was not a significant feature of the Ghanaians and other West Africans obliged to leave Nigeria, as it was in Uganda. Membership questions nevertheless still had a bearing in this episode. The Nigerian expulsion challenged notions of regional membership or citizenship developing within the Economic Community of West African States whose treaty set out the notion of "Community citizens", entitled eventually to freedom of movement, residence and employment within the Community. Progress towards this goal was stymied by the soured relations among West African neighbours engendered by the expulsion.

The expulsion of migrants from Nigeria was related more to a contraction in the economy and the labour market generally than to enduring changes in the structure of the labour market; in terms of the framework suggested in Chapter 2, it derived from the proximate rather than the structural domain. Challenge to national integrity – real or imagined – was more a feature of the Ugandan case where the loyalty of Asians was called into question, than in the Nigerian case, where there were nevertheless concerns surrounding crime attributed to migrants and the alarming "porosity" of borders. As in the Uganda case, the diversion of popular attention from acute economic and political difficulties was a strong imperative for the ruling regime. An additional proximate factor was the Nigerian government's electoral concerns, which figured significantly in generating the migration crisis.

The Middle East: fall-out of the Gulf crisis

Oil wealth was again the background to migration upheaval in the Middle East in the early 1990s. Up to 5 million people were uprooted in the wake of the Gulf crisis of 1990-91, one of the largest mass displacements in recent times, and perhaps the most far-reaching since the Second World War in terms of the number of countries affected. The crisis recast the complex patterns of migration and displacement in a region long used to population upheaval. Many forms of forced migration were generated. As well as refugees fleeing their homelands, large numbers of migrant workers and professionals were expelled or obliged to leave their countries of residence; others were unable to return to the countries they habitually lived in; large numbers of people were internally displaced; and smaller though substantial numbers were rendered stateless, or made the transition from prisoners-of-war to refugees (Van Hear 1993). This section focuses on the migrants obliged to move in the course of the Gulf crisis.

It is thought that the oil boom of the 1970s had attracted more than 5 million foreign workers to the oil-producing countries of the Middle East by the mid-1980s. Estimates vary greatly, but perhaps half of these expatriates were drawn from other Arab countries – principally they were Egyptians, other North Africans, Yemenis, Jordanians and displaced Palestinians. Most of the remainder were from South and Southeast Asia. Expatriate workers in Iraq and Kuwait may have accounted for more than one-third of the total in the region (Amjad 1989; Birks, Seccombe & Sinclair 1988; Owen 1985).

This pattern of migration was profoundly disrupted by the mass exodus following the invasion of Kuwait by Iraq on 2 August 1990. By the end of 1990 perhaps 2 million foreign nationals had left their countries of residence and work as tensions rose in the region. Further outflows of foreign nationals occurred in 1991–92, for the most part after the war itself (Van Hear 1993). The mass displacement involved several hundred thousand nationals of Egypt, Yemen and Jordan, more than 100,000 nationals of India and Pakistan, and more than 10,000 nationals of at least nine other Middle Eastern and Asian countries. The following concentrates on two of the largest migrant communities uprooted in the course of the Gulf crisis – the Palestinians in Kuwait and the Yemenis in Saudi Arabia, whose fate was shaped by what was seen as the pro-Iraqi stance of their leaderships.

The mass exodus of Palestinians from Kuwait

Palestinians in Kuwait before August 1990 were thought to have numbered up to 400,000. In the course of Gulf crisis and its aftermath this population was reduced to less than one-tenth as the Iraqi invasion, impending war, persecution, harassment and changes to residence requirements forced or induced successive waves of Palestinians to leave the emirate for Jordan, the Occupied Territories and other destinations in the Middle East and beyond. Palestinians and Jordanians were also obliged to leave Saudi Arabia, the United Arab Emirates and other states in a partial in-gathering of the diaspora in the region.

The Palestinian population in Kuwait. The Palestinian presence in Kuwait dated from the mass uprooting in the Mandate of Palestine in 1948–49. Their arrival roughly coincided with the inception of Kuwait's oil industry. The 1967 war and subsequent upheavals added to this expatriate population which by the mass exodus of 1990–92 was thus of four decades' standing (Brand 1988; Ghabra 1987; Lesch 1991; Van Hear 1995).

Many in the Palestinian community had lived in the emirate all their lives, and formed a resident migrant community rather than a population of migrant workers. Surveys of those later forced to leave showed that the majority had been in Kuwait (or other Gulf states) for more than 10 years, and more than a quarter had lived there for more than 30 years (Van Hear 1995). Most had brought up their families abroad. Estimates by the International Labour Organisation suggest that the ratio of economically active persons to dependants was about one to four before the crisis (International Labour Office 1991), again indicating a long-settled community.

While some of the Palestinian community had moved straight to Kuwait after the upheaval of 1948, most came from the Israeli-occupied West Bank; others had come to the emirate via Jordan after the 1967 war. Most of the community were therefore Palestinian Jordanians or Jordanians of Palestinian origin, many deriving their rights to Jordanian residence or citizenship from Jordan's claims on the West Bank until 1988. However a sizeable minority were of Gazan origin and held Egyptian travel documents, giving them an even more problematic status. Despite the Palestinians' long residence in Kuwait and their substantial economic contribution, their economic, civil and political rights in the emirate, as in other Gulf states, were much restricted; entitlements such as access to education or health services were greatly circumscribed, and often linked to employment status (Brand 1988; Nour 1993; Peretz 1993). In terms of citizenship and residence status and of social and economic rights, the Palestinians in Kuwait therefore constituted a semi-permanent community of "denizens" in the sense introduced in Chapter 1.

The population has typically been characterized as a wealthy class of middlemen and professionals. Many in the Palestinian community indeed conformed to the profile of a "middleman" or "auxiliary" minority, as outlined in Chapter 2, akin perhaps to some communities of South Asians abroad or of the overseas Chinese. They certainly did include many who ran businesses, although there were constraints on their commercial activities. Kuwaiti law meant that they had to have a Kuwaiti majority partner or a *kafeel* to run businesses; *kafeel* translates broadly as guarantor, but can carry the implication of dependence and even servitude. As well as somewhat dependent business people, the Palestinian community included professionals, technicians, managers and administrators in Kuwait, but it also included less well-off labourers, drivers, artisans and other semi-skilled workers in the emirate. Up to one-third of the Palestinian population in Kuwait may have fallen into the latter category. The characterization of the expatriate Palestinians as a wealthy community thus obscures diversity of wealth and social status among them. All the same, even those who had not accumulated wealth on any substantial scale had led relatively comfortable lives in Kuwait and other Gulf states, a way of life profoundly disrupted by the invasion of Kuwait by Iraq and by the extraordinarily ill-advised support of the Palestinian Liberation Organisation for Saddam Hussein's adventure.

The mass exodus of 1990–92. There were several waves of Palestinian displacement in the course of the Gulf crisis and its aftermath. First, in the wake of the invasion of Kuwait by Iraq in August 1990, large numbers of Palestinians, along with hundreds of thousands of other Arab and Asian workers, fled the chaos of the Iraqi occupation and for fear of impending war. Around 200,000 – perhaps half the pre-August 1990 population – may have left during this period, the largest wave of displacement. Leaving behind them property, assets and livelihoods that had made for relative prosperity, the majority travelled overland in convoys of cars through Iraq to Jordan in a chaotic mass departure.

A second wave of Palestinians left after the defeat and ejection from Kuwait of the Iraqi forces. People fled as a result of persecution by Kuwaiti militia groups avenging alleged collaboration with the Iraqis during the occupation. Even though some Palestinians had helped the Kuwaiti resistance, the community as a whole was treated as guilty by association with the pro-Iraqi stance of the PLO – and indeed of much of the Palestinian population outside Kuwait. Detention, torture and killings continued after the restoration of the al-Sabah regime in Kuwait, despite the critical attention of human rights groups (see for example, Lawyers Committee for Human Rights 1992, 1993). Internationally criticized trials of alleged collaborators increased the insecurity of Jordanians, Palestinians and other foreign nationals still in the emirate and induced many to leave.

Human rights abuses gradually diminished, but Palestinians continued to leave because of harassment and insecurity fostered by the Kuwaiti authorities as part of the restored regime's attempts to reduce the emirate's dependence on foreigners. Palestinian teachers and others were unable to resume jobs held before the occupation; as welfare assistance was not available to non-Kuwaitis, day-to-day survival became increasingly difficult. Access to education for Palestinian children was curtailed, partly as a result of the loss of subsidies formerly received through the PLO. Denial of access to employment, education or health services precipitated further out-movement (Graham-Brown 1994; Van Hear 1993).

Another wave of displacement gathered momentum with the enforcement of new residence regulations in Kuwait. Deadlines for the renewal of residence permits for non-nationals in Kuwait after the al-Sabah restoration were extended a number of times in late 1991 and early 1992. From August 1992, however, the documentation required for residence was enforced more rigorously. The authorities demanded sponsorship by a Kuwait national and Palestinians had to prove that they had not collaborated with the Iraqis. Those without residence permits were subject to substantial fines. Application of these measures, which was much left to the discretion of officials, a continuing hostile social and political atmosphere, and the depletion of community solidarity all reinforced insecurity among the Palestinians and encouraged more to leave, so that towards the end of 1992 it was estimated that perhaps only 30,000 remained. The majority of these were Palestinians of Gazan origin who held Egyptian travel documents and who had nowhere to go (Graham-Brown 1994).

The mass departure of Palestinians and others from Kuwait after the restoration of the al-Sabah regime was tantamount to an expulsion, since flight was first induced by harassment and torture, or fear of it, and later on by denial of access to work, education and health care and the enforcement of new residence rules. Interviews I conducted with returnees to Jordan in 1993 reflected this range of compelling inducements to leave. One man in his late 30s, born in Nablus on the West Bank but who had lived in Kuwait almost all his life, described how his wife had "escaped into the desert and disappeared" after the invasion. One of his sons was killed when Kuwaiti forces burned down his house. He claimed his hand was disfigured by torture, after which he fled with another son to Jordan. Others described how there was "no work, no bread, no life", after the invasion, a miserable state of affairs that continued after the al-Sabah restoration. For still others it was fines imposed for not holding residence permits that were impossible to obtain, the absence of schooling for children, and the generally tense and oppressive atmosphere that precipitated the decision to flee. Many of those who had wished to stay in Kuwait after the al-Sabah restoration appear to have reached the conclusion that a reasonable life was no longer possible there. The Kuwaiti authorities' objective appeared to be to erode the Palestinian population resident in the emirate to about one-tenth of its former size, in line with their stated intention drastically to reduce Kuwait's foreign population (Graham-Brown 1994; Van Hear 1993).

Most of the Palestinians holding Jordanian passports went to Jordan, which may have received 360,000 such people in all. Some of these – perhaps 30,000–40,000 – moved on to the Israeli-occupied West Bank. However there were substantial numbers of Palestinians long-settled in Kuwait who could not make claims on these destinations for refuge. They may have numbered 60,000 and included those from the Gaza strip with Egyptian travel documents, but whom, for the most part, the Egyptian authorities would not allow to enter; they also included many whose documents had expired. Of those with Egyptian travel documents who attempted to go to Egypt, few succeeded and many were stranded at borders or in airports for long periods. Some people of Gazan origin and some of those without documentation moved to Iraq, Sudan or Yemen. Some with wealth and connections managed to emigrate to the US, Canada, Europe, Latin America and Australia. Later chapters detail further this reluctant homecoming to Jordan and the enhancement of the Palestinian diaspora resulting from the uprooting of 1990–92.

Mass exodus and the migration order. The exodus of 1990–92 was another episode in a long and disturbing tradition of Palestinian uprooting. The Palestinian community in Kuwait formed after the uprooting of 1948–49, with later cohorts arriving after subsequent upheavals in the tortuous history of the Palestinians over the last half century. While reactive, forced migration was the persistent and dominant theme in this population's migration history, in a sense, mass expulsion from Palestine in the late 1940s and after transmuted into a proactive economic migration to Kuwait and other Gulf states, before their compulsory departure in 1990–92. Forced movement associated with the emergence of Israel combined with large regional economic disparities associated with oil wealth to generate this migratory order.

While more homogenous than the Ugandan Asians in terms of place of origin, since most came from the West Bank, the Palestinian population in Kuwait, as elsewhere, was diverse in terms of nationality status (Van Hear 1995). Most Palestinians there held Jordanian nationality by virtue of having been residents of the West Bank; others had limited rights of residence in Jordan, some held Lebanese or Syrian papers, some had Egyptian travel documents, but with no right of abode in Egypt, and still others had no documents at all. As in the Ugandan Asian case, this diverse and ambivalent nationality status contributed to doubts about Palestinian loyalty, in turn prompting the pogroms and challenges to residence precipitating the later waves of Palestinian exodus from Kuwait. However it was the right of residence rather than citizenship that was challenged in this episode, whatever moral claims Palestinians may have had in terms of their length of stay in Kuwait and their contribution to its economy.

Demographic balance was also of considerable concern in Kuwait around the time of the Gulf crisis. Around 1990, the roughly 400,000-strong Palestinian community was equivalent to about two-thirds of the population of Kuwaiti citizens – about 600,000; other non-nationals made for a total population of about 2 million. Concern at the size of the foreign population in the emirate was often expressed by the authorities; in the case of the Palestinian community there was also a high proportion of dependants. The reduction in the Palestinian population in the course of the Gulf crisis to about one-tenth of its previous size was therefore seen by the Kuwaiti regime as a useful outcome (Russell & al-Ramadhan 1994; Van Hear 1995).

The mass exodus of Yemenis from Saudi Arabia
While international attention was focused on the plight of migrants moving from Iraq and Kuwait and their evacuation to their countries of origin, the Gulf crisis was generating another, largely unnoticed mass exodus from Saudi Arabia. From mid-

August 1990, deepening tension between the two countries arising from what the Saudis saw as the Yemen government's support for Iraq drove increasing numbers of Yemenis to leave Saudi Arabia. The Saudi authorities began to implement far-reaching changes to the rules governing work and residence for the large Yemeni community in the kingdom. The changes, planned for some time but not implemented, removed many of the exemptions enjoyed by Yemeni migrants, and put more pressure on them to leave.

Arbitrary arrest, detention, torture and widespread harassment induced many more Yemenis to depart, adding weight to the view that the exodus was more of a mass expulsion than a simple deportation of illegal immigrants. By the end of 1990, 800,000 Yemeni expatriates may have returned to Yemen, mainly from Saudi Arabia, but also from Kuwait and other states of the region. The mass repatriation put great pressure on the new nation-state formed just months before from the unification of former North and South Yemen.

Yemeni migration to Saudi Arabia. In recent years labour has been one of Yemen's principal exports, mainly to the booming economies of oil-rich neighbours. Substantial emigration, principally to Saudi Arabia, dated from the oil boom starting in the 1970s. Greatly increased revenues, particularly after the oil price rises of 1973–74, prompted the launch of large scale development projects in the kingdom, whose demand for labour could only be satisfied by migrants. Emigration from Yemen was driven by its underdeveloped economy, marked by poor infrastructure and limited employment opportunities outside agriculture, and exacerbated by intermittent civil war and conflict. By the mid-1970s perhaps one-third of the male labour force was employed abroad, not least because rural emigrants could earn six or seven times in Saudi Arabia what they could at home (Findlay 1994).

Estimates vary, but by the 1980s there were perhaps 1.5 million Yemenis living and working in other parts of the Middle East, mainly in Saudi Arabia and to a lesser extent in Kuwait (see Birks Sinclair and Associates 1990 and Findlay 1987b on the difficulties of estimating the Yemeni population abroad). The collapse of oil prices in the mid-1980s did not result in a large scale repatriation of migrants as anticipated, but rather a fall in migrants' earnings. Despite declining from the mid-1980s, workers' remittances nevertheless contributed a large proportion of the foreign earnings of both the Yemen Arab Republic ("North Yemen") and the People's Democratic Republic of Yemen ("South Yemen") until the crisis of 1990, which occurred just months after the two long antagonistic states were unified to form the Republic of Yemen.

The Yemeni population abroad comprised both short term migrants and long-established expatriates. It included migrant workers who might have been away intermittently for five years or more. It also included what should be regarded as more or less settled migrant communities of foreign residents, rather than migrant workers. Many of these had been in Saudi Arabia for decades, and their children had been born and brought up abroad. These long-established communities were of two types: a middleman minority of traders, merchants and those engaged in services, and a lumpen population who made a living in the informal sector. Their emergence in part reflected changes in the Saudi economy as demand for wage labour contracted and many Yemenis set up their own businesses in the service sector (Birks Sinclair and Associates 1990; Findlay 1987b). Some of the longer term residents were also refugees from Yemen's civil wars.

According to a report on the Yemeni expatriates by the Yemen government (Republic of Yemen 1991), three-fifths of those surveyed had been abroad for more than 10 years. That there was a large proportion of long stayers was borne out by respondents interviewed by the author in 1993: nearly four-fifths had been abroad for more than 10 years and approaching half for more than 20 years; one-fifth of respondents had been born abroad (Van Hear 1994). The length of stay abroad was reflected in the numbers of dependents left in Yemen or accompanying migrants abroad. This proportion varied, reflecting differing patterns of long and short-term migration; for example, a greater proportion of migrants from the coastal region of Yemen known as the Tihama had been living abroad with their families on a long-term basis, while many of those from the Highlands of the interior migrated for shorter periods. The age profile of the returnees surveyed also suggests long stays abroad, particularly for migrants from the Tihama region, where 30 per cent of returnee respondents were aged 45 and over (Republic of Yemen 1991) – again in contrast with the pattern of migration of single young men usual elsewhere.

Migration drew Yemenis from rural backgrounds into a range of urban wage labour, skilled work, business and services. According to the government survey mentioned above, the greatest proportion of respondents, about one-fifth, were general labourers, followed by drivers who accounted for just over 10 per cent of the total (Republic of Yemen 1991). Construction-related work featured strongly, building labourers and artisans comprising 15 per cent of employment abroad. Traders and merchants accounted for a little less than this proportion of employment, and the service sector figured substantially. There were also significant numbers of office workers, three times the proportion in this category before migration. Interviews by the author in 1993 broadly confirmed this sectoral distribution, but also underlined the informal nature of much of the employment, particularly among unskilled labourers, typified by those who stated their job was "carrying things" for supermarket shoppers, in the *suqs* or in the street. In addition to waged or salaried employment, Yemenis owned and ran large numbers of businesses; just over a quarter of respondents in 1993 had done so. These were mainly small to medium scale enterprises in the retail and service sectors, but some controlled substantial mercantile and commercial interests (Van Hear 1994).

The mass exodus of 1990. Until 1990, Yemenis were not subject to the regulations that applied to other foreign residents working in Saudi Arabia. As in Kuwait, foreign participation in the Saudi Arabian economy was restricted through insistence on majority Saudi partnership in businesses, and through the *kafeel* or guarantor system, under which Saudi employers were responsible for their foreign employees' legal and financial affairs. Yemenis were not required to obtain visas (*iqamas*), work permits, sponsorship from a Saudi *kafeel* to work, or a Saudi majority partner to set up businesses in the kingdom. This set them apart from other migrants for whom progressively more stringent immigration rules were introduced in the 1980s.

Reconsideration of the relaxed migration regime for Yemenis, as for other migrants, was prompted by changes in the Saudi economy. By the later 1980s many construction projects were completed or near completion, leading to a shift in demand for labour from construction to services. While many Yemenis adapted to this, the lax regulation of their presence was becoming increasingly unpopular as unemployment began to grow significantly among Saudis for the first time (Findlay 1994). Early in 1990, under pressure of economic contraction and growing unemployment among nationals, the Saudi authorities decided to remove the Yemenis' exemption from visa, work permit and *kafeel* requirements (Birks Sinclair and Associates 1990; Van Hear 1994). But this change in the migration regime was not implemented until after the invasion of Kuwait by Iraq, when economic and political expediency appeared to coincide. Tensions between Saudi Arabia and Yemen had long festered, particularly over border demarcation and claims to oil-bearing territory. The Gulf crisis deepened this intermittent animosity. At the time Yemen had the misfortune of an unusually prominent international profile by virtue of representation on the UN Security Council. Despite assertions of neutrality, Yemen was associated with the pro-Iraqi camp which also included the PLO and Sudan, and suffered the consequences accordingly.

As the crisis intensified, Yemenis were given until mid-November 1990 to regularize their status under the new work and residence rules or leave. All Yemeni migrants were required to apply for work permits and those owning businesses were required to sell a majority share to a Saudi national. In addition to the extension to Yemenis of the regulations on working or running businesses, the Saudi authorities fostered a climate of insecurity among the Yemeni population. Harassment was widespread and several hundred Yemenis were detained and tortured (Amnesty International 1990).

Few of the Yemeni returnees I interviewed in 1993 had suffered torture or direct persecution, though many had undergone harassment and most felt a keen sense of insecurity. One construction worker in his 30s in Saudi Arabia for 15 years complained that he and his friends were repeatedly arrested and interrogated "for nothing"; "We could not stand it so we left." Another man, a butcher in Saudi Arabia for seven years, claimed that Saudis used to intimidate him in his shop, throwing his meat on the floor. For others it was the threat to their children's education that made them decide to leave. But for most it was the inability or unwillingness to secure a Saudi *kafeel* or sponsor that prompted the decision to leave: "We didn't like the idea of having a *kafeel* like Egyptian migrants", "they will say you are their slave". The decision to go was often made quickly, but not taken lightly: "I made my decision in 12 hours and left 35 years behind me", said one man in his 40s.

The mass exodus was thus precipitated by a combination of the removal of Yemeni expatriates' privileged status, the physical persecution of a minority of Yemenis, more widespread harassment, wounded pride, and the feeling among the Yemeni expatriate community as a whole that life was being made impossible for them (Van Hear 1994). Many lost savings and investments as they were obliged to sell their assets at prices well below their value. While never articulated as explicit policy, the Saudi move put severe pressure on the newly unified Yemen against the background of that country's apparent support for Iraq as the Gulf crisis deepened (Addleton 1991; Edge 1992; US Committee for Refugees 1991); at the same time the move had the effect of removing part of Saudi Arabia's surplus labour force.

As the exodus gathered pace from Saudi Arabia, Yemenis also returned under duress from Kuwait and other Gulf states after the Iraqi invasion. The government report on the returnees recorded a total of 731,800, based on a survey of 318,569 returnee respondents; of these, about 90 per cent came from Saudi Arabia and about 7 per cent from Kuwait (Republic of Yemen 1991). Since there is likely to have been some under-counting during this survey – which was conducted while the mass exodus was under way, could not cover all the border crossings and is likely to have missed those Yemenis who were on holiday in Yemen at the time of the expulsion – the commonly cited estimated total of 800,000 returnees does not seem unreasonable (Van Hear 1994). While returning migrants were a routine part of Yemeni social and economic life, the sudden arrival of this mass of people, many of them born or long-settled abroad, was on a completely different scale.

Mass exodus and the migration order. The mass expulsion of 1990 represented a serious rupture in the migratory order spanning Yemen, Saudi Arabia and other Gulf states. Like other migrant populations investigated in this book, the Yemeni community in Saudi Arabia was a mixed population comprising both short-term migrants and long-established expatriates. Both types of expatriate were drawn by oil wealth and the great disparities in living standards it generated. The emergence of an established Yemeni expatriate community in part reflected changes in the Saudi economy as demand for wage labour contracted and many Yemenis set up their own businesses in the service sector. The longer-stayers made their homes and brought up their families abroad, so that an increasing proportion of the total expatriate population of Yemeni origin had little direct experience of their country of origin.

Yemeni residents may have added about 7 per cent to the population of Saudi Arabia – about 15 million in 1990 (Van Hear 1994). This is a substantial proportion, and given that many were long-established, there was a considerable number of dependants in this community. But while there was discussion about the desirability of "nationalizing" the workforce, particularly among recent Saudi graduates seeking employment, curiously a reduction of the numbers of Yemenis for reasons of demography was never explicitly articulated by the Saudi authorities.

Disputed membership status, if not actual citizenship, played a part in the exodus from Saudi Arabia. The change in work and residence rules which relegated Yemenis to the status of other foreign residents in Saudi Arabia and precipitated the mass exodus (Van Hear 1994) rankled against Yemeni notions of a community of peoples in the Arabian peninsula. On the other hand, doubts about the Yemeni origins of some of those expelled – some were thought to have been hajj-visitors of African descent who had stayed on informally in Saudi Arabia – raised the question of the dumping on Yemen by the Saudi authorities of unwanted persons of indeterminate nationality.

As in the Nigerian episode, the two Middle East cases featured the involuntary return of large populations from regionally dominant, oil-powered economies to their labour-supplying peripheries. Cumulative changes in the structure of demand for labour underlay the desire to reduce the substantial foreign presence in the labour force; the heady era of expansion in both Kuwait and Saudi Arabia, seen particularly in construction, was coming to an end and demand for labour supplied by unskilled or semi-skilled migrants was diminishing. Pressures on spending, relative at least to the 1970s and first half of the 1980s, were also beginning to limit largesse. The Gulf crisis was the event, seized upon opportunistically, allowing realization of this hitherto vaguely articulated end of reducing the foreign population in both Kuwait and Saudi Arabia. In addition, concern about threats to national integrity posed by the migrant community were prominent in Kuwait, where misgivings intermittently expressed about the Palestinian presence were thrown into relief by the Iraqi invasion and its aftermath. In both countries, while the foreign labour force was reduced, the redistribution of employment among migrant nationalities was also ultimately more the outcome. Neither expelled migrant community was able to return to their erstwhile place of often long-term residence where they had made a relatively good living and life.

South and Southeast Asia: citizenship disputed

The mass exodus of the Rohingyas from Burma/Myanmar
South and Southeast Asia were the location of two contemporaneous forced mass departures involving disputed nationality in the early 1990s. Over several decades, large numbers of Muslims, known as Rohingyas, have periodically been forced to flee from their homes in Arakan state in western Burma (known since 1988 as Myanmar). Two major exoduses have taken place in recent times. In 1978, some 200,000 Rohingyas fled persecution accompanying a pre-census check on nationality status in Arakan state. Most of these subsequently repatriated, many of them in controversial circumstances; others

moved to the Middle East and other parts of Asia. In 1991–92, another exodus of more than 260,000 Rohingyas took place, precipitated by conscription into forced labour and other persecution that accompanied a heavy-handed military presence in the state. Most of these people subsequently repatriated, again to an uncertain future. Behind both mass exoduses lay issues of disputed nationality: many Rohingyas claim citizenship deriving from their residence when the Union of Burma became independent in 1948, while successive governments of Burma/Myanmar have disputed their citizenship, claiming that much or most of the Muslim population were illegal immigrants from Bangladesh with whose population they share ethnic affinity.

The Rohingya presence in Arakan. Long-standing migration to Arakan from both within the region and from the Middle East accounts for the very mixed origins of the Muslim population in the state. The Muslim presence was established by Arab or Persian traders and clerics who arrived not long after the emergence of Islam (Elahi 1987; Reid 1994). The flourishing commerce and culture of their descendants was periodically invigorated by immigration of other Muslims, mainly from Bengal, over the following centuries. Many were agricultural labourers who migrated from Bengal to the Arakan region in the nineteenth century, including those brought as labourers by the British (Weiner 1993a; Piper 1994). Further involuntary movements from Bengal to Arakan accompanied the partition of India and continued after the emergence of Bangladesh from the 1971 conflict (Ahmed 1996; Reid 1994). Much subsequent migration has been impelled by economic circumstances; much of the more recent migration has been unauthorized, and it is the proportion of more recent arrivals that has been at issue.

The Muslim population of diverse migratory origins became known as the Rohingyas, while people partly of the same ethnic stock, but who were Buddhists, were known as the Rakhine. Arakan or Rakhine state is one of seven ethnic minority states demarcated by Burma's 1974 constitution on the periphery of the ethnic Burman majority core. Several of the ethnic groups, including the Arakanese, straddle international borders (Smith

1991, 1994). There have long been serious tensions among Burma's diverse ethnic groups, and between the periphery and the ethnic Burman core. Much of this antagonism derives from British colonial governance – including classic divide and rule strategy – and particularly from experience during the Second World War, when different groups sided with the British and Japanese. Large numbers of Arakanese Muslims were forced to flee in 1942 after attacks by Rakhine nationalists and Buddhists. In the late 1940s and 1950s the communist party and various ethnic groups, including the Rakhine, took up arms against central government (Elahi 1987; Reid 1994; Smith 1991).

Separatist aspirations and violence were thus much in evidence before and after independence in 1948, particularly among the Arakanese. Under the regime of General Ne Win's Burma Socialist Party (1962–88) policies of ethnic, cultural, religious and linguistic assimilation provoked further secessionist demands and conflict. As political chaos intensified and the economy crumbled, the State Law and Order Restoration Council (SLORC) took power, but the violence grew worse after as the regime countered ethnically-based insurgents with heavy repression: the result was a growing exodus of refugees into neighbouring countries. The moves in Arakan state have been part of this repression, specifically against Muslim insurgents, but also reflecting long standing Burmese central government animosity towards the Muslim Rohingya population generally (Smith 1994). The Rohingyas have suffered from economic neglect of Arakan as a whole, as well as from more targeted harassment and persecution.

In mid-1991 – roughly the time of the second mass exodus – Myanmar's population was estimated at 42.8 million (World Bank 1993). The population of Arakan state may have been 3.5-4.5 million around this time. Of these, a majority, perhaps 2.5 million in 1991, were Buddhists, while the Muslim population of Arakan was estimated at between 1 and 2 million. Thus while the Rohingya population was small in relation to Myanmar's total, it was significant in Arakan, and particularly in the north of the state adjoining Bangladesh. Although in a minority, Arakan state had the greatest concentration of Muslims in Myanmar (Piper 1994).

Much of this population were poor, unskilled labourers and farmers, but there were also prosperous traders and business-men among them. Indeed, Muslim traders and businessmen were alleged to dominate the economy and to be engaged in large scale smuggling of rice; they appeared prosperous relative to the Buddhist Rakhine, who accused them of taking over land (Reid 1994). Local antagonism between the two principal ethnic groups in Arakan coupled with potent wider conflicts between centre and periphery of Myanmar thus underlay the two migration crises experienced by the Rohingyas in recent times.

Mass exodus in 1978 and 1991-92. The Rohingya Muslims resident in Burma at the time of independence had a good claim to be considered citizens of the Union of Burma under the 1948 con-stitution. More recent immigrants have a weaker case. But the citizenship status of all Rohingyas has repeatedly been called into question, particularly by the military governments in power since the early 1960s. The Burmese authorities have periodically launched campaigns, ostensibly against illegal immigrants, challenging Rohingyas to prove their citizenship.

Very often associated with security concerns surrounding insurgencies, one such spate of measures culminated in early 1978 with Operation Dragon King. This was ostensibly a pre-liminary check of nationality status prior to a full national census. The exercise was particularly sensitive in Arakan, given its long running insurgency, the alleged massive immigration from Bangladesh, and the lack of a census there since 1962. Police backed by the army entered the state in February 1978 and picked up several hundred suspect illegal aliens. Protests led to further arrests and persecution. Torture, rape and robbery were alleged, and there were reports of the burning of villages and eviction at gunpoint. As an exodus of Rohingyas gathered pace, the Burmese authorities predictably claimed that it was illegal aliens wishing to escape scrutiny that fled, although many held evidence of long-term and legitimate residence in Burma. As elsewhere, flight was induced by the persecution of some and the widespread fear of persecution among many more in the intimidating presence of the security forces. The upshot was the flight of some 200,000 Rohingyas across the Naaf river into Bangladesh between April and July 1978 (Elahi 1987; Piper 1994; Reid 1994).

Despite the heightened tension between Burma and Bangladesh precipitated by the mass exodus, the two countries reached an agreement on repatriation surprisingly quickly, in July 1978. Repatriation was slow to take off, but as is shown in Chapter 6, it suddenly accelerated as conditions in camps accommodating the refugees rapidly deteriorated. The voluntary nature of the repatriation was thus called into question. By the end of 1979, just over 187,000 refugees had repatriated (Aall 1979; Reid 1994).

Despite the repatriation the Rohingyas' status in Burma was rendered still less secure after the expulsion of 1978. The drafting of a new citizenship law in 1980 proposed two categories of citizenship, one for members of indigenous Burmese groups, and another for those of Pakistani, Chinese or Bengali origin; the Rohingyas were included in the latter category, members of which were excluded from government office and from some sectors of the economy (Elahi 1987; Reid 1994). The citizenship law came into force in 1982. It limited full citizenship to those who could prove ancestry in Burma dating before control by the British in 1824; "indigenous races" such as the Burman, Shan and Karen were exempted, so the law effectively targeted the Chinese, Indian and Rohingya populations who could not prove such ancestry (Smith 1994). While this increased insecurity among the Muslim and other non-indigenous populations – and made some of them play down their ethnicity – the law does not appear to have been acted upon during the 1980s (Reid 1992).

After the trauma of the 1978 expulsion, a period of uneasy but relative quiet prevailed in Arakan, as civil war ebbed and flowed in other parts of Burma's periphery. In 1988, however, the centre plunged into upheaval, as, against the background of political chaos and a devastated economy, a democracy movement mobilized, involving students, workers and monks. The movement was heavily suppressed, but the demonstrations nevertheless continued, and partly as a result the SLORC took over in September 1988, banning opposition parties and arresting their leaders. In general elections held in May 1990 the main opposition party won a substantial majority, but the SLORC would not accept the results or hand over power (UN ECOSOC 1994).

Conditions in Arakan state deteriorated rapidly after the SLORC took power. As in other states featuring ethnic minority insurgency, military intervention was stepped up. Forcible relocation for urban redevelopment and counter-insurgency led to the uprooting of large numbers of people. A border development programme was launched in Arakan with military backing in September 1991; Rohingyas alleged they were forcibly removed from the border area. Muslim villages were destroyed and Muslim-owned land and property confiscated and allocated to Burman or Rakhine Buddhist newcomers. According to the accounts of refugees collected by human rights organizations, many thousands of Muslims, including children and the elderly, were conscripted to work unpaid on the border development projects, sometimes on land they had been forced to leave. Forced labour had long been exacted in Burma, but it reached intolerable levels in Arakan during this period. Two refugees' testimonies collected by Amnesty International typified the Rohingyas' experience at this time:

> I was in a group of 300 people as porters, taken 50 to 60 miles northeast from Taungbazaar to military bases . . . In the last three months more than 50 men died. I saw twenty men who were kicked and died like this. It was impossible to help them because I was carrying my heavy load too . . . If a village does resist sending porters the village is attacked. This happened in my village when twelve houses were burnt down because the men had run away.

> We had to walk for about seven days, and were given only the tiniest bit of rice a day . . . many of the porters became weak... We were all beaten if we could not manage our loads. My brother was beaten with the butt of a gun – two of his teeth were knocked out, and my arm was broken (Amnesty International 1992b: 10, 12).

As well as appalling ill-treatment in the course of this forced labour, particularly associated with porterage, there were frequent reports among refugees of extrajudicial killings, torture, beatings and rape, the confiscation of land, other property and livestock, the closure or destruction of mosques and cemeteries, and arrests on religious and political grounds (Amnesty International 1992b; Piper 1994; Smith 1994).

Rather than any particular incident, it appears to have been the cumulative effect of these escalating human rights abuses associated with a greatly increased military presence – and in particular the conscription of forced labour for building and porterage – that precipitated the mass exodus from Arakan of 1991-92. The precedent of Operation Dragon King in 1978 must have also weighed heavily on the minds of the Rohingya population. It is unclear whether it was the intention of the SLORC to drive out the Muslim population once again, or whether the interventions in Arakan were just part of the nation-wide pattern of intimidating dissidents and ethnic minorities with a tradition of insurgency, particularly in the wake of the 1988 democracy agitation. Both motivations may have been at play. The regime claimed that the greatly increased military presence was in response to insurgent activity, although the activities of the various insurgents were limited in Arakan at this time. As in the 1978 episode, the government claimed that the mass exodus was of illegal immigrants fearful of checks on their residence status. Documents indicating legitimate residence were seized or destroyed in the course of flight. Among the tacit motivations for the escalating repressive activity in Arakan was the attempt to divert the attention of the majority Burman and Rakhine Buddhist populations from the ailing economy and the volatile political situation nation-wide, some indication of which was the reported resettlement of Burmans and Rakhine on land formerly held by Muslims (Piper 1994; Smith 1994).

The mass exodus began in the second half of 1991 and gathered momentum towards the end of the year, so that by July 1992, a year after the beginning of the exodus, there were more than 260,000 Muslim refugees from Arakan state in Bangladesh. Almost all of the refugee population came from four subdistricts in the north of the state (Piper 1994; Smith 1994). As after the mass exodus of 1978, the governments of Bangladesh and Myanmar very rapidly reached agreement on repatriation of the uprooted Rohingyas. The repatriation is considered in detail in Chapter 6. There were again doubts about its voluntary nature, but it proceeded nevertheless. By mid-1995, just 55,000 remained in camps in Bangladesh (UNHCR 1995a), implying that about 200,000 refugees had by then returned to Myanmar – or had melted into Bangladesh's population for fear of repatriation.

After the mass exodus of 1991–92, the Rohingyas' citizenship status became still more indeterminate. The UNHCR appeared to concede the Myanmar government's argument that the Rohingyas were not citizens of Myanmar, for its memorandum of understanding with the Yangon government in November 1993 termed the refugees not citizens but "residents" of Myanmar or Rakhine state, leaving their status in Myanmar open to question (US Committee for Refugees 1993). UNHCR reaffirmed this in 1995: "Most of the Muslims of Rakhine State (around 700,000 people) are not entitled to citizenship under Myanmar's citizenship laws", the organization stated (UNHCR 1995a: 4), noting that returning refugees could apply for the second-tier status embodied in the 1982 law, or for citizenship by naturalization. Although the two episodes in the late 1970s and the early 1990s had similar outcomes, the issues underlying them – primarily the Rohingyas' citizenship status – were not resolved, suggesting that the mass exodus of Rohingyas in 1991–92 may not be the last. As one human rights organization observed, "the refugee problem will not be solved until and unless the Rohingyas are recognized as citizens by the Burmese government and granted the rights they are currently denied. They will remain a vulnerable group, always ready to flee if the alternative is to suffer further abuse" (Human Rights Watch Asia 1996).

Mass exodus and the migration order. The Muslim population in Arakan is somewhat similar in origin to the South Asian presence in East Africa, although more ancient in terms of initial settlement. As the above account showed, early Muslim settlers from the Middle East were supplemented over several hundred years by movement of Muslims from Bengal. Among some of the later arrivals – including agricultural labourers and others brought by the British – migration was involuntary. Forced migration into Arakan continued with the partition of India and after the emergence of Bangladesh in the wake of the 1971 conflict. Forced migration of various kinds, including upheavals associated with the violent reconstitution of nation-states at independence and after, thus shaped the migration order between Bengal (and later Bangladesh) and the Arakan region of Burma/Myanmar. To this extent the events of 1978 and 1991–92 were only an aberration in terms of the direction of the migratory flow.

While the Rohingya minority forms a substantial part of the population of Arakan, there is little evidence that the expulsion had a demographic motivation. Nor does the socio-economic position of the Rohingyas figure prominently in the migration crisis of 1991–92. Although some Rohingya traders and businessmen were alleged to dominate sections of the economy and generated resentment, it appears to have been rather the poorer sections of the community that were targeted for expulsion – in contrast to the Ugandan Asian case.

The roots of the Rohingya migration crisis lie in issues of membership and in the challenges to national integrity this population were thought to pose. These anxieties derive from Burma's long standing tensions between centre and periphery and its never resolved ethnic differences, manifested in pro-tracted conflict between successive ruling regimes and armed factions of diverse ethnic groups. There were the added ingredients in the Rohingya case of a Muslim presence in a pre-dominantly Buddhist country and the calling into question the legitimacy of the presence within Burma's borders of this com-munity of migrant origin. A proximate factor in the transfor-mation of the migration order was the 1988 democracy agitation in the Burman core – leading to the emergence of Aung San Suu Kyi as a focus of the movement – which developed amid great political turmoil and serious economic degeneration. Among the tacit motivations for the escalating repressive activity in Arakan and the precipitation of the mass exodus were attempts to divert the attention of the majority Burman and Rakhine Buddhist populations from the ailing economy and the volatile political situation nation-wide – a motivation found in many of the episodes covered in this book.

The expulsion of ethnic Nepalis from Bhutan

In an episode contemporary with the exodus of Rohingyas, and with striking parallels to it, tens of thousands of ethnic Nepalis fled the Himalayan kingdom of Bhutan, where most had lived all their lives and most had a strong claim to citizenship. As in the mass exodus of Rohingyas, the crisis hinged on the disputed origins and length of settlement of the ethnic Nepali population. The Bhutanese authorities alleged that the ethnic Nepalis were mostly recent immigrants and feared their increasing demographic impact, while the ethnic Nepalis claimed much longer settlement and citizenship of Bhutan. These issues gathered momentum with the introduction of a revised citizenship law of 1985, a census of 1988 in southern Bhutan to identify "Bhutanese nationals", and measures of cultural assimilation. Dissent against these moves precipitated arrests, repression and the flight of refugees, so that by 1995 some 110,000 ethnic Nepalis had fled, most of whom were accommodated in camps in southeast Nepal.

The ethnic Nepali population in Bhutan. Significant numbers of Nepali-speakers began to settle in southern Bhutan from the late nineteenth century, part of a wider migration that accompanied the expansion of Nepal from the eighteenth century. Migrants were pushed from eastern Nepal by heavy taxation, bonded labour and other exactions, and pulled by the development of the tea industry to Darjeeling and Assam where ethnic Nepalis made up much of the workforce on British tea estates. This movement of indentured and wage labourers extended east and northwards into Bhutan. Nepali settlement in southwest Bhutan was encouraged by the Bhutanese authorities responsible for the southern part of the kingdom in the late nineteenth century, and Nepalis rapidly cleared forest and established themselves as cultivators. There was thus a substantial presence of Nepalis in southern Bhutan from the early twentieth century with official sanction. The legitimacy of their presence was confirmed by the 1958 Citizenship Act which granted citizenship to those settlers who held land in that year and who had been resident for ten years (Baral 1996; Hutt 1994; Sinha 1994).

Migration into Bhutan continued subsequently, much of it probably from the large Nepali community in India. The increased flow of development assistance into Bhutan, particularly from the 1970s, stimulated higher living standards and greater immigration. In addition to this unregulated migration, tens of thousands of Nepali labourers were imported each year for road development in the 1970s and early 1980s; many of these may subsequently have merged into the local community (Shaw 1994).

Most of the southern Bhutanese or ethnic Nepali population were tenant farmers who cultivated cashews, fruit and other crops (Hutt 1996); the more recent additions to this long-standing population, some officially sanctioned, others illicit, made for a mixed population of farmers and labourers, factory workers, carpenters and other artisans, and shopkeepers and petty traders. There was also a sprinkling of professionals among the ethnic Nepalis. Despite their economic importance – the south supplied much of the country's food – the position of the ethnic Nepalis in the economy does not appear to have been at issue in the mass exodus of 1991–92.

The proportion of ethnic Nepalis within the kingdom's population has been more of a matter of contention. A 1969 census came up with a population of over a million for Bhutan, but this figure was later acknowledged to be a notional one, settled upon when the country applied for UN membership. In 1990, the king declared the total population was actually 600,000, a figure that entered into the nation's planning deliberations, appearing for example in its Five Year Plans. The proportion of Nepali-speakers has been contested: they were thought to comprise between a quarter and a third of the total population, which would make them number between 150,000 and 200,000 (Hutt 1994). While not articulated explicitly, there had long been anxiety about being overrun by Nepalis, which was among the factors which precipitated the expulsion of the early 1990s.

The mass exodus of 1991-92. The crisis which led to the mass exodus derived from increasing tensions in the 1980s between the Buddhist peoples of the north of Bhutan, collectively known as the Drukpa, and the Nepali-speaking and mainly Hindu peoples of southern Bhutan, known as the Lhotshampa. The attitude of the Drukpas of the north to the Nepali-speaking southerners had long been ambivalent, coloured by fears of ambitions for a "Greater Nepal", compounded by demographic anxiety. Neither fear was wholly unfounded. The fates of Sikkim and Tibet, swallowed up into India and China, were salutary lessons for the Bhutanese authorities, as was Nepali agitation in Sikkim, Assam, Nepal and Bhutan itself; in Sikkim and Nepal this agitation had led to the downfall of feudal kingdoms similar to that of Bhutan.

The ambivalence of the ruling Drukpas towards the Lhotsampas was manifested in changes in the kingdom's citizenship laws. The granting of citizenship to the Lhotsampas in 1958 had marked a period of gradual integration. The citizenship act embodied a relatively liberal interpretation of citizenship, which could be based on descent through the male line; through marriage, if a woman, to a Bhutanese national; and through five years government service combined with the residence qualification. Nepali Bhutanese were recruited into the administration, some occupying senior positions; there was some intermarriage between Drukpas and Lhotsampas; and, with Dzonghka (the Drukpa language) and English, Nepali became one of Bhutan's three national languages (Hutt 1996; Martensen 1995).

This era of tolerance was eroded by legislative and administrative changes which introduced more stringent conditions for citizenship; it dissolved completely with a new Citizenship Act of 1985, which introduced far-reaching changes in qualifications for Bhutanese nationality. Citizenship by birth could now only be claimed through both parents instead of through the father alone; citizenship by registration required evidence of permanent residence in Bhutan before the end of 1958; citizenship by naturalization required evidence of fluency in the Drukpa language and knowledge of Drukpa traditions and history that many illiterate southern Bhutanese could not provide. Absence from Bhutan and from the citizenship register for a year could mean that citizenship was forfeited. Disloyalty to king and country was also grounds for removal of citizenship. Not unreasonably, ethnic Nepalis interpreted these conditions as making it difficult for them to prove the legitimacy of their presence in Bhutan. There were sporadic protests about the retrospective nature of the law, restrictions on marriage, and the 1958 cut-off date for citizenship by registration (Hutt 1996; Strawn 1994).

Worse was to come. Reports that there were more than 100,000 illegal migrants in the south, most of them Nepalis working on development or infrastructure projects, prompted a campaign of deportation in the name of national security and self reliance. Nepali and Indian manual workers on development projects were among the first targeted, especially those on road building and maintenance; many were reported to have overstayed their permits and settled (Hutt 1994, 1996; Strawn 1994).

Then, in 1988, a campaign was launched to identify "Bhutanese nationals" in the south of the kingdom. The population was placed into seven categories: genuine Bhutanese citizens; returned migrants, meaning people who had left Bhutan and then returned; dropout cases, meaning people not present at the time of the census; non-national women married to Bhutanese men and their children; non-national men married to Bhutanese women and their children; adopted children; and non-nationals, including migrants and settlers. This so-called "census" gave ethnic Nepalis further grounds for insecurity, but particular resentment arose from the excessively stringent demands for documentation in the course of the campaign. Many of those who could not prove residence in the year 1958 were categorized as returned migrants or non-nationals, regardless of documentation that showed otherwise. Protests at the conduct of the census by prominent southern Bhutanese and human rights activists were met by arrests and detention (Amnesty International 1992a; Hutt 1996).

Compounding the implementation of the census were measures of cultural assimilation introduced under Bhutan's sixth Five Year Plan running in 1987–92, which asserted a policy of "one people, one nation". It was decided that the culture and traditions of the northern Bhutanese, called *driglam namzha*, should be upheld throughout the country. Among the requirements of this policy was the wearing of traditional Drukpa dress for public occasions, including visits to government offices and buildings; behaviour during formal occasions was also stipulated. Failure to observe these conditions was punishable by a fine. Shortly after the introduction of the dress code, the teaching of Nepali was discontinued in Bhutanese schools. Not surprisingly, ethnic Nepalis saw the dress code and language measures as an attack on their cultural identity (Amnesty International 1992a; Hutt 1996).

Unrest at the national integration policies and the implementation of the Citizenship Act through the census spread from early 1990, culminating in a series of demonstrations in September of that year. Some of the protest was violent, with both government officials and property targeted; there were atrocities against people alleged to be collaborating with the census takers. The protest was met with further repression by state forces (Amnesty International 1992a; Hutt 1996).

Arrests and imprisonment of protesters followed the suppression of the demonstrations; batches of these prisoners were later released under royal amnesties and then made their way to Nepal. After this, people who had been categorized as bona fide citizens during the census found themselves the targets of eviction because they had a relative in prison or abroad; the loyalty condition of citizenship was invoked. As Hutt remarks, "This provision seems in practice to have been extended to all those who opposed, or were related to others who opposed, the government's new policies" (Hutt 1996: 406).

The level of repression escalated. Refugees reported imposition of martial law, school closures, military raids on villages, the burning of houses, detentions, labour conscription of young men and women, beatings, looting of possessions and rape. Schools were turned over to the army as barracks and access to health services was restricted. Ethnic Nepalis were served notices to leave because relatives had already left, because relatives were said to be "anti-nationals", or because they could not produce documents sufficient to satisfy officials.

Many claimed that they were forced to sign papers saying they were leaving Bhutan voluntarily, relinquishing claims on land and homes. They were offered scant compensation for land and property left behind; a condition for compensation was the surrender of citizenship documents, land tax receipts or other papers which might prove citizenship (Amnesty International 1994; Hutt 1996; Ruiz 1992; UNHCR 1993).

Testimonies by refugees collected by Amnesty International reflected these abuses ranging from the confiscation of documents to rape and other violence:

My father and uncle migrated to live in Bhutan, and I was born there. Our family went together to the census team on two occasions. The first time I did not take my citizenship document with me. The second time the census team asked for my land receipt of 1958 and my identity card. The land tax receipt was in my uncle's name. The census team said that I could not have my identity card returned because the 1958 land tax receipt was in my uncle's name. I was categorised F7 [non-Bhutanese], and the census officer told me that I had to leave the country within six days or pay a fine of 6,000 rupees or go to jail for six months. Since I am a poor person, I left the country (Amnesty International 1994: 9–10).

Seven or eight soldiers came to our house... They arrested me and my brother, and tied our hands behind our backs. They took us to Thoemba school which had been turned into an army barracks. An army contingent of 200 to 300 soldiers had come to the village and arrested two or three people from each house. About 200 people were arrested that day. We were all herded together outside the school compound, and made to sit with hands tied behind our backs and heads down. Army personnel then selected eight young women including me and dragged us inside. Those who resisted were kicked and when some of the women fell down, the soldiers hit them with their rifle butts... I was slapped, forced on to the floor and raped by five soldiers. Afterwards I was brought back to the

compound where they kept me for two hours...I was told
to leave the country and that if I stayed in Bhutan I would
be killed ... One week later, we left Bhutan with other
households from our village and came to Nepal (Amnesty
International 1992a).

As already observed in other cases, a significant minority
suffered direct abuses, but these were enough to provoke fear
and flight in the remainder of the targeted population. Ethnic
Nepalis started to flee from Bhutan to Nepal at the end of 1990.
The mass exodus peaked in mid-1992, then gradually declined
during 1993 and 1994 to a trickle in 1995 (Amnesty International
1994; Hutt 1996; UNHCR 1993). At the end of 1995, some 88,600
refugees were living in camps in southeast Nepal, with perhaps
another 18,000 living outside these settlements (US Committee
for Refugees 1996). No prospect of a resolution of the position of
the refugees appeared in sight.

Mass exodus and the migration order. The migration order encompassing Nepal and Bhutan was of several generations standing.
The proportion of the southern Bhutanese population that
derived from early migration compared with later arrivals,
particularly after the cut-off year of 1958, was the matter at issue
in the crisis that emerged in the late 1980s. Apart from some
indentured labour and economic compulsion, this migration
had been largely free and uncontentious until the crisis of 1990,
which was thus a substantial rupture in the migration order.

Like the mass exodus of the Rohingyas, the expulsion of the
ethnic Nepalis from Bhutan exhibits many of the ingredients
that have precipitated the mass exodus of minorities elsewhere –
disputed nationality, demographic anxiety, allegations of illegal
immigration, and attempts at the cultural homogenization of
minority groups through language, dress and other means.
Threats to national integrity as articulated by the ruling
Drukpas thus underlay the migration crisis of the ethnic Nepalis
in Bhutan. The challenge to national integrity was held to hail
from without; Bhutan had long been fearful, with some
justification, of the threat of a greater Nepal which would
swallow up the kingdom. A manifestation of this threat was

held to be evident within – in the form of the substantial population and the different culture of the ethnic Nepalis. Bhutan moved from a relatively tolerant, multi-ethnic state in the late 1950s to an assertively assimilationist one in the late 1980s, culminating in the migration crisis of the early 1990s.

Conclusion

Comparison between these and other cases is pursued further below, but I offer some preliminary observations here. The six cases provide examples of long-settled communities of migrant origin and more recent migrants: there are parallels between the experience of the Ugandan Asians and the Palestinians in Kuwait, between the experience of the Ghanaians in Nigeria and some of the Yemenis in Saudi Arabia, and between the experience of the Rohingyas in Burma and the ethnic Nepalis in Bhutan. A feature common to these populations and to others considered below is their mixed origins and socio-economic character. Also notable is the difficulty in estimating the size of their communities and the numbers obliged to leave – a problem that recurs in the cases explored in the next chapter.

The six episodes of mass exodus were different in form. The African episodes were more explicitly expulsions, ordered by government decree, and supplemented by intimidation and harassment of the migrant communities. The mass exodus of Yemenis from Saudi Arabia was arguably an expulsion, since the Saudi authorities suddenly changed the rules governing the migrants' right to stay, and fostered a climate of insecurity through harassment, detention and torture. By contrast, although there was harassment and abuse of the foreign workforce while Kuwait was under Iraqi occupation, the flight of expatriates was prompted more by fear of the new regime and of the war that the occupation might provoke. Subsequently, persecution and harassment of the Palestinian community left in Kuwait induced their departure in what was again arguably a mass expulsion. In the two Asian cases, expulsion was not explicitly decreed, but engineered by a series of repressive measures against the minority community. In all of the cases, much of the flight was in anticipation of persecution, harassment or intimidation, or of instability, civil conflict or war. Flight was predicated on the calculation that a tolerable life was no longer possible under such conditions. As will be shown below, this configuration of circumstances is common among migrant populations expelled from or induced to leave their country of work, residence or settlement; such a mix of conditions feature in the migration crises drawn from Europe, Central America and the Caribbean that I review in the following chapter.

FOUR

Migration crises in Europe, Central America and the Caribbean

In this chapter a further four episodes of mass exodus in three regions are considered. Two of these – the exodus of ethnic Turks from Bulgaria and of Albanians from Greece – are directly associated with the demise of the communist bloc and the end of the Cold War, a key moment in the transformation of the world migratory order. A case drawn from the Caribbean – the exodus of Haitians from the Dominican Republic – was contemporary with these episodes. The fourth case – the exodus of illegal Mexican workers from the US in 1950s – is outside this period, but is included to demonstrate that mass expulsion is not the preserve of the former communist bloc or the developing world. As in the previous chapter, for each case I outline the history of the migration order, give an account of the migration crisis, and place the crisis in comparative perspective. I conclude the chapter by drawing on the 10 episodes to offer a comparative review of the character of migration crises.

Southern Europe: two Balkans episodes

The expulsion of ethnic Turks from Bulgaria
In 1989, more than 300,000 ethnic Turks long-settled in Bulgaria were obliged to leave that country, against the background of a campaign to deny their Turkish identity and to assimilate them into the majority Slav society. The mass exodus was the

precursor of others that took place against the wider background of the dissolution of communist regimes in Europe. About 310,000 Bulgarian Turks had arrived in Turkey by August 1989, making it, until subsequent events in Yugoslavia, "one of the largest European mass exoduses since the close of World War Two" (US Committee for Refugees 1990: 66). Up to half of those who departed subsequently returned to Bulgaria after the fall of the communist regime there; the rest remade their lives in Turkey.

The Turkish presence in Bulgaria. Turks settled in the area that is now Bulgaria from about the fourteenth century, their presence a legacy of Ottoman domination of the Balkans until the latter part of the nineteenth century. The decline of the Ottoman Empire and the emergence of the Balkan states saw a concomitant reversal of the status of Turks: from people deriving privileged status from the erstwhile ruling power, they were now a vulnerable minority subject to forced migration. Since the last quarter of the nineteenth century ethnic Turks have been induced or compelled to move from various parts of the former Ottoman Empire to the "homeland" in Turkey. With the largest Turkish minority in the Balkans, Bulgaria's ethnic Turks have been very much part of this "in-gathering".

The Turkish population has been moving out of Bulgaria since the end of Ottoman rule in 1878. Successive waves of Turkish emigration occurred in periods of ethno-religious tension, despite efforts to safeguard the rights of the ethnic Turkish Muslim minority in an Orthodox Christian country by treaty and through the League of Nations in the inter-war years (Vasileva 1992). Several hundred thousand Turks left Bulgaria for Turkey during the Balkans and First World Wars, and in the course of population exchanges during and after those conflicts (Kostanick 1957; de Zayas 1988). The two countries signed a convention in 1925 covering the voluntary movement of people between them, which set the pattern for subsequent Turkish emigration from Bulgaria in the inter-war years (Kostanick 1957). There was also a general emigration of Bulgarians to the US, Australia and other parts of Europe as a result of economic crisis in the early 1930s (OECD SOPEMI 1994).

Communist rule after the Second World War ended most emigration from Bulgaria, but further bilateral agreements were negotiated – albeit acrimoniously – in the early 1950s and late 1960s to regulate the outflow of Turks. There was also some state-controlled labour migration mainly to sympathetic states in the Middle East (OECD SOPEMI 1994). Heavy taxation, state control of agricultural marketing, collectivization of privately held farm land, nationalization of private minority schools and measures against Turkish culture in the name of modernization built up great pressure to emigrate and, when exit restrictions were relaxed in 1950, many ethnic Turks applied to leave. In August 1950 the Bulgarian government announced that 250,000 ethnic Turks had made applications to emigrate and pressured Turkey to accept them within three months. The Turkish authorities said the country could not accept these numbers in such a short time and closed Turkey's borders intermittently over the following year, amid unsuccessful negotiations between the two countries to resolve the issue. In what was tantamount to an expulsion (Kostanick 1957), pressure for ethnic Turks to leave continued, so that 155,000 had quit Bulgaria by late 1951. Most had to abandon their property or to sell it at well below its value. Once in Turkey however these appear to have been settled successfully, helped by the distribution of land, seed and farm equipment, and the provision of housing. That this influx was a continuation of the long pattern of return migration to Turkey assisted integration, since the new arrivals joined communities composed of prior returnees (Kostanick 1957; Poulton 1994; Simsir 1986). Another agreement between the two countries was reached in 1968 which allowed the departure of relatives of those leaving up to 1951. This agreement expired in 1978; during this period some 52,400 people left, the bulk of them in 1969–74 (OECD SOPEMI 1994; Poulton 1994). After this emigration all but ceased until 1989.

Despite the emigration, substantial numbers of Turks remained in the land in which they were long-settled, concentrated in two regions in north and southeast Bulgaria. Their greater birth rate relative to the Bulgarian Slavs largely made up for the loss of population through emigration, so that the Turkish proportion of Bulgaria's population declined only marginally, from about 10 per cent after the First World War to about 9.5 per cent in the late 1980s. Concern over the threat to demographic balance posed by the Turkish population has preoccupied Bulgarian regimes of all complexions this century (Vasileva 1992). The population of Bulgaria in mid-1989 was just under 9 million (World Bank 1991), of which the ethnic Turks numbered just under 850,000.

Because of their higher birth rate and correspondingly more youthful population, ethnic Turks figured strongly in the work force. Large areas of the countryside, particularly important tobacco and wheat growing areas, were increasingly populated by Turks (Poulton 1994). While most lived in the countryside, many were urban dwellers. Most had low levels of education and skills, but there were still significant numbers of educated and skilled people among them (Scott 1991).

There were other reasons than anxiety about demography for the regime's animosity towards the Turks. Five centuries of Ottoman rule were deeply etched on the national psyche, and there was a general Bulgarian fear of assimilation by neighbouring states, a fear with some foundation given the experience of other Balkan nations. The Turks' adherence to Islam and use of the Turkish language were seen by the Bulgarian communist party as inimical to nation-building and modernization (Poulton 1994).

These issues came to head in 1984. Under a programme of national revival and socialist renewal, a heavy-handed campaign was launched forcibly to assimilate the ethnic Turks, principally by demanding that they change their Turkish names to Slav ones, by banning the public use of Turkish language and the wearing of Turkish dress, and by circumscribing the practice of Islam. Compliance was enforced through the issue of identity cards, through employment, and through dealings with bureaucracy and financial institutions. There was substantial resistance, including hunger strikes, to these measures, but it was heavily repressed (Poulton 1994). Thereafter sporadic resistance and sullen acceptance among the Turks prevailed until the late 1980s.

The mass exodus of 1989. As the impact of *glasnost* permeated through the eastern bloc, particularly through the relaxation of control over radio transmission, opportunities for dissident groups to organize, including those representing ethnic Turks, began to open up in 1988. Hunger strikes and demonstrations gathered momentum from May 1989. Again they were violently suppressed, involving many deaths, and leaders and activists of the dissident groups were expelled. This outflow quickly mutated into a generalized mass exodus, as, similar to the early 1950s, the authorities relaxed exit controls, urged ethnic Turks to leave, and called on Turkey to open its borders to them. Relaxation of passport regulations and exit requirements also precipitated the departure of many other Bulgarians, relieving strong pent-up pressure to emigrate (OECD SOPEMI 1994).

A human rights organization gathered the testimony of some caught up in the early waves of expulsion. One woman, a 22-year-old student, said she was expelled because she had participated in a demonstration. She was summoned to the mayor's office and told to leave the same day: "Go to Turkey. Now that you have participated in the demonstration see what it is really like in Turkey", she was told. She estimated that her village had a population of 850 families, and that each Turk expelled came from a different family. She was allowed one bag of personal possessions and one hour to say good-bye to her family. Another man, a 53-year-old economist who had opposed the name-changing campaign in 1984–85 and participated in demonstrations in 1989, was called to the police station and told, "Your language is different. Your religion is different. You always wanted to go to Turkey. So now you are going." The police warned him that if he did not leave within four hours, they would forcibly expel him (Zang 1989: 31–33).

While political activists and dissidents suffered direct expulsion, most of the ethnic Turks appear to have calculated that it was no longer worth living in Bulgaria given the assimilation campaign and repression, and that Turkey with its more vibrant economy offered better prospects. As well as the promise of greater earnings and a better life, there was the possibility of migration to western Europe (Vasileva 1992). Nevertheless, it was for most a hurried and chaotic mass exodus. Many abandoned houses and other property or were obliged to sell them at low prices before they left on foot, by car or train with whatever personal possessions they could take with them (Kirisci 1996; Poulton 1994; Zang 1989).

About 310,000 Bulgarian Turks had arrived in Turkey by August 1989 (US Committee for Refugees 1990). Although the sudden arrival of this large number placed great strain on Turkey, it relaxed entry procedures, provided reception facilities and announced that the refugees would be accepted immediately as citizens without the usual residential qualifying period. However, faced with an inflow that continued unabated, the Turkish authorities later closed the border and reimposed visa entry requirements for ethnic Turks, trapping many on the Bulgarian side of the border (Kirisci 1996; Poulton 1994).

In November 1989, a day after the fall of the Berlin wall, the hard-line leadership of the Bulgarian communist party was ousted, partly as a result of the forced assimilation debacle and the mass exodus. Political liberalization followed, and dissidents, including ethnic Turk activists, were released. Against the background of continuing agitation, the assimilation policy was dropped. The change of regime and liberalization precipitated a large return movement of the ethnic Turks, a substantial number of whom had in fact already gone back for lack of employment opportunities and housing in Turkey. Other motivations for return included reunification of families separated in the course of the mass exodus; attempts to recover property; and, compared with Bulgaria, harsher working conditions, the lack of employment for women, a higher cost of living, and the absence of social security entitlements in Turkey (Poulton 1994; Vasileva 1992). More than 130,000 had returned by January 1990 (Poulton 1994); within a year 155,000 may have returned, about half of those who left in the mass exodus (Vasileva 1992).

While the campaign against the Turks was not widely supported by the Bulgarian population at large, the policy turnaround was not welcomed everywhere and provoked a nationalist backlash. Some had benefited from the mass exodus by buying up cheap property left by the Turks. Bulgarians in areas with a Turkish majority were fearful and nationalist demonstrations spread through much of the country in late 1989 and early 1990 (Poulton 1994). Nevertheless measures were introduced to restore Turkish names (although the procedures were cumbersome and costly), press freedom, religious freedom and the teaching of Turkish in schools. These measures continued to draw protest from Bulgarian nationalists. Their fears were magnified by the emergence on the political scene of an adeptly led party representing the ethnic Turks, the Movement for Rights and Freedoms, which held the balance of power after elections held in October 1991 (Poulton 1994).

In the meantime, further waves of Bulgarian emigration gathered momentum in 1990–91 to western Europe, principally asylum-seekers to Germany, and to the US and Canada (OECD SOPEMI 1994). Another wave of ethnic Turkish emigration, this time economically motivated, took off from 1992. As elsewhere, economic liberalization resulted in strain on local economies and societies. The price of tobacco, a principal cash crop of ethnic Turkish farmers, dropped sharply; the privatization of land meant that many Turks unable to buy the farms they worked were rendered landless; unemployment among them rose steeply as state subsidies on enterprises were removed; and removal of subsidies on consumer goods led to further hardship. By comparison, Turkey was economically buoyant. By mid-1992, 80,000 ethnic Turks had left and another 140,000 were reported to have applied to emigrate to Turkey. The new exodus weakened the ethnic Turk party's electoral base and contributed to the fall of the government in November 1992 (OECD SOPEMI 1994; Poulton 1994). The outflow continued. Early in 1997, some 200,000 ethnic Turks from Bulgaria were reported to have arrived in Turkey on tourist visas since the beginning of 1993. Claiming that the economy could no longer absorb the newcomers, the government threatened to cease issuing visas and to induce the migrants to return to Bulgaria, although there were suggestions that such measures might be tempered with provision for dual citizenship (Associated Press 25 February 1997).

Mass exodus and the migration order. Like some of the communities examined in the previous chapter, the ethnic Turks of Bulgaria were a long-settled population, a manifestation of previous Ottoman domination of the Balkans. But the migration order that has prevailed for the last century or more has been one of emigration from Bulgaria, as the Turkish population has been moving out of the country since the end of Ottoman rule. As the above account showed, successive waves of Turkish emigration occurred, peaking in the first part of the twentieth century and in the early 1950s, when what was effectively a forced mass exodus was instigated by the Bulgarian authorities. The still larger expulsion of 1989 thus had ample historical precedent in the turbulent Bulgarian emigratory order. While it can be seen as a discrete episode, in longer perspective, the mass exodus of 1989 can therefore be viewed as an accentuation of a process long under way and which continued on a substantial scale afterwards. The mass exodus of ethnic Turks is thus rather different from other episodes considered here since the migration crisis accelerated a migratory flow that had already been in motion for more than a century.

The roots of the mass exodus of 1989, as of previous outflows, lay in demographic anxieties and in threats to national integrity that the Bulgarian authorities thought were posed by the ethnic Turks. The substantial Turkish population, concentrated in two regions of the country, a constant proportion despite more than a century of emigration, and with a higher fertility rate than the majority Slavs, had long concerned Bulgarian governments. Their ethnic, religious and cultural compatibility with the majority population was called into question: their adherence to Islam and use of the Turkish language, among other traits, were perceived as obstructions to socialist modernization and nation-building. In the late 1980s these concerns were thrown into sharp relief by a political economy in upheaval as the grip of the communist regime weakened. The expulsion thus has to be seen within the wider context of the changes under way in eastern Europe as communist regimes came under severe strain in the later 1980s. There is a convincing case for seeing the measures against the Turks as a kind of a safety valve mechanism for containing potentially greater socio-economic conflicts in Bulgaria that were emerging throughout the communist regimes of eastern Europe and the USSR in the 1980s.

Albania, Greece and Italy:
mass emigration, mass forced repatriation
In contrast to the long standing migration between Bulgaria and Turkey, migration from near neighbour Albania was of recent origin. After more than four decades of isolation, the disintegration of Albania's communist regime in 1990–91 precipitated massive emigration of Albanians, mainly to neighbouring Greece and Italy. While early arrivals were tolerated for a short time, both countries, hitherto largely countries of emigration rather than those of immigration, became increasingly alarmed at the unregulated incursion. Italy returned several thousands of Albanian arrivals by boat, while Greece deported several hundred thousands in two operations in 1991 and 1994, and intermittently deported large numbers between and after those dates. Albanian emigration to both countries has nonetheless continued unabated as Albania has lurched from crisis to crisis, raising the prospect of further mass deportations.

Exodus of Albanians after 1990: a new migration order. There was some migration of Albanians to other parts of southern Europe and the US prior to establishment of the communist regime at the end of the Second World War, but for the subsequent 45 years emigration was almost completely halted. The explosion of migration from the end of 1990 with the undoing of the communist regime was thus a novel phenomenon, as Albania moved rapidly from closure to mass out-migration. The mass exodus was precipitated by and contingent on liberalization during and after the demise of the communist regime, coupled with economic deterioration and social unrest among ethnic Greeks and the Albanian population at large.

The migration order of Greece was also in transition from the late 1980s. Having long been a country of emigration, it was increasingly becoming a transit destination for asylum-seekers from the Middle East, hopeful of resettlement in the West. Greece had also been receiving ethnic Greeks or Pontics from the former Soviet Union, a form of in-gathering referred to in Chapter 2. Further, as a member of the European Community, the pan-European debates on migration, the Dublin convention and the Schengen agreement impinged on Greece, where new asylum procedures were introduced early in 1990 (Black 1994a, 1994b; Voutira 1991). In addition to these new developments, Greece also had long-standing concerns about the substantial population of Greek origin in southern Albania.

The Albanian exodus to Greece was initially mainly of people seeking asylum. The first wave of Albanian boat people landing in Italy were also treated as asylum-seekers. But before the end of 1991 the official perception in both receiving countries was that this was an issue of undocumented economic migration.

At first, 90 per cent of those entering Greece were of ethnic Greek background; this proportion declined later in 1991 to about 50 per cent (US Committee for Refugees 1992). Reception centres in the border areas of Epirus and western Macedonia were reported to have assisted 15,000 migrants in the first eight months of 1991. Some of these entrants were issued work permits for between six months and a year; it was reported that they could earn in a day one third of their monthly pay in Albania (National Foundation for the Reception and Resettlement of Repatriated Greeks nd). However, several thousand of this first wave were returned to Albania, amid UNHCR complaints that the organization had not been consulted. Greece subsequently strengthened its migration regime by tightening entry and deportation procedures.

Mass expulsions of Albanians, 1990–94. The Greek and Italian authorities then took more vigorous action. In an operation known as the "Broom", some 82,000 Albanians were expelled from Greece in the latter part of 1991; there were nevertheless thought to be 150,000 Albanians still in the country at that year's end. Meanwhile, most in a second wave of Albanian arrivals by boat to Italy were summarily sent back, against a clamour of international concern about the legality and morality of this action (US Committee for Refugees 1991, 1992; Poulton 1994). The compulsory returns were accompanied by the provision of assistance in Albania by both Italy and Greece, the latter through the National Foundation for the Reception and Resettlement of Repatriated Greeks, set up to assist the Pontic in-gathering (Voutira 1991).

Elections in March 1992 changed the political complexion of

Albania, ending the regime of reformed communist Ramiz Alia and bringing Salih Berisha to power as president. Further political and economic liberalization was promised, but if anything the tensions leading to mass exodus subsequently heightened, particularly among ethnic Greeks. The economy continued to deteriorate, with real GDP declining by 9.7 per cent in 1992, even though remittances from the new emigrants worth $150 million entered the economy in that year (Economist Intelligence Unit 1994; *The Economist* 17 September 1994). Industrial production slumped and there were frequent breakdowns in power and water supply. Inflation was reported to be running at 500 per cent a year, and unemployment at 40 per cent (Pettifer 1992). Not surprisingly, mass emigration continued, but, drawing on its tighter migration regime, the Greek authorities turned back or expelled large numbers of migrants and would-be migrants: estimates vary between 350,000 and nearly 380,000 (Glytzos 1995).

The desire to migrate was now well established among the Albanian population (Pettifer 1992). A survey undertaken by the International Organisation for Migration (IOM) in December 1992 found that nearly three-fifths of the one thousand interviewed wished to migrate. While the aspiration was to go to Germany, Italy or the US, Greece was the most common actual destination. Of the 10 per cent who had resided abroad, nearly nine-tenths had lived in Greece, with the remainder in Italy, former Yugoslavia (i.e. Macedonia or Kosovo), Germany and France. Almost all of these had left since 1990. More than half had relatives abroad, most of whom were in Greece and Italy, with the remainder in Germany, the US and former Yugoslavia. Of these relatives, four-fifths had left in 1990–92, and 13 per cent before or just after the Second World War (International Organisation for Migration 1993).

A further survey undertaken in 1995 revealed similar results, but with some significant changes. The proportion of Albanians wishing to migrate had declined to 44 per cent. The US had superseded Italy and Germany as the most popular destination, but Greece was still the most common actual destination, and more were making their way to Italy than in 1992. Economic problems as motivations for migration were less prominent than in 1992, although unemployment was more so; corruption, crime, and personal security were cited as reasons for wanting to leave. Friends and relatives abroad – of whom more had of course accumulated by 1995 – were now the most important sources of information on migration. Most migration was illegal and clandestine, and use was made of traffickers, particularly on a well-organized motorboat route to southern Italy. Many of those who left were well-educated and skilled. Many declared the aspiration to return to Albania after a few years (International Organisation for Migration 1995).

Against the background of upheaval in the Balkans, and particularly as the crisis in neighbouring former Yugoslavia deepened, the position of Albania's Greek minority had meanwhile become a matter of considerable concern. The size of the population involved was disputed: the Albanian authorities estimated the ethnic Greek population at 60,000, while Greece put it at 350,000 – although this figure probably included all those who were adherents of the Greek Orthodox church (Poulton 1994). Long standing Albanian fears about Greek designs on the southern part of the country, styled northern Epirus by Greek nationalists, continued in the post-communist era. As the twilight communist regime had liberalized, ethnic Greeks had agitated for and largely won the restoration of religious rights, greater press freedom and the restitution of property; attempts to assure the teaching of Greek in schools were less successful. For their part, Albanians believed that ethnic Greeks had better work and business opportunities, were benefiting from land privatization and had better access to medical care across the border in Greece (Nazi 1994). Ethnic Greek agitation focused around the pressure group Omonia ("Concord"), set up in 1989–90. Albania alleged Greek government involvement in stirring up the ethnic Greek movement, and was apprehensive of being squeezed at the same time by Serb destabilization in the north of the country, involving Albanians in Kosovo and in Macedonia; indeed a Serb–Greek alliance was feared. For its part, Greece had long protested at the treatment of the Greek minority in Albania, its fears heightened by the precedents of ethnic cleansing being set in neighbouring former Yugoslavia. Expulsion of ethnic Greeks to make way for the settlement of Albanians was feared.

Matters came to a head with the expulsion from Albania in June 1993 of an ethnic Greek cleric alleged to be fomenting dissent. Greece retaliated by expelling up to 26,000 Albanians. Immigration nevertheless continued and there were still said to be about 300,000 Albanians in the country (de Waal 1995). Ironically, Albania was by now economically buoyant. By 1993, remittances were worth $330 million, more than twice Albania's officially recorded export earnings; remittances had been almost nil in 1991. Having been written off as "clinically dead" in 1992, real GDP grew by 11 per cent in 1993 and was projected to grow 6 per cent in 1994 and 1995 (Economist Intelligence Unit 1994). A further irony was that Greek investment may have helped this turnaround, since Greek companies were involved in road and other infrastructure contracts, and Greek textile plants had relocated to southern Albania to take advantage of low wages (*The Economist* 17 September 1994).

Tension flared again in 1994 with the arrest by the Albanian authorities of members of the ethnic Greek movement and their jailing on spying and arms charges. Greece responded with the expulsion of more Albanian illegal migrant workers – up to 70,000 of the 150,000–300,000 estimated to be working in Greece were expelled in another Operation Broom (*The Economist* 17 September 1994; US Committee for Refugees 1995). Emigration pressure in Albania nevertheless appeared unrelenting: shortly afterwards, 15,000 Albanians were thwarted in an attempt to flee by ship.

Illegal immigration had meanwhile become almost a structural feature of Greece's society and economy. Most of the Albanian population in Greece were seasonal agricultural labourers or engaged in domestic service. Albanian workers were widely employed at low rates of pay on farms and building sites in Greece; despite low pay, migrants could earn 20 times or more in Greece than they could in Albania (de Waal 1995). It was suggested that illegals may have accounted for three-quarters of total immigration and for 8 per cent of the workforce (Glytzos 1995). The ethnic Greeks among them may have been of higher social status in terms of occupation and resources than other Albanian migrants. The IOM surveys of Albanian "potential migrants" in 1992 and 1995 found that about a quarter were white collar workers, civil servants, professionals or private business people (International Organisation for Migration 1993, 1995).

Late in 1995 the Greek government claimed that a million migrants, mainly Albanians, had entered Greece illegally since 1990, but this figure only seems plausible if it includes would-be immigrants turned back at the border. An estimate of 300,000 Albanians in Greece at any one time was consistent with earlier estimates. The government claimed to have spent $30 million on detaining and expelling illegals over the past four years. It had set up a task force combining the police, army, navy and coast guard, and sought assistance from the European Union to support its surveillance programme. The authorities claimed that 2,000 illegals were being deported daily, and that, in the first nine months of 1995, the Greek police had arrested and deported 175,000 Albanian illegal immigrants (*Guardian* 16 November 1995; Voice of America 2 November 1995).

Emigration to Italy also continued unabated. The Italian authorities deployed 500 troops along Italy's southern coastline in an attempt to thwart the thriving traffic in illegal migrants brought across the Strait of Otranto by speedboat (*Guardian* 11 May 1995; Reuter 23 August 1995). While most of the 15,000 apprehended were Albanians (US Committee for Refugees 1996), a growing number were Kurds, Chinese and other Asians, indicating that Albania was itself being transformed into a country of transit for third country would-be migrants into the European Union.

Apart from attempting to police the frontiers more rigorously, both the Greek and Italian governments continued investment in Albania to assist economic reconstruction in a bid to stem emigration. The investment was directed towards job creation in small scale ventures in rural areas and industry and in education and training (Glytzos 1995). As with other assistance of this kind, it appeared unlikely that in the short term such investment would discourage emigration from Albania, and the pattern of deportation and periodic expulsion from Greece and Italy seen in 1990–94 looked set to continue. Perhaps in recognition of this in March 1996 Greece and Albania signed a treaty under which Albania allowed the establishment of Greek schools for its ethnic Greek population, while Greece undertook to offer an amnesty to illegal immigrants from Albania (*Migration News* May 1996).

Late in 1996 Albania plunged into another crisis as a series of pyramid investment schemes collapsed, depriving huge numbers of Albanians of their savings. Nationwide unrest at this disaster escalated into armed rebellion in the south of the country, and a new exodus gathered momentum as people fled the chaos. By the end of March 12,000 Albanians had fled to Italy and 3,500 to Greece. While Italy had little choice but to accommodate most of the arrivals on a temporary basis at least, the presence of criminals among them, and the involvement of criminal organizations in their passage by sea, prompted repatriation of some Albanians and the establishment of naval patrols to turn back Albanian vessels (*Refugee Reports* March–April 1997).

Mass deportation and the migration order. Like the exodus of Bulgarian ethnic Turks, the mass emigration of Albanians to Greece and Italy was part of a series of exoduses precipitated by the Europe-wide demise of communist regimes. Unlike the exodus of Bulgarian ethnic Turks, however, this was a migration order very recently set in motion. As Albania's communist regime crumbled and the country emerged from isolation, closure and forced immobility swiftly gave way to an explosion of emigration from the end of 1990. As the communist regime unravelled, liberalization, economic deterioration and social unrest precipitated the mass exodus. The Albanian exodus initially took the form of seeking asylum, but rapidly became an issue of undocumented economic migration. Driving this incipient migration order was both economic necessity and long pent-up pressure for emigration, released from 1990. Subsequent mass exodus from Albania is attributable to the failure of democracy and a market economy convincingly to take root. The expulsions from Greece and Italy in 1990–94 can be seen as interventions attempting to roll back the emergence of this new migration order, part of the response of both countries to their transformation from countries of emigration to ones of immigration.

There were thought to be between 150,000 and 350,000 Albanians in Greece at any one time in 1991–94, the period of successive expulsions of illegal immigrants. The population of Greece was about 10 million at this time (World Bank 1994), so that at most Albanians would have added 3.5 per cent to the population in the country. Perhaps 200,000 were deported over the period, although many more may have been turned back at the border.

The Greek authorities' intermittent campaigns to deport Albanians reflected their ambiguous attitude towards Albanian immigration, which was seen as both economically beneficial and as a threat to national integrity. Issues of national integrity also featured insofar as Greece's concern about the fate of co-ethnics in Albania figured strongly in its relations with its neighbour; issues of membership figured insofar as nationality (if not citizenship) was an important question for the ethnic Greek minority in Albania. Greek and Italian concerns centred on the legitimacy of the Albanians' presence rather their demographic impact or their role in the economy, although, as elsewhere, there was anxiety, well-founded or not, about crime associated with immigrants. By investing substantially in Albania, both Greece and Italy hoped to halt the exoduses that challenged their fledgling immigration regimes, whose weak development necessitated the use of crude forms of immigration control like mass deportation.

Central America and the Caribbean: migrant worker expulsions in the 1950s and 1990s

Operation Wetback: the expulsion of Mexican migrants from the US

Expulsions of migrant workers are not confined to developing countries or to former communist states, nor are they only a feature of recent history. In 1954 the US authorities launched Operation Wetback, a campaign to deport illegal Mexican migrants from southern states of the US against the background of increasing concern at the volume of illegal migration that accompanied the legal import of Mexican workers under the Bracero Program. The US authorities claimed that 1.3 million illegal migrants left the US in fiscal year 1954, as a result of publicity before the campaign, in the course of Operation Wetback itself, or through routine deportations during the year. Some have cast doubt on this figure, but whatever the true number, several hundred thousands of Mexican migrants were compelled to leave the US in 1954.

Mexican migration to the US. Migration from Mexico to the US has a long history. There was a very large movement of migrants north towards the end of the nineteenth century drawn by railway construction. During recession Mexican migratory flows were curtailed and migrants were squeezed out; there was a mass deportation of Mexican workers during the 1930s (Balderrama & Rodriguez 1995). Mobilization in the US during the Second World War diminished sources of domestic labour, raised wage levels and increased pressure by employers for renewed import of Mexican workers, particularly for farm work in the southern states. An agreement was signed between the two countries in July 1942, and the first workers were admitted under what became known as the Bracero Program in September of that year. Although envisaged as a wartime contingency measure, the programme lasted 22 years until 1964 and involved the import of between 4.5 million and 5 million Mexican workers (Calavita 1995; Garcia 1980).

Under the agreement, the US Agriculture and Labor Departments signed contracts with individual Mexican workers, engaging them in specified occupations, usually in agriculture, for a specified period – usually one year, after which they were to return to Mexico. Certain minimal conditions of work and pay were guaranteed. However, applicants for bracero contracts far exceeded official labour requirements – one estimate was that only one in ten applicants received a contract – so that the Bracero Program was accompanied by a large unregulated exodus of workers from Mexico to find work. Such movement had been under way for decades, but was given new impetus. The Mexican government saw the programme as a means of

NEW DIASPORAS

making this outflow more orderly, but in the event it acted as a pump-primer for increased Mexican emigration (Calavita 1992, 1995; Garcia 1980).

The migrants were mainly single young men, mostly from small communities; most were landless, although they were not the poorest of the poor. More than nine-tenths of braceros employed went to Texas, California, Arizona, New Mexico and Arkansas, with California and Texas employing most. While legal entrants ran at between 45,000 and 200,000 annually in the first decade of the programme, illegal entrants were thought to number hundreds of thousands. That illegal migration burgeoned is borne out by apprehensions and deportation of illegals recorded: expulsions rose from about 57,000 in the first half of the 1940s to 856,000 in the latter half of the decade (Garcia 1980).

Not surprisingly, given the surplus of labour supply, the conditions of labour contracts were often not honoured, and there were frequent complaints of abuse and exploitation. These abuses by employers encouraged legal migrant workers to "skip" their contracts and join their many compatriots in the illegal labour market. The population of illegals was also swollen by those who had overstayed their contracts (Garcia 1980).

While the bracero programme was welcomed by the farm lobby, not all interests welcomed it. Among the opponents were organized labour, social and human rights organizations (including some Mexican-American groups), some religious organizations and small farmers who argued the case for the domestic migrant over the immigrant worker. As undocumented migration grew, concern about the issue spread to other constituencies, fed by reports in the popular press in the 1950s. Echoing more recent history, opposition to immigration was based on the view that the illegals undermined the country's working community, threatened social, political and economic stability, and violated immigration laws. Those who favoured unrestricted entry argued that undocumented workers were essential for the labour needs of agriculture. Indeed, by the 1950s, undocumented workers were entering in such large numbers that many employers chose to engage them in

128

preference to braceros, because the illegals had no rights and employers had no contract obligations to meet (Garcia 1980).

Operation Wetback, 1954. In 1954 the US authorities resolved to tackle the burgeoning problem of illegal immigration, but ambivalence over what should be done was widespread in Congress and among officials in Washington, reflecting the diversity of interests and views about the issue. A mass round-up and repatriation of illegal aliens was nevertheless called for. The campaign, which became known as Operation Wetback, has been described in detail by Garcia (1980), on which the following draws.

Army assistance was sought to implement the round-up, but the military was lukewarm to the proposal. Nevertheless, military consultants were brought in and the operation was planned along military lines. The cooperation of the Mexican authorities to remove deportees from its border areas was gained, although, fearful of adverse popular reaction, the Mexican government was content to cede responsibility for the campaign to the US. The operation was widely publicized in advance to pressure migrants to leave – partly because the Immigration and Naturalization Service (INS) did not have the resources to mount an operation large enough to apprehend and deport all of them. The advance publicity appears to have worked, for thousands of migrants began to leave California, Arizona and Texas.

The drive was directed at illegal aliens entering the country, in transit or already employed on farms or ranches. As well as the Border Patrol, other law enforcement agencies were enlisted, so that, unlike routine activity against illegals, the drive against them this time took the form of a large scale, coordinated campaign. The police were asked to apprehend and hold illegals on charges of vagrancy until they were dealt with by the INS. A "buslift" of illegals was organized to move them south to the border with Mexico, where between 1,000 and 2,000 deportees arrived daily. Later many apprehensions took place along the border, suggesting that efforts were by then directed to stopping migrants coming in rather than deporting those who had already entered illicitly.

Operation Wetback was launched first in California and Arizona, and then moved to Texas, where many growers had made little use of the Bracero Program, preferring to utilize undocumented and unregulated labour. The first deportations by ship began. The ironically named SS *Emancipation* and another vessel made 26 trips carrying 800 aliens per voyage; many of those boat-lifted were "repeaters" who had been expelled and managed to re-enter. By this time the campaign was drawing to a close, partly because it had exhausted INS funds and partly because the growing season was over; demand for labour had diminished and with it the incentive to enter the US illegally.

The operation was declared a great success. Commissioner of Immigration and Naturalization Joseph Swing claimed triumphantly in his annual report, "The so-called 'wetback problem' no longer exists ... The border has been secured" (US Department of Justice 1955, cited in Garcia 1980: 225). The much-touted success of Operation Wetback was used to good effect by the INS, which lobbied for and won significant increases in its funding vote from Congress. Images of a wetback invasion if vigilance was not maintained continued to prompt increases in appropriations in following years.

Closer scrutiny casts doubt on the success claimed. There are wide discrepancies in the numbers claimed deported. The INS claimed that voluntary departure begun before the deportation campaign, Operation Wetback itself, and routine deportations had resulted in the departure of 1.3 million illegals during the fiscal year 1954. However the number of apprehensions during Operation Wetback made up only a small proportion of the total number said to have departed; the INS claimed that the campaign resulted in just over 84,000 apprehensions and deportations in California, just over 23,000 in Arizona, and just over 80,000 in Texas (Garcia 1980). Although it seems unlikely that more than a million other migrants were induced to leave, a figure of several hundred thousand involuntary departures during the year – including those deported by state agencies and those indirectly induced to leave – does not seem implausible.

Although it slowed migration for a time, Operation Wetback

did not bring illegal migration from Mexico to an end, as subsequent history shows; at best it temporarily disrupted the inflow. Subsequently there were increases in the number of braceros engaged, but contracts began to decline after 1960 and the number of illegals apprehended rose again. Garcia argues that even the temporary decline in illegal migration is illusory, since many of the braceros contracted were apprehended wetbacks who legalized their status – the so-called "dried out" wetbacks. Meanwhile employers again began to hire undocumented workers in large numbers, even before the end of the Bracero Program in 1964 (Garcia 1980). While its effectiveness was questionable, Operation Wetback and its aftermath set the precedents for the struggle between migrants and the state over control of the border that has been under way ever since.

Operation Wetback and the migration order. Operation Wetback ruptured a migration order that by the 1950s was more than half a century old, substantial migration from Mexico to the US dating from the end of the nineteenth century. As the above account showed, in the first half of twentieth century migration flows broadly followed the economic health of the US; immigrants were encouraged during boom and ousted during recession. Shortages of domestic labour during the Second World War led to greater state intervention into migrant labour supply, culminating in the Bracero Program negotiated between the US and Mexico. The programme gave added impetus to the unregulated immigration that had been going on for decades. Both the legal and illicit migration was driven by economic necessity and the sharp economic disparities between the two countries. While the bulk of this migration was temporary, there was a substantial population of Mexican–Americans of long standing. The mass deportation of 1954 can be seen as perhaps the most far-reaching direct intervention attempted by the US authorities into the migration order, of many such interventions undertaken before and since.

It is difficult to estimate the numbers of Mexican migrants in the US at the time of Operation Wetback. If we accept the INS figure of 1.3 million departures during 1954, we might assume that the number of Mexican migrants in the US before the exodus to be of the order of 2 million. But as suggested above, the INS figure may well be an exaggeration. Whatever the current size of the Mexican migrant population in the US, it was small relative to the total US population of 155 million in 1954, although more significant when set against the population of the states involved – principally California (4.4 million in 1954), Arizona (456,000) and Texas (7.1 million) (US Department of Commerce, Bureau of the Census 1956).

Most of the Mexicans in the US at the time of Operation Wetback were seasonal farm workers, although some sought other work in industry and services. Many of the latter found employment in hotels and restaurants. The attitude of the host community to these migrants varied considerably. While many farmers, growers and other employers benefited from and defended their presence, labour organizations were among the interests that mobilized against foreign in favour of domestic migrant workers in the run-up to Operation Wetback. Of the mass exoduses considered in this book, the mass deportation of 1954 was probably the most hotly contested among diverse sections of the established population.

Citizenship was not an issue among the Mexicans removed from the US under Operation Wetback, except for those Mexican–Americans caught up in the deportation drives, and among whose community generally insecurity was heightened. For the majority of Mexican migrants, as for the other migrant workers reviewed in this book, it was rather the legality of their presence that was at issue. While anxieties about employment among US workers were among the factors shaping the drive towards intervention into Mexican immigration, probably more important were the issues of national integrity that surfaced in the shape of concern about control of the border with Mexico, galvanized by the growing thrust of state intervention at the time.

The expulsion of Haitians from the Dominican Republic
Like Operation Wetback, the last migration crisis considered here involved expulsion of foreign workers whose migration was long established. Following heavy international criticism of

the treatment of foreign workers and of child labour in particular, in mid-1991 President Balaguer of the Dominican Republic ordered the expulsion of all foreign workers employed in the sugar industry under the age of 16 or over the age of 60. Within three months, some 50,000–60,000 people of Haitian origin had left; while up to 8,000 people were deported under the provisions of the decree, the majority left for fear of what might happen to them as round-ups, arrests and deportations proceeded. The mass influx into Haiti helped precipitate the overthrow of the government there led by Jean-Bertrand Aristide. The mass deportation was wound down the day after the coup in Haiti, and a counter-flow of refugees to the Dominican Republic from the new Haitian military regime was set in motion, resulting in the return to the Dominican Republic of perhaps two-thirds of the Haitians only just expelled.

Haitian migration to the Dominican Republic. Like many other countries receiving migrants, the Dominican Republic's attitude to migration has been ambivalent. On the one hand migrant labour has been welcomed: indeed, the Dominican Republic's sugar industry has long been dependent on the exploitation of cheap labour from neighbouring Haiti, since Dominicans have been unwilling to cut cane because of its associations with slavery (Ferguson 1992). On the other hand, anti-immigrant sentiments have periodically precipitated violent moves against Haitian residents in the Dominican Republic. This antagonism has been fuelled by Dominican assertion of racial superiority deriving from Haitians' history of slavery, and anxiety about the dilution of the Dominican Republic's light-skinned, Spanish-speaking population by dark-skinned, Creole-speaking Haitians. A shared history of war, invasion and occupation has deepened the persistent rancour between the two countries.

Migration of Haitians to work in the sugar industry began in earnest in the 1930s. While the sugar companies welcomed the labour, the Dominican authorities were apprehensive about the influx of Haitians and its impact on the Republic. These tensions took violent form in 1937 when a dispute with Haiti escalated into a massacre of between 15,000 and 20,000 Haitians, mainly sugar workers, on the orders of the repressive General

Rafael Trujillo. In what became known as *El Corte* (the cutting), men, women and children were marched into the cane fields and slaughtered by the army (Ferguson 1992; Kirk 1992). But while *El Corte* was etched on Haitian historical consciousness and profoundly shaped Haitians' relations with the Dominican Republic, the massacre did little to deter migration.

After the Second World War, labour recruitment was regulated by bilateral agreement between the two countries. Three categories of Haitian labourers subsequently emerged in the Dominican Republic. The *congos* were those recruited through the official channels; the term is also used to describe first-time or freshly recruited cane cutters. Many of these stayed on after their contracts to become *viejos* or old hands. These were more or less permanent residents, some of whom married Dominican women. Few became citizens, but their children could become Dominican nationals by virtue of having been born on Dominican soil. In a third category were illegal workers who illicitly crossed the 300 kilometre porous border between the two countries (Ferguson 1992). The proportion of long term and more recent migrants is unclear.

With the fall of the Duvalier regime in 1986, the bilateral recruiting regime fell apart. As a result a labour shortage developed in the Dominican Republic, leading to the forced recruitment of labour for the sugar industry, including the plantations run by the Consejo Estatal del Azucar (CEA), the State Sugar Council (Ferguson 1992). Two main methods of forced recruitment were used. The cane companies, including the state-owned CEA, engaged Haitian recruiters known as *buscones* to recruit workers by deception in Haiti: the recruits were bussed to the border, then arrested as illegal immigrants by the Dominican military or police and taken forcibly to the sugar plantations. Alternatively, forced recruits were picked up by the military in periodic sweeps of Haitian *viejos* or illegals working in construction, gardening or as domestic workers in the Dominican Republic. The forced recruits were obliged to live in poor conditions in camps or barracks, known as *bateyes*, on the sugar plantations (Ferguson 1992; Kirk 1992).

As a result of this migration and unofficial settlement, a substantial population of Haitian origin, many of them *viejos* and their descendants, became permanent residents of the Dominican Republic. According to the Dominican authorities, there were more than a million Haitians in the Dominican Republic in the early 1990s. This total probably includes Dominico–Haitians and children of Haitians with a claim to Dominican nationality from birth in the Dominican Republic. A more plausible figure for the Haitian population resident in the country in about 1990 was 500,000 (Ferguson 1992; Kirk 1992). In mid-1991, the population of the Dominican Republic stood at 7.2 million (World Bank 1993), so the population of Haitian descent was a significant proportion of the Dominican Republic – up to 7 per cent. Many lived permanently in the country without papers because their status had never been regularized (Americas Watch 1992).

Fears of "swamping" and ethnic dilution by an influx of Haitians were often articulated in vitriolic terms by the authorities of the Dominican Republic. In 1984, president-to-be Balaguer wrote of "the erosion of Dominican national identity, steadily under way for more than a century through dealings with the worst of the Haitian population" (quoted by Ferguson 1992: 90). The hardening of such sentiments presaged the expulsion of people of Haitian origin in 1991 and after.

The expulsion of 1991. The mass exodus of 1991 has the dubious distinction of ostensibly being precipitated by human rights reports. Criticism from international human rights groups about forced recruitment and the labour conditions of Haitian sugar workers was taken up in the US Congress and threatened trade relations with the Dominican Republic. Some reforms followed, including undertakings to issue individual contracts to Haitian cane cutters, to regularise the status of resident Haitians and to improve conditions on the *bateyes* (Ferguson 1992). But abuses continued, and further evidence of forced recruitment and employment of child labour fed further criticism by human rights organisations, widely reported in the US media (Amato 1991; Americas Watch 1991, 1992; Americas Watch/National Coalition for Haitian Refugees 1990). The Dominican government's response this time was cynical. In June 1991 President Balaguer ordered the expulsion of Haitians under 16 and over

60 years of age, on the pretext of complying with the demands for the protection of the young and old from abuses. The decree was characterized by the Dominican Republic's ambassador to the US as "a humanitarian measure designed to solve any isolated problems that may have existed concerning the employment of Haitian children" (quoted by Lawyers Committee for Human Rights 1991: 4). Interestingly, President Balaguer also justified the measure by referring to US maltreatment of Dominicans – in particular their deportation from the US mainland and Puerto Rico (Ferguson 1992; Kirk 1992).

The round-ups and deportation began as the 1991 harvest was drawing to a close. The population targeted by the decree was quite small; all foreigners working in the sugar industry of the specified ages. But "foreigners" effectively meant Haitians. The decree did not distinguish between those legally resident in the Dominican Republic and illegals or undocumented people. It also appeared to disregard the government's recent undertakings to regularize the status of Haitian workers (Americas Watch 1992; Lawyers Committee for Human Rights 1991).

Moreover, implementation of the decree disregarded its own terms, for many of those deported were not of the specified ages, nor were they only sugar workers. Claims to Dominican citizenship were ignored by the Dominican police or military, who targeted anyone black, of Haitian appearance or accent; those expelled included dark-skinned Dominicans. Many of those arrested were beaten, racially and otherwise abused, robbed and had their documents seized or destroyed (Americas Watch 1992; Lawyers Committee for Human Rights 1991). These measures precipitated the flight of many more Haitians, Dominicans of Haitian descent and black Dominicans, fearful of deportation and mindful of the troubled history of Haitian migration. In particular, the memory of the 1937 massacre, *El Corte*, was deep.

Those forced to leave included people born in the Dominican Republic of Haitian parents, known as Dominico–Haitians, and people of mixed Dominican and Haitian parentage, known as *arrayanos*; both of these categories had a claim to citizenship because children born in the Dominican Republic of Haitian or mixed parentage had the constitutional right to Dominican nationality (Americas Watch 1992; Lawyers Committee for Human Rights 1991). Many with strong claims to citizenship or residence chose to leave in the atmosphere of persecution accompanying the implementation of the decree. Many of these had little or no experience of or connection with Haiti, and no resources with which to reconstruct their lives.

As well as workers in the sugar industry, human rights groups reported the targeting for expulsion of construction workers, carpenters, painters, masons and others in the building trade, domestic workers, store-keepers and people running small businesses (Americas Watch 1992; Lawyers Committee for Human Rights 1991). A 31-year-old man who had lived in the Dominican Republic for 15 years told a human rights organization:

> I was there at the time of the harvest and cut cane for eight years. Then I went to Santo Domingo to learn a trade. I worked in construction. I was on my way home when some Dominican soldiers asked me for my papers. I showed them my *cedula* (ID) and my birth certificate. They tore them up. They arrested me. I was taken to [San Cristobal detention centre] and kept in jail for seven days. Then I arrived here. I don't know anyone. I left everything I had in Santo Domingo (Americas Watch 1992: 17).

As well as habitual concerns, articulated in scarcely veiled racial terms, about the threat Haitians were alleged to pose, the Dominican authorities cited economic grounds to justify the expulsion:

> We would like to point out that the problem is not merely one of immigration and demographics. It is more serious still, as it has numerous economic, labor, social and health implications. First, estimates are that there are more than one million Haitians in our country. They represent a very competitive labor force that displaces Dominican workers. Finally, the problem has enormous political and economic significance, considering the tremendous burden that this

vast number of immigrants represents for the Dominican state, especially in the midst of this crisis that grips our country as it does so many others, when we have to restore the health of our economy ... (response of the government of the Dominican Republic, 1 July 1991 to the cable of the Inter-American Commission of Human Rights, 26 June 1991, reproduced by Henckaerts 1995: 229–39).

However, the prime determinant of the expulsion was the Haitians' ethnicity rather than their position in the economy.

Between 50,000 and 60,000 people may have fled to Haiti between June and the beginning of October 1991 (Americas Watch 1992; Kirk 1992; UNHCR 1991). The mass influx put great pressure on the Haitian government led by Jean-Bertrand Aristide, which was already under considerable strain. In a speech to the UN General Assembly, Aristide condemned the treatment of Haitian workers in the Dominican Republic; days later he was overthrown in the coup of 29–30 September (Ferguson 1992). Significantly, the repatriation was wound down the day after the coup and a counter-flow of refugees to the Dominican Republic from the new Haitian military regime began almost immediately. Church groups estimated that two-thirds of those who left in the expulsion returned, together with many first time cane cutters, so that there were more Haitians in the *bateyes* in 1992 than there were before the expulsion (Kirk 1992). This counter-movement is explored further in Chapter 6.

Expulsions of undocumented migrants continued in subsequent years. Early in 1996, 2,000 Haitians were repatriated after an army round-up of undocumented aliens (Reuter 30 April 1996); then, invoking the 1991 decree, a further 1,000 people of Haitian origin were expelled in the middle of the year in conditions similar to the mass expulsion of 1991 (US Committee for Refugees 1996). Early in 1997 the Dominican Republic launched another campaign to detain and deport Haitian immigrants. The government's suggestion at the end of 1996 that recruitment of several thousand Haitian cane cutters might be needed for the harvest provoked a backlash, nationalist, anti-Haitian and racist in tone. The official response to this reaction was to order another mass deportation, and in an exodus again similar to the expulsion of 1991, some 15,000 Haitians and Dominicans of Haitian descent were forced to leave the Dominican Republic. The deportation was again carried out by the Dominican army which conducted sweeps of neighbourhoods where Haitians and Dominico–Haitians were concentrated. People of Haitian appearance were once more arrested, detained and sent to the border. As in 1991, they could not collect personal belongings or notify their families; their identification papers were ignored or destroyed; families were split and children separated from their parents (National Coalition for Haitian Rights 1996, 1997). The mass exodus was greeted by outrage in Haiti and protest by the Haitian government, but the two governments came to an agreement early in February under which Haiti agreed to try to control the outflow of its nationals while the Dominican Republic undertook greater coordination with Haiti over the deportations. As in the previous expulsions, those affected included second and third generation children of Haitian immigrants who were entitled to Dominican citizenship, and Haitian cane cutters and their families brought into the country legally since the 1950s whose status has never been regularized.

Mass expulsion and the migration order. The expulsion of 1991 was just the largest in a recent series of such episodes which have temporarily disrupted the migration order. Migration of Haitians to the Dominican Republic was long-standing, beginning in earnest in the 1930s, driven mainly by poverty in Haiti and drawn by the sugar industry in the Dominican Republic. As in the US, the Second World War marked a change in the migration order, as labour supply became regulated by bilateral agreements. As in other cases reviewed here, the population of Haitian origin resulting from this migration over several decades combined a long-established community with more recent arrivals. The recruiting regime fell apart in the later 1980s and the ensuing labour shortage led to the emergence of forced recruitment of labour for the sugar industry and the presence in the Dominican Republic of more Haitians of uncertain status. The mass expulsion of 1991 had a bloodier precedent in the massacre of Haitians in 1937. As then, the upheaval only temporarily reversed the migratory flow, for many of the migrants returned as refugees from Haiti almost immediately after the mass exodus; the migration order was sustained, only changing in that forced recruitment of labour was no longer necessary.

The decree that precipitated the mass exodus from the Dominican Republic was ostensibly targeted at "foreigners", but as well as recent and long-settled Haitian migrant workers, those expelled included many who had Dominican citizenship or a claim to it. Although the challenge was never made explicit, the claims to Dominican citizenship of Dominico–Haitians, the rights of residence of long-settled people of Haitian origin, and the legality of the presence of more recent Haitian migrants were all challenged in the course of the migration crisis of 1991 and after.

Economic motivations were at play in the expulsion, which occurred after the end of the sugar cane harvest. But this was a relatively weak motivation, a relatively minor adjustment to the labour supply and a partial removal of the irritant of an under-class engaged in the informal sector. A rather stronger politico-economic motivation, as elsewhere, was to provide a diversion, a scapegoat, for the strain economic austerity was putting on the population at large. Also powerful were issues of national integrity, in particular the alleged threat posed by Haitian migration to race and nation, which had long been a theme among the Dominican Republic's rulers. The international arena was also significant in this case. The expulsion was an unsubtle response to international pressure, a snub to international human rights groups. It also had the effect of helping to destabilize the neighbouring, already teetering government of Jean-Bertrand Aristide, with which the Balaguer regime had little sympathy.

Of the ten episodes of mass exodus examined, the expulsion of Haitians from the Dominican Republic was the most short-lived, and its disruption of the migration order the least enduring. Indeed, by enhancing the insecurity of the migrant community of Haitian origin, the episode reinforced that very migration order, which has featured similar mass expulsions of Haitians in subsequent years.

Conclusion: comparing the character of migration crises

The ten cases reviewed in this and the previous chapter illustrate the range of migration upheavals that have occurred as changes have permeated the world migratory dispensation, particularly in recent years. While only two episodes – those in the Balkans – were directly associated with the end of the Cold War and the dissolution of the communist bloc, five others – the Middle East, Asian and Caribbean cases – were all contemporary with these events, suggesting that the beginning of the 1990s was a pivotal moment in the world migratory order.

The effects of the crisis on each migration order varied. For some, the crisis did mark a fundamental enduring shift in the migration order. For others, the shift was fundamental but only partial, in that the previous migration order resumed, although more weakly than before. For still others, the crisis marked only a temporary shift in the migration order, which rapidly resumed its prior shape. For still others, the crisis marked an accentuation of what was already under way. For some, the migration crisis was the culmination of a long-term process; for others it was a sudden rupture. These different outcomes are explored further in the following chapters.

As I indicated in Chapter 2, such crises throw into relief the working of migration orders. Common processes can be seen at work in the cases sketched in this and the previous chapter. To conclude the exposition of the 10 cases, I summarize and compare the character of the migration crises by drawing out the features of the migration order and of each migrant community that came to be at issue during each episode.

Force, choice and the migration order

The migration orders outlined featured long-settled communities of migrant origin, short-term migrant populations and intermediate categories in which long settlement was overlain by more recent arrivals. For some, like the Ugandan Asians, the ethnic Turks, the Rohingyas and the ethnic Nepalis, their migratory background was of several generations standing. For others, like many of the Palestinians, some of the Yemenis and some of the Haitians, migration had occurred in the previous generation. For the Ghanaians, some of the Yemenis, the Albanians, some of the Haitians and the Mexicans, migration had occurred in the lifetime of the migrant population itself. Several of the long-settled populations were joined by later arrivals, usually of cognate origin, making the community's collective migration biography complex. Moreover, different waves or cohorts of arrivals may have migrated under different circumstances. Some of these prior migrations involved greater choice than others. Several populations – notably the Palestinians in Kuwait, the ethnic Turks in Bulgaria, the Rohingyas in Burma, and the Haitians in the Dominican Republic – had previously experienced force at various stages of their migratory careers. Forced migration has thus been an important feature of some of their migration histories, even prior to the migration crises reviewed here. The types of migrant community and their varying status prior to exodus are summarized in Table 4.1.

The migration histories of these communities indicate how developments in the political economy and in the evolution of nation-states shaped the context in which individual and household decisions to migrate were made, how connections between

Table 4.1 Status of migrant communities prior to exodus

	Temporary migrants	Long-term residents	Nationals
Asians in Uganda 1972		+	+
Ghanaians in Nigeria 1983	+		
Palestinians in Kuwait 1990		+	
Yemenis in Saudi Arabia 1990	+	+	
Ethnic Turks in Bulgaria 1989			+
Albanians in Greece 1991	+		
Rohingyas in Myanmar 1991	+	+	+
Ethnic Nepalis in Bhutan 1991	+	+	+
Mexicans in the US 1954	+		
Haitians in the Dom. Rep. 1991	+	+	+

countries of migrant origin and destination were established, how migration regimes developed and changed, and how migrant networks which sustained migratory flows emerged. Most of the movements involving migrant workers were predicated on substantial economic disparities between the place of origin and destination. But economic determinants were by no means the whole story, and political and strategic factors were often just as important in shaping migration orders. The following sections focus on the features of these unfolding migration orders and of the migrant communities they encompassed that became areas of strain: these cluster around issues of demography, socio-economic status, and membership.

Demography. Demographic concerns played a strong part in several of the episodes reviewed, although these concerns did not always match demographic reality. Indeed, given that demography was often an arena of contention, it is often not certain what those demographic realities were. Table 4.2 presents the demographic data in so far as they can be known or estimated. As the table shows, the size of these migrant communities, both absolute and in proportion to their host populations, varied considerably. Only in half of the cases did

Table 4.2   Size and proportion of migrant communities prior to exodus

	Size of migrant community	Total population of host country (millions)	Proportion (per cent)
Asians in Uganda 1972	74,000	10.0	<1.0
Ghanaians in Nigeria 1983	c. 1 million	90.0	1.0
Palestinians in Kuwait 1990	400,000	2.1	20.0
Yemenis in Saudi Arabia 1990	c. 1 million	14.9	7.0
Ethnic Turks in Bulgaria 1989	850,000	9.0	9.5
Albanians in Greece 1991	150–300,000	10.0	<3.0
Rohingyas in Burma 1991	1–2 million	43.0	2.0–4.0
Ethnic Nepalis in Bhutan 1991	200,000	0.6	33.0
Mexicans in the US 1954	2–3 million?	155.0	1.3–2.0
Haitians in the Dom. Rep. 1991	500,000	7.2	7.0

Sources: migrant community populations, as in text; total populations of host countries, World Bank, *World Development Report*, various years; US Department of Commerce, Bureau of the Census 1956.

the migrant communities account for more than a small proportion of the total population, although in some cases concentration of the populations of migrant origin pushed the proportions in particular regions higher.

The table shows that the size of the migrant community involved in migration crisis relative to the host society was substantial in the cases of the ethnic Turks in Bulgaria, the Palestinians in Kuwait, the Yemenis in Saudi Arabia, the ethnic Nepalis in Bhutan, the Albanians in Greece, and the Haitians in the Dominican Republic; the Rohingyas were numerically significant in Arakan state in Burma. Demographic concerns were particularly significant in helping to generate the migration crises in Bulgaria, Kuwait, Bhutan and the Dominican Republic. They were most explicit in the case of the ethnic Turks in Bulgaria, but the demographic balance between nationals and foreigners was also a pressing matter in Kuwait at the time of the Gulf crisis. The demographic balance in Bhutan was an underlying concern rather than an explicitly articulated one, although there had long been anxiety in Bhutan about being over-run by Nepalis or absorption into a "Greater Nepal". The danger of ethnic dilution by Haitian migrants has also often been expressed in the Dominican Republic. Perhaps surprisingly, given the numbers and proportions involved, such concerns were not explicitly articulated in the Yemeni, Rohingya and Albanian episodes. In the case of the Asians in Uganda, the Ghanaians and other West Africans in Nigeria, and the Mexicans in the US, the numbers involved may have been substantial, but the proportions can hardly be said to have been significant, although in the latter two cases, as in others, fears about unbridled immigration and anxiety that control of borders was being lost were concerns often articulated.

Socio-economic status. The socio-economic status of migrant communities and their place in the political economy – summarized in Table 4.3 – had a strong bearing in generating several of the migration crises.

As with demography, perceptions of the migrant community by the larger society were often at some variance with reality. There was also a circularity to the social and economic margin-

Table 4.3 Socio-economic composition of migrant communities prior to exodus

Asians in Uganda	Middleman or auxiliary minority of traders and business people, technical, administrative and managerial staff; teachers, storekeepers, petty traders and artisans
Ghanaians in Nigeria	Unskilled and semi-skilled labourers, artisans, petty traders, business people, professional, administrative and managerial staff, teachers
Palestinians in Kuwait	Middleman or auxiliary minority of business people and traders, technical, administrative and managerial staff; teachers, storekeepers, petty traders artisans and semi-skilled workers
Yemenis in Saudi Arabia	Unskilled labourers, semi-skilled labourers, drivers and artisans, petty traders and store-keepers, restaurateurs and bakers, office workers, merchants and business people
Ethnic Turks in Bulgaria	Mainly peasant farmers, some clerical, sales and service workers, some professionals and technical staff
Albanians in Greece	Seasonal, unskilled and semi-skilled farm and construction workers, domestic workers
Rohingyas in Burma	Mainly peasant farmers and labourers, a few professionals and business people
Ethnic Nepalis in Bhutan	Mainly peasant farmers, some artisans and labourers, shop-keepers, traders and a few professionals
Mexicans in the US	Mainly seasonal farm workers, some industrial and service workers
Haitians in the Dominican Republic	Sugar workers, construction and domestic workers, artisans, storekeepers and small business people

alization that fed antagonism against the migrant communities. Some, like the Ugandan Asians and to some extent the Palestinians in Kuwait, were alleged to dominate particular markets, occupations or sectors of the economy to the detriment of the majority populations. Some – the Ugandan Asians again, the Rohingyas, the ethnic Nepalis and the ethnic Turks – were accused of failing to integrate into the wider society, and their loyalty was called into question. Some, like the Ghanaians in Nigeria, the Albanians in Greece and the Haitians in the Dominican Republic, were held responsible for crime and other social and political instability. While these allegations were sometimes founded in part, more often they were manifestations of the search for scapegoats at times of political, economic or social strain. By a process of generalization, the shortcomings of one section of the migrant community were extended to the whole of it, belying the fact such communities were often socioeconomically diverse, as the table shows.

Their position came under the particular gaze of the majority society at such times of stress in the political economy. In the two African cases, the background to mass exodus was severe economic strain accompanied by social and political unrest that threatened the ruling regime. In the Middle East it was a regional political upheaval, coupled with longer term economic changes, that precipitated the migration crisis. Explanation of the migration crises in the Asian cases are to be found more in the arena of challenges to national integrity than in the economy, although strains were certainly evident there. Political economy in upheaval and national integrity under threat were evident in mixed proportions in the two Balkans episodes and in the cases drawn from Central America and the Caribbean.

The question of membership. Often closely related to socioeconomic status, issues of membership came to prominence at times when national integrity – usually as represented by the ruling regime – was under real or imagined challenge, either from within or from without. Ambivalent membership status that led to questioned loyalty often derived from the diverse origins and development of the migrant communities. Questions of membership, belonging and integration underlay attitudes to and treatment of the Asian population in Uganda, the Rohingyas in Myanmar, the ethnic Nepalis in Bhutan, the ethnic Turks of Bulgaria, and the people of Haitian origin in the Dominican Republic. Membership questions were manifested in different ways. Citizenship and nationality issues were particularly significant in the Asian cases, while for other long-settled populations it was more the right of residence that was at issue. For more recent migrants it was the very legality of their presence that was challenged. Argument over the legitimacy of a

Table 4.4   Nature of the challenge to the migrant communities

	Legality of presence challenged	Rights of residence challenged	Citizenship disputed	Ethnicity/ cultural challenge
Asians in Uganda 1972		+	+	+
Ghanaians in Nigeria 1983	+			
Palestinians in Kuwait 1990		+		
Yemenis in Saudi Arabia 1990	+	+		
Ethnic Turks in Bulgaria 1989				+
Albanians in Greece 1991	+			
Rohingyas in Myanmar 1991	+	+	+	+
Ethnic Nepalis in Bhutan 1991	+	+	+	+
Mexicans in the US 1954	+			
Haitians in the Dom. Rep. 1991	+	+	+	+

migrant community's presence was often couched in ethnic, religious or cultural terms.

The pretexts for inducing mass exodus clustered around these four main dimensions of membership: the legality of the migrant community's presence; the right of residence; citizenship claims; and cultural compatibility. As Table 4.4 shows, these dimensions were often combined. Thus the rights of residence of Ugandan Asians were challenged, their citizenship was disputed, and their cultural and ethnic compatibility with the majority population was questioned. In the cases of the Ghanaians in Nigeria, the Albanians in Greece and the Mexicans in the US, the challenge was to the legality of their presence. For the Palestinians in Kuwait and the Yemenis in Saudi Arabia, it was the right of residence that was undermined or removed. The challenge to the ethnic Turks in Bulgaria was to their ethnic, cultural and religious compatibility with the majority population. All four dimensions figured in the cases of the Rohingyas in Burma, the ethnic Nepalis in Bhutan, and the Haitians in the Dominican Republic, with religious difference playing a significant part in the Burma and Bhutan cases.

The moment of upheaval: precipitating migration crises
If these were the ways in which antagonism to migrant communities was manifested, the intentions of governments

towards migrant communities in their territories were not always transparent. For example, as was indicated in Chapter 3, it was not clear if the SLORC intended to expel the Rohingyas, as in 1978, or if the regime's intervention in Arakan was part of the nation-wide intimidation of dissidents in response to the 1988 democracy movement and contingent upheaval. Similarly, it is not clear that the Bhutanese authorities set out in the mid-1980s with the intention of ridding the country of its ethnic Nepali population. More likely, there was a cumulative escalation of moves against this community; this successively provoked reaction and protests that in turn led to the decision substantially to reduce the ethnic Nepali population. Opportunism or pragmatism were perhaps the overriding features of the Kuwaiti authorities in the mass exodus of Palestinians. While concern had been expressed about the level of the foreign population in general and of the Palestinians in particular, the Gulf crisis presented the opportunity to realize the tacit aspiration to remove part of the foreign population regarded as of doubtful loyalty through the mass departure of Palestinians. Similarly the Gulf crisis provided the Saudi authorities with the pretext to implement measures against Yemeni migrants under consideration for some time.

The degree of force and the way it was deployed also varied considerably. In most of the cases – those of Uganda, Nigeria, Saudi Arabia, Kuwait, Bhutan, Greece, the Dominican Republic and the US – decrees were promulgated, legal measures were undertaken, or other administrative action was instigated to direct migrant-origin populations to leave. These were direct or "hard" expulsions (see Chapter 1 and Henckaerts 1995). In the cases of Bulgaria, Myanmar and the early waves of departure from Kuwait, the pressures were more indirect, though nonetheless compelling. In all of the episodes, inducing people to leave involved varying combinations of harassment, intimidation, persecution and actual violence. But while intimidation, persecution and violence could be widespread, sparing application of abuse could yield disproportionate results, for fear was as potent a means of inducing people to move as actual violence. Indeed, the majority of the people in these episodes moved, not because they were directly persecuted or because of actual violence against them, but because they felt that life was no longer tolerable in the place they were trying to make a life. In terms of the framework I laid out in Chapter 2, these people were left with little choice but to move. I turn to the consequences of such movements for the making and unmaking of transnational communities in the following chapters.

FIVE

Consequences of migration crises

Having examined the character of the 10 migration crises in Chapters 3 and 4, I turn in this chapter to some of the socio-economic consequences of these migration crises. Pursuing the question "crisis for whom?", I look at the effects of migration crises on the three principal parties involved in them: the migrant communities themselves; the territories and established populations receiving those communities; and the territories the migrant communities were obliged to leave. Since the data available varies greatly among the 10 cases, examples are used selectively in this chapter.

The effects of migration crises on migrant communities

Migrants' testimonies of their experience during mass exodus portray the atmosphere of tension and panic that prevails when ethnic rivalry, racism or xenophobia are heightened. They show how fear is a powerful means of inducing people to move, particularly when memories of earlier episodes of violence and upheaval are touched off. Among Haitians in the Dominican Republic, for example, the folkloric memory of the 1937 massacre of Haitians was deeply held: "In 1937 they tossed babies into the air and caught them on bayonet points. I didn't want that happening to my kids", a black Dominican laundress told Reuter news agency, after fleeing with her Haitian-born husband and five children (Reuter 10 September 1991). Likewise, the memory among Rohingyas of Operation Dragon King in 1978 was still fresh in the early 1990s.

Testimonies also show how physically and psychologically traumatic are the effects of mass exodus on the people forced to move. As well as suffering the fear and indignity of being rounded up by the police or army, physical assaults by the security forces or members of the majority community are routine. Arbitrary treatment leaves a lasting sense of injustice. Documents are often confiscated or torn up, and less tangible dimensions of identity destroyed. Households are split up, and children separated from their parents. People are obliged to leave behind their livelihoods and possessions, or to sell their assets at knock-down prices; belongings may be stolen or lost, and wages owed forgone; and the prospect of recovering assets is a forlorn one. A lifetime's effort may be lost, a way of life destroyed. An ethnic Nepali woman factory worker expelled from Bhutan told Amnesty International:

During the census operation in Chhukha district in 1993 I was classified as F7 (non-national) because I did not have a land tax receipt for 1958. I surrendered the land tax receipts that I did have in my possession to the census team. I was born in Bhutan, but I do not know whether my parents were born in Bhutan or not. I was a factory worker and I was due two weeks' wages which is why I remained in my house. One day five soldiers came to my house and asked me why I had not left. They grabbed me and pushed me to the ground. My 15-year-old daughter was so afraid that she ran away into the forest. I was so scared that I left Bhutan immediately with my three children (Amnesty International 1994: 10).

Similar stories were told by Haitian expellees from the Dominican Republic:

I left Haiti with my parents when I was 7 months old. I was living in Santo Domingo and worked there as a house painter. I was sick and was coming out of hospital when soldiers asked me if I was Haitian. I showed them my papers. They arrested me. I was taken to San Cristobal [detention centre] where I spent six days before coming here, I learned that my wife had also been arrested and sent here. I've lost track of her. Everything I owned was left in Santo Domingo.

I come from Belladere and spent six years in the Dominican Republic. I was a cane cutter. The working conditions were hard. I escaped to Santo Domingo from a *batey*. I had been working as a mason's helper. I was crossing the street when about six Dominican soldiers aimed their guns at me. They said I'm Haitian and they were going to arrest me and send me to my president. They took me to a large bus as if I were a thief. They told me I was going to San Cristobal for a few days before being sent home. I spent nine days in San Cristobal. I have only the clothes on my back (Americas Watch 1992: 17, 19).

Rohingyas forced to flee Myanmar experienced greater brutalization:

We didn't come here happily. We came here because we were suffering in Burma … The government was constructing a road from Buthidaung to Tang Bazaar … Each person was to build [12 feet] of road. Those who were unable to work because of fatigue were taken to the bushes and beaten … The women were not spared. They were also forced to work and were raped by soldiers at night (Lambrecht 1995: 8).

I came here after my sister … was raped and killed by the army. She was taken away and then the next day they dumped her body on the rubbish tip outside the village, I was the first person to find her. When I saw my sister, I just ran away and came right here (Amnesty International 1992b).

Even where expellees do not suffer actual violence, the

debilitating effects of expulsion are profound. In his memoir of the Asian exodus from Uganda, Mamdani records the unsettling and depressing character of forced departure:

> Every day busloads of people departed for the airport. In the confusion, there was never time to see more than a few people before departure. For those who were staying behind, it became a daily ritual to go to Airways House in the evening and say goodbye to any familiar faces there. This was, however, not a usual goodbye, for everybody would be leaving sooner or later. Yet, in most cases, there were no addresses to be exchanged. One wondered if one would ever see the friend again. After each bus had left there was the same gloom, the same feeling of hopelessness and despair. Soon we stopped going to Airways House (Mamdani 1973: 65).

The journey out of the country itself involves hardship, privation and often physical danger. Transport costs are inflated by profiteers, and agreements over destinations are frequently not honoured, with expellees being dumped at borders to fend for themselves. Border crossings themselves present further hazards, where forced migrants are prey to extortion by officials and others. Some of the confusion involved in the upheaval is conveyed in this account by a young Ghanaian woman caught up in the expulsion from Nigeria in 1985:

> They were arresting people ... they said that if they see any Ghanaian they will arrest the Ghanaian. My sister and myself, we had to hide, because the soldiers were coming ... Then one day they said they were sacking people and we didn't believe it. They gave a deadline and we didn't have money so we said maybe before the deadline we will get some money and transport ourselves. The date was getting near when a driver came that would take us. He looked at all our luggage and he checked all the amount and we all paid. He took the things to his house in his lorry. Then he said the next morning he would come and pick us and bring us. Three days went by and

the two of us, we went to his house and enquired about him ... All the luggages were lying there in the house. Ashantis, Ghanaians, some of them with children on their backs, they were all lying in that house. Then we asked of the man. They said he had gone out and he would come and meet us. When he came, we just started crying, saying we wanted our money. So he gave us our money, to us without any deduction ... Then we went to look for transport ... Tomorrow would be the last day of the date [the deadline], so that afternoon we left. I was charged 150 naira [a very large sum at the time]. [The lorry driver] said he was going to leave us at Accra. We didn't get to [the border] and it was night. Many people were sleeping and the lorry goes halt. The front tyre went off so the vehicle went into the bush. So we slept till the next morning. The driver took the tyre to get it mended. We were lying in the bush there ... All this time on that road, rain is beating you there, everything is beating you there...

The expellees were then made to return to Lagos and corralled at the Murtala Mohammed International Airport, from which several hundred broke out and rioted. Those who were left were ordered to board a ship, which they refused to do. This woman and some friends later found another truck to take them to the border:

At [the border] there are always soldiers, so if you do not pay money, you do not collect your things. And even if you have money you have to put down your luggage and remove what they want before they let you go ... [This time] the driver was a Ghanaian, he suffered to bring the vehicle from Nigeria ... Truly when we came to Benin, we kept our luggages in some house. And before we came back to Benin, people stole most of our things. When we went to Accra, everywhere we went, they were giving us food, [but] they were not giving us money. Accra, I didn't know anybody, three days. We were sleeping in the timber market. And a lorry came and the man said he was going to charge us, but when we came home then he [would] take his money. So that was what we did and we came [home] to Tamale ... (interview, Tamale, Ghana, 1987).

Even after arrival and relative security is attained, for many the prospect of reconstructing a life is daunting. For many Palestinians, the exodus from Kuwait was their second or even their third uprooting. As one elderly returnee to Jordan put it: "In 1948 I was 22 and I was able to start again. In 1967 I was 41 and I was able to start again. In 1990 I was 64 and now I am unable to start all over again" (interview Amman 1993). For others, there was little prospect of remaking home: a sign erected by Bhutanese refugees outside a refugee camp in Nepal stated:

Bhutan is our homeland. We had been there for genera- tions. We had land and house to live. We were productive farmers, self reliant and peace loving people. We want to go back to our home early. It is our plea to our well wishers to send us back with dignity, safety, security and assurance of our human rights, so the money you are spending on us can be saved for future calamities or spare to other destitutes in the world.

While the short term effects of migration crises on the populations involved can be pieced together to some extent from first hand accounts and the reports of human rights organizations and assistance agencies, evidence of the effects after the immediate crisis is more scanty. The rest of this section draws on fieldwork by the author in 1993 among the people received by Jordan and Yemen in the wake of the Gulf crisis designed to elicit the impacts of mass exodus on these popula- tions two or three years on.

The Kuwait Palestinians in Jordan: mixed fortunes
As I noted in Chapter 3, the characterization of the returnees from Kuwait as a wealthy class obscured the diversity of wealth among them. All the same, even those who had not accu- mulated wealth on any substantial scale had led relatively comfortable lives in Kuwait and other Gulf states. A majority of

returnees now found themselves impoverished, relatively or absolutely in Jordan.

Successful reconstruction of lives and livelihoods in Jordan much depended on the recovery of assets and entitlements from Kuwait or other Gulf states. While almost all households were obliged to leave behind some of their assets and property, or to sell their assets at a loss, many were also able to bring or later to recover substantial assets, including work-related entitlements, savings and capital. However, these savings and other assets were often rapidly depleted on living expenses in Jordan.

As savings and assets diminished, Jordan's labour market provided little respite for returnees, a majority of whom remained without work. According to a survey of April 1991, only 16 per cent of those in its sample of returnees seeking work had found employment (Jordan NCERD 1991). Returnees' employment appears to have improved only a little subsequently. Jordan's Ministry of Labour estimated 60 per cent unemployment among returnees early in 1993, which roughly squares with my 1993 interview findings: just over one-third of 100 returnees interviewed in 1993 had found regular employment, and of these, two-thirds were self-employed. Others found occasional work, but more than half of those interviewed were unemployed. This compares unfavourably with estimates of unemployment rates nationally, which ranged between 20 and 25 per cent, having increased from just over 10 per cent in 1989 and 17 per cent in 1990 (Amerah et al 1993; UNICEF 1992).

Living costs were partly obviated for some returnee households by the ownership of housing. The survey of 1991 mentioned above suggested a surprisingly high proportion of home ownership among returnees, but this proportion fell among later arrivals. It is likely that more households in the first wave of arrivals owned housing or had access to family homes than those in subsequent waves who tried to stay on in Kuwait for precisely the reason that they had no such assets to call upon in Jordan. Two years later just under one-third of households I interviewed owned homes, or had a claim to family houses; about 10 per cent of households had bought houses after their arrival. However, accommodation owned was not always accessible, since other family members or tenants might be in occupation. Just over a quarter of households interviewed lived in their own homes, and a smaller proportion in family houses or those of relatives, but the latter arrangement was often far from ideal given the overcrowding that this generated. The remaining households were obliged to resort to the highly priced rental sector; evictions were increasingly common as funds ran out.

Family and kin networks were important for initial support and for finding accommodation: many returnees stayed with relatives at first, and then rented housing. But such support had its limits, could lead to hardship and tension within households, and diminished as a source of supplementing livelihood as time went on. Other, often sporadic, sources of income included borrowing, charity, and recourse to returnee self-help organizations. In a telling reversal of roles, remittances from relatives abroad elsewhere than the Gulf were reported to have become an important source of income for one-tenth of returnee households interviewed.

Two or more years after their arrival, returnees were experiencing very mixed fortunes. While some had managed to rebuild their homes and lives, others were in severe straits. Based on their former occupations while abroad, the following categories of returnee households could be discerned among those interviewed in 1993.

The first category comprised households headed by unskilled workers in Kuwait, including general labourers, storemen, office messengers and guards; some of these had run small businesses in addition to their waged employment. In Jordan none of the households interviewed in this category had members in regular employment. Almost all rented accommodation, which was poor and overcrowded. Health problems were common, and, because of the high cost of health care in Jordan, often went untreated. The modest savings and work-related entitlements of these households were spent on transport from Kuwait, and then rapidly depleted on rent and living expenses.

A second category consisted of households headed by skilled workers, clerks, supervisors, drivers or artisans in Kuwait's public, parastatal or private sector; like other waged workers they might also have run a small business. About half of the households interviewed in this category had one or more members in work after coming to Jordan. Some ran taxis, grocery, confectionery or hardware stores, bakeries or other small businesses; others had found waged work in offices or shops; the remainder were unemployed. More than half of these households rented costly and often inadequate rented accommodation, while others shared housing with relatives – although often this accommodation could not sustain overcrowding, obliging a move into rented housing. About a quarter of the households interviewed in this category owned their own houses, suggesting that the circumstances of at least some were not as reduced as might be expected. Some, mainly those formerly employed in the public sector or in large scale private firms, had managed to secure work-related entitlements before leaving Kuwait or after arrival in Jordan.

A third category comprised households headed by petty traders and those who had run small businesses in Kuwait, with a Kuwaiti *kafeel* as a silent partner. Members of such households included those who formerly ran haulage and furniture businesses, retail and wholesale traders and second-hand car dealers; these were one-person concerns or staffed by family labour. Few such households interviewed had members working in Jordan, and only one had restarted a business. With no work-related entitlements because of their self-employment, and with recovery of assets unlikely, such households were in a vulnerable position in Jordan. Almost all lived in rented accommodation.

A fourth category comprised households headed by professionals, technicians, administrators and managers in Kuwait, including accountants, doctors and other medical staff, journalists, engineers, translators, teachers and university lecturers. Like the skilled workers and artisans, the circumstances of these households varied. Half of these households had no regular income-earner, and, with assets brought back from Kuwait almost gone, were in a vulnerable state. Of those earning, half were in salaried employment and half had set up small businesses, such as shops, small restaurants or farms, on their own or with returnee partners; this employment was usually unrelated to their former professions and none reported much success with their new businesses. More than half of the households lived in rented accommodation, less than one-third owned their homes, and the remainder shared accommodation with relatives. Some had managed to extract work-related entitlements, some savings or other assets; these funds were often sunk into house building. Alternatively, land for house building may have been bought before the crisis with funds accumulated in Kuwait. Savings left over were often low.

A fifth category included households headed by those who had run medium-scale businesses in Kuwait, such as machine tool shops, driving schools, import-export concerns, supermarkets, transport businesses, and dealerships in textiles, scrap, electrical goods and cars; they had utilized hired as well as family labour. Less than half of those interviewed had restarted businesses in Jordan (only one of which was related to the business in Kuwait) and most had no member in full-time employment. Half rented private accommodation, one-third owned homes and one-fifth lived with relatives. Many had managed to recover liquid assets such as bank account holdings from Kuwait, but had been obliged to abandon work premises, equipment and stock in Kuwait, rendering many of these households in a vulnerable position.

Finally, there was the wealthy minority of households, headed by businessmen, industrialists and professionals. These had largely managed to reestablish themselves in their previous line of business – such as in import and export houses, private health care, real estate, or manufacturing. Almost all had bought or built new houses or extended existing ones formerly used for periods of leave from Kuwait. With substantial savings or capital to cushion them against initial hardship (some had presciently moved or spread some of their assets to Jordan before the crisis), they later invested on the stock market or in their own businesses. However, many of those who had large fortunes in Kuwait had lost them, or were only gradually recovering them; some now lived in much reduced circumstances in rented accommodation, running restaurants or other businesses with which they were unfamiliar.

This categorization shows that general downward mobility among returnees was in evidence, as might be expected following the massive uprooting, but also that former socio-economic status in Kuwait or elsewhere in the Gulf was not a safe guide to such status two years after arrival in Jordan. While the lower and upper strata in the first and last categories remained firmly in their stations, there appeared to be considerable dissolution of intermediate levels. Thus more than half of the skilled workers and artisans in the second category found employment in Jordan, if not as lucrative as they were used to, and owned their homes. Conversely, many professionals and business people in the third, fourth and fifth categories could not find employment, and few of those that did worked in fields for which they were qualified; while some such households owned their homes, many were obliged to rent housing in the expensive private sector. Many of those who had run businesses, including substantial ventures, were unable to recover much of their assets and were in a vulnerable position two years after their arrival in Jordan. Psychosomatic disorders and other health problems were commonly reported among those dispossessed of their wealth, as among the habitually poor returnees, adding weight to the view that dislocation endured across socio-economic divides.

Partly fed by the sense of aggrievement that the uprooting and its consequences generated, there was evidence of organization among the returnee population, in the shape of both formal and informal returnee interest groups (Van Hear 1995). One such organization, the Cooperative Society for Gulf War Returnees, ran an efficient and well-attended clinic, operated a welfare or hardship fund, and was active in publicizing the returnees' case through public meetings and the media. Other less formally organized groupings articulated returnee business interests. One prominent form of lobbying activity was in the registration of claims for compensation for losses incurred in the course of the mass exodus, for submission to the UN Compensation Commission in Geneva, set up under the terms of the 1991 Gulf War cease-fire (Katzman 1993; Van Hear 1995). Claims by returnees to Jordan were thought to total $3 billion. Of those interviewed in 1993, more than half had registered claims for compensation of up to $100,000, while another 15 per cent had submitted larger claims. If fulfilled only in part, these claims would result in a substantial influx of capital, but the prospects of a settlement, at least of the larger claims, were distant. Funding for compensation was supposed to come from UN-supervised sales of Iraq's oil, but there was little sign that Iraq would comply with this. Moreover, the stipulation that compensation would be paid only to those who had left up to 2 March 1991 (the date of Kuwait's restoration to its former rulers) or who could prove their losses resulted directly from Iraq's invasion of Kuwait excluded those in the second and third waves of Palestinian displacement from Kuwait, and by implication absolved Kuwait of responsibility for their uprooting.

Yemeni returnees from Saudi Arabia: the rootless and the rooted
The fate of Yemeni returnees from Saudi Arabia depended largely on the extent to which they had maintained contacts with their communities of origin while abroad. Their experience varied considerably by region. Four broad divisions might be made: the experience of returnees to the plain, known as the Tihama, running along the west coast of Yemen; the experience of those who returned to the Highlands in the interior; that of those who returned to the Hadramawt, in the eastern part of former south Yemen; and that of returnees to Aden and its hinterland in the south of the country.

The Tihama. Of the total of 731,800 returnees enumerated in the government survey of 1991 (Republic of Yemen 1991), 45 per cent returned to the Tihama plain. Most, though not all, of the returnees to the Tihama had been away for long periods – many for 20, 30 or more than 40 years. Some second and even third generation returnee children were encountered by the writer in 1993. Many of these people had effectively made their lives in Saudi Arabia and did not intend to come back to Yemen, links with which they had all but severed, retaining only the knowledge of their family's place of origin. These returnees, predominantly of mixed African and Arab descent, were the least able to reintegrate into Yemeni society and populated shanty settlements in and around the main towns. Unemployment among these returnees was high; otherwise work was casual – usually labouring, porterage, petty trade or hawking – although some returnees had managed to set up shops or other small businesses.

The Highlands. According to the government survey, 35 per cent of the returnees enumerated returned to Highlands regions of Yemen, including the capital city Sanaa. Migrants from the Highlands tended to stay in Saudi Arabia for shorter periods than those from the Tihama; they remitted money, and they made at least occasional visits home, thus keeping up their links with the home community. Most were therefore able to find at least some accommodation on their return, and, albeit with difficulty, some means of livelihood in both urban and rural-based employment. Farming, shopkeeping, taxi-driving and construction work were among the most common occupations, but employment was again often casual.

The Hadramawt. About 13 per cent of the returnees enumerated in the government survey returned to the Hadramawt region in the former People's Democratic Republic of Yemen. Many returned from Kuwait rather than Saudi Arabia. These tended to be wealthier than other returnees, had maintained links with the homeland and had invested substantially in property and construction. Hadramis in Saudi Arabia were not all subject to the same pressures as other migrants, since, like others from the former PDRY, they had already acquired the requisite sponsors. Their centuries-old tradition of residence abroad also made their position somewhat different from that of other Yemeni migrants; they formed a trader diaspora spread in the Arab world, eastern Africa, and south and southeast Asia (see Chapter 6).

Aden and its hinterland. The area around Aden received 5 per cent of the returnee total, according to the government survey. As a port Aden has always attracted a conglomerate of migrants and nationalities, and received its share of returnees in 1990–91; many lived in very poor conditions in shanty settlements like those of the Tihama. As in the Tihama, unemployment among returnees was high, and where it could be found, work tended to be very casual.

This broad, four-fold regional pattern was rendered more complex by concurrent and subsequent migratory movements. By no means all returnees made for their place of origin, but many gravitated to major towns. Thus many Tihamis were found in Sanaa and particularly in Aden, where they formed new shanty settlements; conversely some people from the Highlands went to the Tihama to settle. There also appeared to be developing a drift of returnees, particularly Tihamis, to the Hadramawt to work in construction financed by Hadrami returnees. Typically such returnees drifted from the Tihama to Aden and then on to the Hadramawt. Returnees were thus embraced by wider currents of rural–urban and other migration within Yemen.

Notwithstanding the efforts of government and non-government organizations, and the lack of formal self-organization among returnees, their reintegration was largely a matter of self-resettlement. Those who had maintained links with their home communities through visits, remittances and other social and economic transactions – principally short-term migrants and better endowed longer-established expatriates – were usually able to effect this transition, albeit with difficulty. In far worse circumstances were those – often Tihamis – who had lost or never had such links, and who now found themselves without social or economic resources in poor shanty settlements in the Tihama and around the main towns of other parts of Yemen.

All returnees suffered a decline in their standard of living, but some more so than others. For short-term migrants the exodus was disruptive, but less of an upheaval than for many of those long resident abroad. Indeed, for a substantial proportion of the returnee population, their length of stay abroad threw into doubt the utility of the terms "return" or "repatriation" to describe their mass arrival in Yemen. Many of the Yemenis long resident abroad had made their lives and brought up families there; many of these, though by no means all, had lost meaningful social and economic ties with Yemen; many of those born abroad had little direct experience of Yemen. This had obvious implications for attempts at reintegration; such people – perhaps a third of the returnee total – were in a much worse position than those who had maintained their ties with home communities through visits and remittances. For the former the notion of *re*integration was a misnomer and models of integration into a new host society were perhaps more appropriate. This was also the case for other migrant-origin communities long-settled abroad considered in this book – notably the Kuwaiti Palestinians in Jordan, the Ugandan Asians in the UK and the Bulgarian ethnic Turks in Turkey.

The effects of mass arrivals on recipient territories

After the effects on the migrant communities forced to move, the most profound impacts of migration crises are felt by the countries and communities receiving sudden mass arrivals. Demographic and socio-economic effects on recipient territories are considered in some detail here.

The numbers of arrivals and their proportion relative to the established populations determined the impact on the countries receiving them. These dimensions are summarized in Table 5.1. As the table shows, the proportion of forced migrants to the total population of the countries receiving them was significant in the cases of Ghana, Jordan and Yemen, which I consider further below. In several cases, where numbers may not have been great relative to the national population, impacts on particular regions may have been significant where there were concentrations of the newcomers: this may have been true of Ugandan Asians in Britain, the Bulgarian ethnic Turks in Turkey, Rohingyas in Bangladesh and the Bhutanese ethnic Nepalis in Nepal, which are each considered below.

As for the other cases, the demographic impact of the forced return on Albania seems significant in total, but its impact was lessened because the forced migration took the form of deportations spread over four years. The total of 200,000–300,000 involved represented between 6.6 and 10 per cent of Albania's population of about 3.3 million in mid-1990 (World Bank 1992). If, as the US authorities claimed, 1.3 million Mexican workers departed from the US during and after Operation Wetback, this would have added significantly to Mexico's current population of about 28 million. As the real total deported was probably

Table 5.1 Some demographic effects of mass arrivals on receiving countries

Expelling country	Receiving country	Number of arrivals	Arrivals: total population %	Demographic profile	Addition to labour force
Uganda	UK	<30,000	0.05*	households	minimal*
Nigeria	Ghana	<1 million (800,000 net)	<9.0	single men and women, 20s–30s	<17.0
Kuwait	Jordan	360,000 (300,000 net)	<10.0	mainly households	<12.0
Saudi Arabia	Yemen	800,000	<7.0	mixture of households and single males	<15.0
Bulgaria	Turkey	300,000 (200,000 net)	0.5*	mainly households	minimal*
Greece	Albania	<300,000	<10.0	mainly single males	minimal**
Myanmar	Bangladesh	260,000	0.2*	households	minimal
Bhutan	Nepal	<100,000	0.5*	households	minimal
US	Mexico	<1.3 million	<3.5	single men	minimal**
Dominican Republic	Haiti	<60,000	0.9	single people and households	minimal

*The additions to the population and labour force may have been insignificant nationally, but were significant locally: e.g. Asians in Leicester, UK; ethnic Turks in some Turkish towns; Rohingyas in Cox's Bazar; ethnic Nepalis in southeast Nepal.

**Addition to workforce minimal because of re-emigration after expulsion.

Sources: migrant community populations, as in text; total populations of host countries, World Bank, *World Development Report*, various years.

substantially lower, the demographic impact is likely to have been correspondingly less. Moreover, as in the case of the Albanians and others reviewed here, substantial numbers of those deported made their way back to the US subsequently. Likewise, the arrival of 50,000–60,000 people of Haitian origin from the Dominican Republic was demographically insignificant when set against Haiti's population in mid-1991 of 6.6 million

(World Bank 1993), the more so since so many of these people returned to the Dominican Republic shortly after the September 1991 coup in Haiti.

As with demography, evidence of the socio-economic impacts of sudden mass arrivals is strongest in the cases of returnees to Ghana, Jordan and Yemen. There is some evidence in the cases of the Ugandan Asians in the UK and North America, the Bulgarian ethnic Turks in Turkey, the Rohingyas in Bangladesh and the ethnic Nepalis in Nepal. Since the mass returns of the Albanians, Haitians and Mexicans were short-lived, there is little evidence of their impact on the countries to which they were expelled.

Ghana: from mass return to economic turnaround

The return of a million expellees from Nigeria to Ghana in 1983 would have increased the country's population by about 9 per cent (World Bank 1985). Most of these were young men and women without their families, adding substantially to Ghana's population of working age. Their arrival seemed to come at the worst time, for Ghana's fortunes were touching their nadir in 1982–83. But while the initial impacts of this mass return on the economy were certainly serious, particularly in the areas of employment and remittances, a case can be made that the beleaguered country may have benefited from the episode in the medium term.

The proportion of the Ghanaian population reckoned to be economically active was thought in the early 1980s to be between 45 and 49 per cent (International Labour Organisation 1990; World Bank 1985). If so, since most of the returnees were of working age the increase in the economically active (or potentially active) population could have been around 17 per cent, a serious blow to an economy which had been severely debilitated by more than a decade of decline and where un-employment was already at record levels.

As with population and workforce figures, estimates of the scale of remittances by Ghanaians in Nigeria are very difficult to make, not least because so little was remitted through official channels. The World Bank estimated annual receipts of workers' remittances in the early 1980s at just $1 million and the

International Monetary Fund at even less (International Monetary Fund 1990; World Bank 1983, 1984, 1985). Given the extremely adverse exchange rate in Ghana at the time, this figure might conceivably have reflected official receipts, but the real level of remittances must have been much higher if a million migrants were working in Nigeria alone. A more credible estimate is that they totalled $300–500 million annually in the late 1970s and early 1980s (Gravil 1985; Tabatabai 1988), an important inflow of private income and capital into the economy. Their loss, coupled with the immediate impact on the labour market of the mass return, was another serious blow for Ghana's ailing economy. However the return of labour power and the influx of unknown amounts of capital may ultimately have been beneficial.

By 1985, two years after the first mass expulsion, several hundred thousand returnees were engaged in agricultural work, and teaching and health posts vacant before 1983 had been filled. The large increase in agricultural labour power, coinciding with better rains, is thought to have boosted food crop production, revived Ghana's ailing cocoa output, and may well have assisted the country's economic recovery in the second half of the 1980s. These improvements may in turn have helped to convince donors to continue backing Ghana's Economic Recovery Programme (Ricca 1989; Van Hear 1992).

Five years after the first mass return of expellees, Ghana was in much better economic shape than it was at the time of the expulsion. Commonly cited World Bank and government figures indicate annual growth in GDP of more than 5 per cent in the second half of the 1980s, until 1990 when growth slowed to 3.3 per cent (Kapur et al 1991). These figures should be interpreted with caution. Adopted as a model reforming economy by the World Bank and the IMF in the 1980s, Ghana continued to receive large amounts of assistance in the form of credits from these and other institutions. There were doubts about the basis, the cost and the sustainability of the recovery (see for example, Toye 1992). Nevertheless, it is generally accepted that Ghana staged a substantial turnaround in its fortunes between the early and the later 1980s.

While there were many other contributory factors, at least some of the credit for this recovery was arguably due to the returnees. It is very difficult to determine to what extent the mass return of migrants contributed to the economic improvements. At the very least it may be said that the returnees were not a net burden. The evidence is not conclusive, but since it is likely that they contributed substantially to Ghana's labour-scarce rural economy (Tabatabai 1988), it is plausible to argue that returnees helped to kick-start the revival of agriculture and the economy more widely in the second half of the 1980s.

This argument is lent support by various local level studies. One such investigated the coping strategies of a small town in southeast Ghana between 1983 and 1989 (Dei 1992). The town absorbed nearly 300 returnees, increasing its population by 5 per cent. Well over half of the returnees engaged themselves in agriculture locally, farming individually and co-operatively using land held communally, bought or rented. Some, in response to favourable market conditions for food crops, engaged themselves in lucrative new ventures growing tomatoes and beans. Others set up as seamstresses, hairdressers or traders; some brought back capital equipment like chain-saws and mini-buses. Still others may have helped to remedy shortfalls in the availability of hired farm labour in the area. The local level evidence also provides a reminder that scrutiny of official initiatives meant to assist integrating returnees should not eclipse the paramount importance of the self-activity of returnees in reintegrating into Ghana's economy and society, with little or no official assistance.

Returnees to Jordan: burden or benefit?

In all, Jordan may have received more than a million people uprooted from Kuwait, Iraq and other states in the region in the wake of the Gulf crisis of 1990–91. Perhaps half of the estimated 865,000 third country nationals passing through Jordan were Egyptians; others were migrants from Yemen, India, Bangladesh, Pakistan, Sri Lanka, the Philippines and Sudan. Most of these "third country" migrants were repatriated within weeks to their homelands in other parts of the Middle East and in south and southeast Asia. Jordan was nevertheless obliged to accommodate in the longer term some 300,000 Palestinian holders of its passports as involuntary "returnees". This held profound consequences for a small country already encountering serious economic problems against the background of long-standing regional volatility.

Return migration to Jordan was gathering momentum in the 1980s due largely to economic changes in the region (Findlay 1987a), but the involuntary mass return triggered by the Gulf crisis was quantitatively and qualitatively of a different order. First, there was a net addition of some 300,000 people within two years, the majority within months of the invasion of Kuwait by Iraq in 1990. This added between 9 and 10 per cent to Jordan's population, estimated in 1990 at between 3.2 and 3.45 million, and rising to nearly 4 million in 1992 (Central Bank of Jordan 1992, 1993; World Bank 1992, 1994). Second, perhaps two-fifths of the returnees were less than 15 years of age. Of those interviewed by the author in 1993, 28 per cent had been born abroad or had been infants when their parents migrated. Adding those born or brought up abroad to those who moved straight to Kuwait from the West Bank suggests that a majority of those who arrived in Jordan in 1990–92 had never lived there before, making the term "returnee" problematical when applied to them.

Both the government and international agencies initially regarded the mass arrival of Palestinians from Kuwait and the Gulf as yet another blow to an already beleaguered economy. Economic slow-down and recession in the 1980s had come to a head with a currency crisis in 1988–89, forcing the government into a range of austerity measures overseen by the International Monetary Fund and the World Bank. Structural adjustment and debt rescheduling programmes were blown off course by the Gulf crisis, particularly by the disruption it brought to trade and aid. The returnees seemed to add a further, enduring burden (Central Bank of Jordan 1990, 1991; UNICEF 1992).

As Table 5.1 shows, one of the principal impacts of the mass arrival was on the labour market. Jordan's labour force was estimated at 630,000 in 1990 (Jordan, Ministry of Labour 1991). If the estimate of the ILO (1991) that one in four of the Palestinian population in Kuwait were economically active is extrapolated to the 300,000 net arrivals in Jordan, some 75,000 economically active people would have been added to the labour force, a figure that broadly conforms with Jordanian government figures. This would have added 12 per cent to the labour force, immediately and substantially exacerbating unemployment.

Estimates of the rate of unemployment varied greatly. Ministry of Labour estimates put unemployment at 19 per cent at the end of 1991 (Amerah et al 1993; Jordan, Ministry of Labour 1991), but the ministry's figures included only the registered unemployed and the real total was certainly higher. Unsurprisingly, unemployment increased immediately after the mass return, thereafter declining marginally from perhaps 25 per cent at the beginning of 1992 to 20 per cent by that year's end; subsequently it began to rise again (UNICEF 1992). These figures obscure important sectoral features, one of the most significant being graduate unemployment, estimated by the Ministry of Labour at 23 per cent in 1992. Exacerbated by the mass return, unemployment among new graduates in Jordan helped to fuel resentment of the newcomers.

Demand on educational, health and other social services greatly increased following the mass arrival; thousands of new places had to be found in a school system in the throes of reform (UNICEF 1992). Take-up increased of free or subsidized health care. Vehicles brought back by returnees heavily increased traffic congestion and pollution. Of the pressures put on Jordan's resources, the impact on water supply may turn out to be critical, for demand for water in Jordan far exceeded supply even before the returnee influx (Edge 1993). The mass arrival contributed to the overall spread of poverty in Jordan (UNICEF 1992), not least because those formerly reliant on remittances from Kuwait not only saw those remittances disappear, but also had to support returning relatives as well as themselves.

While the immediate consequences of the mass arrival were indeed negative and disruptive, some longer term potential benefits to the national economy were already becoming apparent by 1992. First, the mass arrival meant that large numbers of professional and skilled people entered Jordan's labour market, which was likely ultimately to be beneficial even if they could not all be absorbed at once. Returnees had a high standard of education, with half or more having pursued secondary level and beyond; between 10 and 15 per cent of the returnees to Jordan were reported to hold university degrees, including substantial numbers with qualifications in engineering, medicine and other professions (Jordan, Department of Statistics 1992; Jordan, NCERD 1991).

Second, the return meant that there was a large inflow of financial resources into Jordan, although in future years remittances (at about $600 million in the late 1980s) were greatly reduced. Estimates of the inflow of funds in 1991 were put at the equivalent of $1.2 billion (*Middle East Economic Digest* 3 July 1992). Central Bank of Jordan estimates of workers' remittances and of savings transferred to Jordan in 1990–92 (including assets like cars and furniture brought back) totalled the equivalent of $3.5 billion (Central Bank of Jordan 1993), of which the bulk was attributable to involuntary returnees from Kuwait and the Gulf. To put this figure into perspective, this was equivalent to about 40 per cent of Jordan's foreign debt in 1991 of $8.64 billion (World Bank 1993).

The capital inflow was evident among Jordan's banks, whose deposits doubled in 1991–92 (*Middle East Economic Digest* 15 January 1993). The abundance of capital also manifested itself in frenetic stock market activity, in which returnees featured strongly. The annual volume of trade on Amman stock market more than doubled in 1990–92, to the equivalent of nearly $1.3 billion, and share prices trebled in value in the same period. The volume of trade increased markedly in 1992, as a boom in real estate tapered off (Amman Financial Market 1993).

Whether or not this capital influx was used productively is arguable. As with the inflow of skilled labour, the impact of increased availability of financial resources depends on the existence of opportunities to invest, and in turn on the uses to which such resources are put. Moreover, it bears repeating that the wealth brought in was highly unevenly distributed. Evidence of the capital inflow was most obvious in construction activity, much of which was attributable to returnees, and in ancillary industries such as quarrying, cement and steel bar manufacture, woodworking and furniture-making (Peretz 1993). Other evidence of returnees' investment was mixed. Returnees' intentions, asserted soon after arrival (Jordan, Department of Statistics 1992; Jordan, NCERD 1991), to invest in small to medium scale businesses – mainly in commercial ventures and services, but also in agricultural and industrial enterprises – did not appear to have been translated into substantial investment in viable ventures two years later. Many small scale shops and businesses were set up with capital brought back, but few returnees reported much success with these. While industrial activity increased substantially in Jordan in the early 1990s (Central Bank of Jordan 1992), participation of returnees in large scale industrial ventures was slight. Some large scale trading companies which relocated from Kuwait to Jordan were in a position to acquire large industrial or commercial assets (*Middle East Economic Digest* 7 August 1992). But the returnees' principal contribution to industrial development, as to other forms of economic activity, came rather in the form of making capital available for others to invest in industry.

There was probably more returnee involvement in agriculture. Livestock ventures were reported to be popular among returnees. Returnees also rented land to set up arable farms, while others bought and reclaimed land to farm olives, fruit and vegetables. Nationally, agricultural production and the area brought under cultivation increased markedly between 1989 and 1992: production of cereals, fruit and vegetables nearly doubled, and livestock and dairy products registered similar large increases (Van Hear 1995). While part of the increase was due to better weather than in recent years, some of the credit for the improvement may be attributed to returnees.

Despite the ambivalent impact of returnee investment, the aggregate effect of increased activity in construction, agriculture and services, together with other developments, was a "surprise economic boom" reported towards the end of 1992 (Edge and Dougherty 1992; Morland 1993). Against expectations of 3 per cent GDP growth in 1992, GDP actually grew by an exceptional 11 per cent, with 6 per cent growth projected for 1993 and 5 per cent subsequently; given the exceptional population increase in 1990–92, per capita GDP growth was of course lower, but it was still substantial. The relative importance of the returnees' contribution and of the government's structural adjustment programme, overseen since 1989 by the IMF and World Bank, was a matter of debate. Government officials stressed the stability of the currency, lower inflation rate and reduction of the budget deficit, which they attributed to the adjustment programme; this had created the conditions for returnees and others to invest in Jordan, they claimed. On the other hand, since the recovery was led by construction, agriculture and services – all sectors in which returnees featured strongly – it is not unreasonable to suggest that their contribution was considerable.

Wealthy returnees interviewed were strong advocates of the benefits that they had brought, both in terms of expertise and experience and in terms of capital. Some spoke of a "brain-gain" for Jordan. Many of Jordan's burgeoning private universities were funded and staffed by returnees from the Gulf. Expertise from Kuwait's well-developed medical sector – largely staffed by Palestinians – could make Jordan the centre of gravity for the region in terms of health care, claimed some health specialists. Others spoke of Jordan's potential, with the help of returnees' expertise and investment, for becoming the Hong Kong of the Middle East. This was not as fanciful as it sounded, for despite its paucity of natural resources, Jordan had advantages in its highly educated and trained labour force, its good infrastructure and its relative political and economic stability. Indeed, the economic conditions generated by structural adjustment and by the influx of returnee skills and capital led one business analyst to describe Jordan as a potential "Singapore in the desert" (Morland 1993). The realization of such a vision obviously depended on many factors, not least developments in the regional political arena, but its very articulation represented a great shift from the gloomy prognosis that accompanied the arrival of the returnees during the crisis of 1990–91.

Macro-economic indicators suggest that, contrary to expectations, a remarkable economic turnaround accompanied the arrival of 300,000 Palestinians from Kuwait and the Gulf. The precise weight of the returnees' contribution to this recovery is open to debate, and may be impossible to disentangle from other concurrent factors, notably the impact of structural adjustment. In terms of human development, the picture after the mass return was less clear. Of course, growth in GDP is hardly a reliable indicator of human well-being. The positive macro-economic indicators co-existed with trauma and tragedy, unemployment and spreading poverty. Many of the returnees, like many of the wider population, were marginal to the economic recovery and benefited little from it. For many returnees, as for many of their relatives and dependents long in Jordan, the consequences of the events of 1990–92 were unambiguously negative. Poverty and vulnerability of households increased; unemployment remained stubbornly high and rising; social, educational, health and welfare services were put under great strain; pressures on housing, water supply and other resources greatly increased; socio-economic differentiation was accentuated; the cohesiveness of Jordanian society diminished as rivalries between the established population and the newcomers increased; and anxiety and uncertainty over the future grew, accentuated by the stop–go movement of the Israel–Palestinian peace process. All of this reinforced the ambivalence Palestinians felt towards their new home in Jordan, an ambivalence explored further in later chapters.

Returnees to Yemen: opportunities missed
The Republic of Yemen that emerged in 1990 from the unification of the Yemen Arab Republic (known as North Yemen) and the People's Democratic Republic of Yemen (known as South Yemen) was classed as a low income nation, with GNP per capita of $520 in 1991 (World Bank 1993). Since this figure captures only the recorded economy, some caution is in order – real income per capita was almost certainly much higher. Other indicators nevertheless confirm the picture of under-development. Yemen ranked 130th out of the 160 countries in the UNDP's Human Development Index for 1992: life expectancy at birth in 1990 was 52 years, only 39 per cent of the adult population were literate, only 35 per cent of the population had access to health services, and only 46 per cent had access to safe drinking water (UNDP 1992).

The mass return exacerbated many of these indicators of human well-being, as well as greatly increasing the numbers of job-seekers in the labour market. If the estimate of 800,000 returnees was accurate, Yemen would have absorbed a 7 per cent increase to its population – estimated at 11.3 million in mid-

1990 (World Bank 1992) – within three months in that year. Like the movement of Palestinians to Jordan, the forced return to Yemen involved a substantial proportion of dependants.

The total workforce was estimated at about 2.5 million in mid-1990 (Republic of Yemen 1992). If the 318,569 respondents surveyed by the government late in 1990 are assumed to have been returnees of working age, their return would have added nearly 11.5 per cent to the 1990 workforce. This is certainly an underestimate of the additional workforce, since those described in the survey as dependants included both men and women of working age. An estimated addition of 15 per cent to the workforce (Overseas Development Institute 1991) therefore does not seem unreasonable.

Loss of remittances is held to be one of the main damaging impacts on Yemen's economy of the mass return (Abdalla 1991; Addleton 1991). In the early 1980s, remittances were the main source of foreign exchange for both North and South Yemen. Remittances were already on the decline from the mid-1980s; estimates vary, but from a peak of perhaps $1.7 billion for both Yemens in 1983, they plummeted to a combined total of between $440 and $505 million in 1989, and were set to fall further in 1990 (Birks Sinclair and Associates 1990; Edge 1992). The long-term decline was partly due to falling wage levels and incomes from Yemeni businesses in Saudi Arabia as construction and other opportunities contracted; to declining absolute numbers of Yemeni migrants as Asian workers or Saudi nationals replaced them; and to the increased proportion of long-term Yemeni migrants who settled with their families and therefore no longer remitted part of their income. Nevertheless, the earnings of Yemeni workers abroad still accounted for much of Yemen's official foreign receipts (Edge 1992), as well as a large volume that did not pass through official channels.

To speak of the "loss" of these remittances is a little misleading. The mass return appears to have had a positive impact at the macro-economic level, with a dramatic positive effect on Yemen's current account balance, which has habitually recorded a heavy deficit. This turnaround was almost wholly due to a near three-fold increase in private transfers by returnees, to the equivalent of about $1.3 billion in 1990 (*Middle East Economic*

Digest 31 July 1992). As substantial amounts were remitted through unofficial channels, it is not unreasonable to suppose that total transfers were substantially greater than the officially recorded figure. In addition, goods and equipment said to be worth $374 million at current official rates of exchange were brought back by returnees – mainly motor vehicles, household furniture, electrical items, work-related equipment and commercial goods (Republic of Yemen 1991).

While the impact on the current account balance was temporary, the longer term impact of this injection of cash and capital equipment may not have been negligible. Annual remittances of between $400 million and $500 million (the levels of the late 1980s) were not forthcoming in subsequent years. On the other hand, since the equivalent of three years' worth of remittances was received in a single year, the subsequent shortfall was in a sense already accounted for. Moreover, since it was unlikely that all of this large sum would be used for consumption, a substantial amount – much more than that in "normal" years – could have been available for investment.

By early 1993, this potential had hardly been realized. The impact of returnee investment was limited, both by region and sector. As already indicated, returnees to the Hadramawt were reported to have begun investing their capital accumulated or recovered from abroad, largely in construction. This reportedly began to draw returnees languishing in camps and shanty settlements in the Tihama to the Hadramawt as labourers. The construction sector elsewhere also afforded some limited employment opportunities for returnees.

Returnees had a considerable impact on agriculture in certain areas, but the national picture was much less clear. About 40 per cent of respondents in the government survey had been farmers, shepherds or in other rural occupations before migration. Of the 12 per cent respondents in the government survey who had found work after return, about a quarter declared themselves to be peasant farmers, and a small number of others were engaged as shepherds, hunters and in other rural occupations. After the return, farmers represented just 3 per cent of the total of returnee respondents and a still smaller proportion of the total returnee population of working age (Republic of Yemen 1991).

Among the returnees interviewed by the author in 1993, the proportion of returnee farmers relative to those in rural occupations before migration was also small, confirming the impression of just a modest return to the rural sector.

The evidence from overall agricultural output is more equivocal. The area of land under cultivation and gross agricultural output actually declined sharply between 1990 and 1991, that is, in the first year after the mass return, but both the area under cultivation and total output revived markedly between 1991 and 1992 (Van Hear 1994). Better rains no doubt accounted for some of these increases, but greater labour input by returnees to farming may have had some impact, as may have the great increase in demand precipitated by the mass return. It is nevertheless difficult to make a convincing case that by 1993 returnees had had a significantly positive impact on Yemeni agriculture nationwide.

More than two years after the mass arrival, investment and employment creation by returnees did not appear to have made significant inroads into the greatly increased unemployment the mass return had precipitated. As indicated above, only 12 per cent of returnee respondents were employed as of the end of 1990 (Republic of Yemen 1991). Those that had found work seem to have returned to the kinds of employment they had pursued before migrating – peasant farming, general labouring and driving. The writer's interviews in 1993 indicated that more returnees had found employment as labourers, semi-skilled workers or artisans, and had set up small businesses, although much of this employment was very irregular. Although difficult to quantify because of the informal nature of much employment, by that time unemployment nationally was reported of the order of 40 per cent (*Middle East Economic Digest* 19 March 1993).

In terms of the development of "human capital", modest advances were apparent. Skill levels among the expatriate labour force were moderately enhanced while abroad, which brought potential benefits to the Yemeni economy. The educational standard of returnee household heads, like that of the population at large, was low. According to the government survey, only 17.5 per cent had some kind of school qualification, mostly at just primary level, and 44 per cent were said to be illiterate (Republic of Yemen 1991); these proportions were broadly reproduced among respondents interviewed in 1993. Nevertheless, this was better than the national 62 per cent adult illiteracy estimated for 1990 (UNDP 1993; World Bank 1993). Moreover, the educational level of returnee children, most of whom had had schooling at primary level or beyond in Saudi Arabia, was a marked improvement on that of their parents. These modest changes aside, the mass return put further strain on Yemen's poorly developed education, health, other social services and infrastructure, worsening indicators of human and social development already among the poorest in the Middle East (UNDP 1993; World Bank 1993).

The macro-level impact of the mass return was thus mixed. Remittances from abroad, which although on the decline still accounted for much of Yemen's foreign exchange receipts, were greatly diminished. The return greatly exacerbated unemployment, pushing it to levels in marked contrast to the domestic labour scarcity precipitated by the emigration of the 1970s and 1980s. The mass arrival also imposed severe strain on Yemen's under-developed infrastructure, education, health and other social services. On the other hand, the returnees brought in a large one-time influx of capital, equivalent to several years' receipt of remittances. More than two years after the mass arrival, however, evidence of any benefits from this influx was sparse. Returnee investment was seen in parts of the country and the economy – in the Hadramawt and in some pockets of agriculture – but for the minority of returnees who were able to find employment, conditions were uninspiring, and the prospects were grim for those scratching out a living in shanty settlements.

Overall, the evidence of positive economic effects of the mass return on Yemen was less convincing than in Jordan. Indeed, the strains imposed by the mass return were among the factors that increased Yemen's destabilization in subsequent years. The fragile new polity that emerged for the unification of the Yemen Arab Republic and the People's Democratic Republic of Yemen in May 1990 held together for the time being, but it was under severe strain by late 1993. Increasing tension between the government's northern and southern members late in 1993 culminated in the outbreak of civil war in May 1994, four years after unification, and the triumph of the north over the south (Prados 1994). The economy meanwhile lurched from bad to worse (*Middle East Economic Digest* 14 and 21 April 1995). However, since the prospects for re-emigration to Saudi Arabia or elsewhere were very limited, Yemeni returnees had little option but to make the best of the situation in their beleaguered country.

The Ugandan Asians and Bulgarian Ethnic Turks: co-ethnics and subsidies

On the evidence of the Palestinians and the Yemenis long established in the countries from which they were expelled, it might be expected that the Asians and the ethnic Turks settled for generations in Uganda and Bulgaria respectively would have experienced severe difficulties in the countries to which they found themselves uprooted. While difficulties were indeed experienced, integration was accomplished with greater ease than was anticipated.

The experience of a large proportion of the Asians expelled from Uganda was different from that of other migrant communities discussed since so many were resettled in developed countries, principally the UK where they had claims to citizenship. Although the arrivals from Uganda made for a pronounced bulge in UK immigration in the early 1970s (Robinson 1993), which was the subject of much heated discussion, the addition to the total UK population was negligible (see Table 5.1). However, the concentration of Ugandan Asians in cities like Leicester and parts of London did make for a significant local demographic impact. There was negligible demographic impact on the other destinations in North America and South Asia where Ugandan Asians settled.

Coming with little funds and after short stays in camps, many of the Asians in the UK were able to rebuild their lives within a few years of arrival. They bought houses and re-established themselves in their businesses or in their professions, despite the obstacle of having to re-accredit their qualifications gained abroad. The view that the resettlement of

Ugandan Asians was generally successful is supported by a number of studies that take advantage of the hindsight offered by 20 years experience of Ugandan Asian resettlement.

Robinson (1986, 1993) uses a range of national quantitative data to track the long term resettlement experience in Britain of East African Asians, of whom the Ugandan Asians represented a substantial component. He documents the considerable material progress that the Asians made in education, employment and housing, showing that in several arenas the Ugandan Asians out-performed earlier Asian immigrants to the UK, and in some cases the white population. Among the conditions for this progress were the presence of an already-established community of co-ethnics, grasp of the host language, and recognition of the role of education as a route to social mobility. Such macro-level data is lent support by evidence at the local level. A long-term study by Marett (1988, 1993) demonstrates progress in the spheres of employment, housing and education among Ugandan Asians in Leicester, where one-fifth of the Ugandan Asians in Britain settled. Similar success was reported in the US by Strizhak (1993) in the ostensibly inauspicious setting of South Carolina. Among the conditions for this success were acceptance and approval of the resettlement programme by local business interests, the demand for skilled and semi-skilled labour, and a fund of good will on the part of both the newcomers and the host community. Ugandan Asians also made good in Canada where some 6,000 were resettled.

Needless to say, this socio-economic advancement should not be over-stated, nor was it easily won. While signalling the significance of East African Asian high achievers in public service or private business, Robinson (1990, 1993) cautions against too glib a stereotyping of the Asians as success stories. Not all the expellees became successful business people or professionals; not all found work appropriate to their skills. There was popular and institutional racism to overcome. Moreover, advances were achieved in conditions very different – particularly in terms of employment – than prevailed two decades later in the 1990s.

As with the Ugandan Asians, integration of the expellees from Bulgaria in Turkey was less painful than might have been expected. The demographic impact of the mass arrival of some 300,000 Bulgarian ethnic Turks in Turkey was minimal, the more so as up to half returned to Bulgaria subsequently; Turkey's population increased from 55 million in mid-1989 to 56.1 million in mid-1990 (World Bank 1991, 1992). However, the impact was disproportionate in large towns like Ankara and Istanbul where many of the new arrivals settled. Successful integration much depended on age, education, skills, qualifications and the presence of networks of assistance – relatives or friends who had previously emigrated. Typically, immigrants of peasant origin made their homes in the suburbs, and found unskilled work as building or road labourers, or in small factories, businesses and shops. Teachers, doctors and technicians were able to find employment in their professions (Vasileva 1992).

A survey of 700 Bulgarian ethnic Turk households, commissioned by the ILO and completed in September 1990, more than a year after the mass arrival, found a surprisingly high level of employment among the new immigrants. Unemployment among those of working age was found to be 10 per cent for men and 13 per cent for women (Scott 1991). Employment rates compared well with those of the established population. There were however great regional variations, those in Ankara and Istanbul faring better in finding employment than elsewhere. While the survey suggests that significant numbers of professional and technical workers, particularly teachers and doctors, found employment in their professions again, many had to take jobs for which they were overqualified; more found employment as production workers in Turkey than had been in this sector in Bulgaria. The earnings of the new arrivals were below the norm, more than half of those in employment receiving less than the minimum wage in Turkey (Scott 1991).

The ILO survey found a relatively high level of education among the arrivals, nine out of ten of the economically active having secondary education or beyond; this compares well with the Turkish population as a whole (Scott 1991). If the survey was representative of the Bulgarian ethnic Turks as a whole, this would seem to contradict other reports that they were mainly drawn from peasant or rural backgrounds. It also suggests that Turkey may have benefited from an influx of relatively educated and skilled workers.

Turkish employers were not slow to take advantage of new sources of relatively well-educated and low paid labour, which again must have done little to endear the newcomers to the established working population (Council of Europe 1991; Vasileva 1992). Indeed, striking a chord with other cases in this book, after initial displays of hospitality among the established population, resentment of the newcomers' competition in the labour and housing markets was reported (Council of Europe 1991). Moreover, if the economic integration of the newcomers was less of a problem than might have been expected, social and cultural integration was more so: differences in educational systems and curricula and in language dialect created some difficulties (Council of Europe 1991; Vasileva 1992).

The otherwise relatively painless integration of the ethnic Turks was at least in part attributable to substantial subsidy. The Turkish authorities provided reception centres and temporary accommodation for the new arrivals, after which those that found employment were encouraged to rent accommodation, subsidized by the government for a year. Others were settled in prefabricated houses and low-cost housing units, part-funded by the Council of Europe's Social Development Fund (Council of Europe 1991, 1994). Funds were also made available for vocational training and job creation (UNDP 1993a; USGAO 1991). The subsidies continued more than five years after the mass exodus (Council of Europe 1993, 1994), assisting the further integration of those who had chosen to remain in Turkey after expulsion from Bulgaria.

The Rohingyas and the ethnic Nepalis: camp life

Both the Rohingyas and the ethnic Nepalis were held in refugee camps for long periods because their citizenship was disputed by both sending and receiving states. Uncomfortably straddling the categories "refugee" and "returnee", integration into the society that received them was not an option that presented itself.

Bangladesh is classed among the world's poorest countries: in mid-1991, around the time of the arrival of the Rohingyas, annual GNP per capita stood at \$220 (World Bank 1993). Bangladesh stood 146th out of 173 countries in the UNDP human development index for 1992; in that year life expectancy at birth was 52.2 years; the adult literacy rate was 36.6 per cent; 60 per cent of the population had access to health services and 32 per cent to sanitation (UNDP 1994). The country is among the most densely populated countries of the world, with more than 800 persons per square kilometre. While the impact of the arrival of 260,000 Rohingyas in Bangladesh was insignificant when set against the country's population in mid-1991 of 110.6 million (World Bank 1993), their impact locally was of greater moment. Most of the refugees were concentrated around Cox's Bazar in southeastern Bangladesh, where substantial numbers of the population were from Arakan.

The first wave of refugees in late 1991 were accommodated by relatives in Cox's Bazar. Thereafter the camp population grew steadily, peaking at nearly 270,000 in mid-1992. As repatriation gathered pace (see Chapter 6), camp numbers began to diminish, so that as of the end of January 1994, 198,353 refugees were accommodated in 17 camps and three transit centres, located mainly in the Cox's Bazar area (UNHCR 1994). Unknown numbers lived among local communities.

Increased pressure on land was one of the main impacts of the refugees' presence. They were concentrated in a region already overcrowded, and where most flat land was under cultivation; the only space available for them was in hills surrounding the paddy fields, in coastal sandy areas or in forest areas. The felling of trees for shelter and fuel wood, extra demand on aquifers by the sinking of wells, and sanitation problems were among the strains put on local resources. Poor nutrition leading to health problems held the prospect of the spread of communicable diseases to the local population (US Committee for Refugees 1992a).

On top of the pressures of population and land scarcity, the area was vulnerable to cyclones and flooding. At the time of the mass influx Bangladesh was still recovering from the impact of devastating typhoons and floods in 1991. Another cyclone hit the Cox's Bazar area in May 1994, centring on Teknaf where many of the refugees were living, and destroying several of the camps, many of which were on low lying terrain and were thus vulnerable to storms (*Independent* 4 May 1994).

Local resentment at the presence of the refugees and calls for their repatriation were articulated by the Rohingya Repatriation Action Committee, probably with the support of local government officials (Asia Watch 1993; *Burma Update* 25 September 1992). Some of the allegations against the refugees were well-founded, while others were not. Locals complained that the refugees were privileged compared with Bangladeshis, and that they wished to stay in camps where they had free food, medicine and shelter. People in communities near the camps complained about price increases associated with the sale of relief items, increased crime, and worsening employment conditions. Conversely, local employers benefited from cheap Rohingya labour, paying about half the local going rate for work in rice fields or brick-making. Officials and police were reported to benefit from payments made by refugees to allow them to undertake illicit employment (Lambrecht 1995).

Environmental degradation associated with the refugee presence was substantial, although not all was attributable to the refugees alone. Collection of firewood exacerbated deforestation. There was said to be considerable illicit trade in hardwood controlled by Bangladeshi businessmen, who employed refugees. Trees were also felled by refugee labourers to fuel brick kilns for Bangladesh employers (Lambrecht 1995).

Both the government and UNHCR were concerned about discontent among the local population and their hostility to the presence of the refugees. Much of the local population was indeed arguably worse off than the refugees. The UNHCR undertook to extend assistance to the local population through improvements to the supply of water; the rehabilitation of health and education facilities; the repair and upgrading of roads and bridges; improvement of sanitation; promotion of agriculture and animal husbandry; and redressing the degradation of the environment. On the latter front, alternative sources of fuel were to be sought to reduce the felling of trees, and land was to be replanted (UN General Assembly 1993). Despite these undertakings, the pressures on the local community exerted by the refugee presence were prominent among the factors driving the repatriation campaign that gathered momentum from 1994, so that by mid-1995 camp numbers had declined to 55,000. This counter movement is explored further in Chapter 6.

As with the Rohingyas in Bangladesh, the impact of the arrival in Nepal of 90,000–100,000 ethnic Nepalis from southern Bhutan was not of great demographic importance set against a total population of 19.4 million in mid-1991 (World Bank 1993); but the mass arrival was significant in the two districts of southeastern Nepal, Morang and Jhapa, where most of the refugees were accommodated. The first ethnic Nepali refugees from Bhutan accumulated in crowded camps with very limited facilities; but as the number of arrivals increased the Nepali authorities requested the assistance of the UNHCR, which subsequently oversaw improvements in shelter, sanitation and water supply. New sites had to be found to accommodate increasing numbers, so that by 1995 there were eight camps on five sites accommodating 88,600 people in the two districts; others lived outside the camps (Baral 1996; Hutt 1996; US Committee for Refugees 1994, 1996).

Conditions in the camps have been described as "basic but decent" (Hutt 1996: 412). Idleness was one of the main problems; means of making a livelihood were limited, and few refugees were paid for work they did within the camps. Keeping of animals was not allowed and there was no access to land. Refugees were allowed out of the camps during the day and could seek work, but had to report back at night or jeopardize their entitlements. Some refugees set up businesses in Morang and Jhapa or moved to other parts of the country. Rickshaw driving was one avenue of employment (Baral 1996; Hutt 1996; Reilly 1994).

As in Bangladesh, the initial welcome for the refugees did not last long. Early in 1993 the Nepali authorities claimed that the refugee presence had increased crime, prostitution and gambling around the camps, and that it would step up security in them to check illegal activity. Refugees were also blamed for causing deforestation by cutting firewood; perversely, they were also said to sell kerosene supplied to them by donors (Baral 1996; US Committee for Refugees 1994). Again as in Bangladesh, the local population viewed the refugees as pampered, receiving free food, health care, education, water supply and other benefits. There was competition for employment and locals claimed that refugees could undercut local wage levels because of the food and other subsistence they received free – wages were therefore at least in part surplus to their subsistence. Against these costs and drains on the local community, the refugee presence brought some benefits, including improvement in roads which serviced the camps and some rehabilitation of the environment, such as tree planting; the inflow of aid funds made possible other modest improvements (Hutt 1996).

There were a substantial number of ethnic Nepalis from Bhutan outside the camps, either by choice or because they had been screened out by the UNHCR and the Nepali authorities as not having a valid claim for asylum. One estimate was that there were some 18,000 Bhutanese living in refugee-like circumstances in Nepal and unable to go back to Bhutan (US Committee for Refugees 1995). More than five years after their forced departure, there appeared no prospect of a resolution of the plight of those in camps any more than of those outside them.

The effects of mass departures on the territories left

Evidence of the effects of mass exodus on countries left is more scanty than that for territories receiving forced migrants. Such that it is, the evidence suggests that the impact of the sudden departure of substantial numbers of people is damaging, particularly in the economic sphere.

In Uganda the departure of Asians yielded some short-term payoffs in terms of stemming one source of capital flight, relieving pressure on the balance of payments, and providing loot for Amin to distribute to disgruntled supporters, but overall the expulsion was economically damaging. Trade and industry was disrupted, professional and technical expertise was lost, and government revenues fell. The wholesale sector, cotton ginning, construction and education were among the sectors worst hit by the departure, while the labour force suffered from a general diminution of skills and experience (Tribe 1975). The appropriation of Asians' assets, through direct looting, auctioning and other disposal, and through the mechanism of the Custodian Board, set up to oversee Asian assets after the expulsion, scarcely made up for these losses. The slide in Uganda's economy continued through much of the following decade and more: after growing at an average of 3.6 per cent annually in 1965–73, GDP fell by an annual average of 2.1 per cent in 1973–83 (Hansen and Twaddle 1988, 1991; World Bank 1985). That the return of some Asians from the later 1980s (see Chapter 6) coincided with Uganda's subsequent revival lends weight to the view that their presence was economically positive.

The expulsion of migrant workers from Nigeria led to labour scarcities and increases in wages in a number of sectors, notably construction, the ports, hotels, catering and domestic service (Van Hear 1983). Already contracting in the early 1980s, Nigeria's economy continued on a downward trend after the expulsions of 1983–85. After average annual growth of 6.1 per cent in 1965–80, the years of oil-based boom, GDP contracted annually by an average of 0.4 per cent in 1980–89 (World Bank 1991). GNP per capita tumbled from $770 in 1983 to $340 in 1991 (World Bank 1985, 1992). While it would be foolhardy categorically to suggest that the mass exodus had a determinant effect on Nigeria's economic performance, the country's economic decline adds weight to the argument that the mass exodus was in the medium to long-term economically damaging.

Since most of those who fled Arakan in Myanmar were poor farmers or day labourers, the mass departure would have removed labour from agriculture and other parts of the economy. However, arguably the conscription of forced labour had already damaged local economies by the withdrawal of labour and by the debilitation of conscripts by widely reported ill-treatment. It appears to have been the poorest who were forced to flee since they did not have the resources to pay off military harassment or conscription into forced labour; aid workers in the camps in Bangladesh reported a low level of education and skills among the camp population. If so, and the better endowed and resourceful stayed behind, Arakan may not have lost much of its skilled workforce. Given the lack of access to Arakan since the mass exodus, there is little evidence with which to assess the impact of the departure.

Evidence of the effects of the mass exodus on Bhutan is likewise scanty. The departure of more than 100,000 ethnic Nepalis is likely to have halved their population, and reduced the country's total population by about one-sixth. Some indication of the impact of this departure might be extrapolated from the impact of the expulsion of foreign labour in 1986–88, just prior to the exodus of southern Bhutanese. To help meet manual labour shortfalls, a national workforce programme was launched, but only 5,000 out of a target of 30,000 people were mobilized. There were also greater calls on the system of labour duty, under which each household had to provide a person's labour for two weeks of the year (Strawn 1994). Ethnic Nepalis were productive agriculturalists, who grew rice, maize, wheat, pulses, oranges, and spices. If 100,000 out of a population of 200,000 left, the agricultural labour force would have been greatly depleted, and there were indeed reports of farms and orchards reverting to forest. There were also indications of social disintegration in southern Bhutan, with reports of banditry in the depopulated countryside, which encouraged further flight (UNHCR 1993).

There were mixed views about the composition of the ethnic Turks expelled from Bulgaria, so that views of the effects of their departure are therefore also mixed. Vasileva (1992) maintains that most of the forced emigrants were of rural origin, with low levels of education, skills and professional qualifications. However the survey of arrivals in Turkey by the ILO suggested that there were significant numbers of educated and skilled people among them: 14 per cent had been in professional or technical occupations, 13 per cent were clerical, sales or service workers, 11 per cent were drivers, 12 per cent were farmers, and the remainder were production or construction workers. Moreover, the survey found that 65 per cent of the expellees were in the age group 15–64, meaning that the ratio of economically active persons to dependents was high (Scott 1991). If those surveyed were at all representative of the Bulgarian ethnic Turk population as a whole, this suggests that

Bulgaria experienced a considerable loss of educated and skilled workers (Scott 1991). Whatever the proportions of skilled and unskilled labour, urban and rural, among the expellees, the mass exodus precipitated a labour shortage in the countryside, since many of those leaving were farmers. Bulgaria was already facing labour scarcity, an impact tacitly acknowledged by the Bulgarian authorities in a decree for "civil mobilization" which demanded compulsory labour in areas affected by labour shortages (Poulton 1994). Agrarian production such as cattle raising and wheat and tobacco production were reported damaged (Vasileva 1992). In addition, the mass departure precipitated capital flight since the Turks withdrew large amounts of savings from banks to take with them (Poulton 1994). The exodus yielded short-term opportunities for the population left behind. Housing and other property were bought up cheaply from departing Turks (Poulton 1994; Vasileva 1992). However these dubious gains were reversed or contested when a large number of the Turks subsequently returned, which precipitated further social, economic and political upheaval (see Chapter 6). The net effect of the expulsion of ethnic Turks from Bulgaria and their subsequent return was to reduce Bulgaria's ethnic Turkish population by just under one-fifth. Overall, the mass departure was followed by a decline in Bulgaria's economy: its GDP is estimated to have fallen by 33 per cent in the three years 1900–1992, bottoming out in mid-1992 (Verona 1993).

In the other cases explored, either substitute labour was found for the departing migrant community or there was a swift return of the community so that disruption of the labour market was short-lived. In Kuwait and Saudi Arabia there was temporary disruption of certain sectors – notably administration in Kuwait and retail in Saudi Arabia – precipitated respectively by the departure of Palestinians and Yemenis. In Kuwait, the departure of foreign labour retarded post-war reconstruction. But gaps in the labour market of both countries were rapidly filled by workers drawn from other Arab or Asian migrants. Egyptians appear to have substituted for the Palestinians in Kuwait; in 1995 there were said to be about 200,000 Egyptians legally present and up to another 50,000 illegals (*Migration News* July 1995). Indians appear to have made up the shortfall in

Saudi Arabia, which continued to shed foreign labour subsequently; more than 100,000 illegal foreign workers were reported to have left late in 1994 and early in 1995 following a crackdown on residency documentation (*Middle East Economic Digest* 10 and 24 February 1995). Moreover, as has been noted, a reduction of the foreign workforce was desired by both regimes, prompted both by security concerns and by changes in the economy and demand for labour in each (Russell & Al-Ramadhan 1994).

Operation Wetback in the US did not appear to precipitate problems of labour supply since, in the short-term at least, legally imported labour was substituted for wetbacks as a result of the campaign. In California, contracting of braceros increased by 25 per cent. In the Rio Grande Valley of Texas, bracero contracts increased from 3,000 to 70,000 after the operation (Garcia 1980). However, this legitimization of labour supply was partly illusory, for significant numbers of these recruits were illegals who legalised their status. The hiring of so-called "dried-out" wetbacks who legalized their position "created the strange situation of the United States expending large amounts of money to oust 'illegals' and then turning around and spending even more money to return many of them to this country as 'legalized' braceros" (Garcia 1980: 220). Moreover, many of the legalized braceros accepted contracts to get back into the US; once in they struck out on their own again. The response of farmer-employers to the campaign was mixed. Many growers in Texas vigorously opposed the campaign and argued for the use of undocumented workers in preference to braceros. Others, mainly in California and Arizona, came round to supporting the campaign. Growers probably calculated, rightly, that the campaign was just a stop-gap move, and that they could manage for the time being with legitimate bracero labour (Garcia 1980). Proponents of the campaign claimed that the round-up had opened up for citizens jobs previously held by illegals. Decent wage levels were said to obtain for citizens since the mass deportation, and earnings were now being spent in the US rather than being remitted to Mexico. The claims of success were used to good effect by the INS itself, which lobbied for and won significant increases in its funding vote from Congress.

Images of a wetback invasion if vigilance was not maintained continued to prompt increases in its vote in following years (Garcia 1980).

As in the US during Operation Wetback, many employers in the Dominican Republic were unhappy with the campaign against people of Haitian origin. The state-owned sugar enterprise CEA protested that migrant workers legally in the country were being rounded up or intimidated into leaving, causing serious labour shortage during the cane harvest. The expulsion was opposed by other landowners and industrialists who stood to loose cheap and pliable labour (Ferguson 1992). However, since so many Haitians returned so quickly after the expulsion and the September coup in Haiti (itself part prompted by the destabilizing effect of the mass exodus), the impact on the economy of the loss of labour was short-lived. The position was similar in Greece following repeated expulsions of Albanians. The expulsions upset some Greek employers, and deprived some Greek households of domestic workers, but the disruption was only temporary as fresh or returning Albanians could readily be hired.

Conclusion: assessing the effects of mass exodus – the problem of "interference"

In this chapter I have examined some of the socio-economic consequences of migration crises, focusing on the effects of the forced repatriation or regrouping of migrant communities. One of the problems of assessing the longer term consequences of such crises on the population forced to move, on the territories receiving them, and on the territories they leave is that the effects have to be disentangled from contemporaneous factors and developments. This "interference" indeed presents major methodological problems when trying to investigate the impacts of mass exodus.

As has been shown, the territories involuntarily left are likely to be undergoing serious upheaval, turmoil or conflict, of which mass exodus is just one part – or consequence. The effects of mass exodus are likely to be inseparable from these other dimensions of upheaval, and so it is difficult, if not impossible to assess the impacts of mass exodus alone. Similarly, territories receiving forced migrants are likely also to be in upheaval, or thrown into crisis by a number of developments, of which a sudden, forced, mass arrival is just one. Here again it is difficult, if not impossible to separate what precisely are the effects of such mass arrivals.

Other, less acute developments may also "interfere" in this way. A feature of several of the countries which received forced migrants in the episodes covered is that they had structural adjustment programmes under way, usually overseen by the International Monetary Fund or the World Bank. Ghana was subject to a wide-ranging structural adjustment programme, whose contribution to subsequent economic performance has been the subject of much debate. Jordan and Yemen likewise had such programmes under way, and both in addition faced trade and other economic sanctions from their rich neighbours. Yemen also suffered a damaging civil war in 1994. All of these developments make tracking the longer term impact of the returnees difficult. In the case of the Bulgarian ethnic Turks in Turkey, the impact of quite substantial assistance from the Council of Europe may have been significant in their apparently successful economic integration.

If the effects of contemporaneous developments and events need to be screened out for an assessment of the impact of mass exodus and influx, this methodological problem becomes more acute as time goes on and as subsequent developments intervene. While the passage of time may present the opportunity to review the longer term effects of mass exodus, interference from subsequent developments makes this task increasingly difficult.

No resolution of this problem has been offered here, but three broad conclusions have been drawn. First, most migrant communities, though traumatised in the short term by mass exodus, show great resilience in rebuilding their lives. Second, the territories receiving sudden, disorderly mass inflows, while suffering in the short term, may in the longer term derive some benefits from such mass arrivals. Third, for the territories left, short-term benefits of mass departure are usually outweighed by longer term damage. Having looked at the consequences of migration crises on the communities and territories immediately affected, the following chapter places the consequences of such migration crises in broader perspective, by looking at how they help make or unmake transnational populations.

SIX

Diasporas made and diasporas unmade

In the previous chapter, the discussion focused on some of the socio-economic consequences of migration crises on the territories receiving substantial populations of expelled migrants, and to a lesser extent the countries expelling these people. These territories were usually immediate or near neighbours. But this is only part of the picture, for just as migration orders straddle several countries and regions, so do the effects of migration crises. In this chapter I examine the wider ramifications of such migration crises for migration orders and for the making and unmaking of transnational communities.

Migration crises of the kind I have described could have three outcomes. First, the population forced to move might stay put in the territory which received them; this outcome was considered in the previous chapter. A second outcome might be movement onwards to another destination. A third outcome might be the return of some or all of the population to the country from which they were expelled. Each of these outcomes occurred among the 10 cases reviewed. Put another way, for the migrant communities involved, migration crises constituted three moments. They might be moments of "de-diasporization", re-grouping or in-gathering when a migrant community returned to its place of origin. They might be moments of diasporization, or re-diasporization, when a migrant community was dispersed, or further dispersed. Or they might mark temporary reversal of diasporization, after which the prior migration order was reasserted or reaffirmed. In terms of the making and unmaking of transnational communities or diasporas, the outcomes of migration crises represented respectively their unmaking, their remaking and their reassertion.

Referring back to the framework of force and choice outlined in Chapter 2, these in-gatherings, onward movements and return migrations involved varying degrees of forced migration. Almost all of episodes examined in Chapters 3 and 4 involved "de-diasporization", the partial unmaking of diasporas, in the form of the reluctant homecomings examined above. However, only in two of the cases, those of the Yemenis expelled from Saudi Arabia and the ethnic Nepalis from Bhutan, did the forced homecoming appear to be enduring for almost all of the population expelled. There appeared little prospect of a return to the country from which mass exodus took place, nor, in the Yemeni case at least, of onward movement to some other destination. In contrast, the expulsion of Asians from Uganda fostered the further dispersal of this already diasporized population – to the UK, other parts of Europe and North America; there was also a limited regrouping of this population, of unknown magnitude, in South Asia; in neither case was there much choice of destination. The mass exodus of Palestinians from Kuwait led in one sense to re-diasporization of this already diasporized population – to other parts of the Middle East, Europe and North America; but it also led to regrouping in the sense that many gravitated to Jordan, which was their country of nationality if not necessarily their home. In other cases regrouping was the main outcome, but there were weak contributions to re-diasporization. As I show below, some Rohingyas from the 1992 exodus, as after the 1978 episode, made for the Middle East and other southeast Asian destinations like Malaysia; more choice was exercised in these movements further afield than in the movement to Bangladesh. Likewise there appears to have been some scattering of ethnic Nepalis from Bhutan to northern India to join prior Nepali-speaking communities there; again, these people appear to have exercised greater choice than those who ended up in refugee camps in Nepal. Expulsion may also have a delayed diasporizing effect: as is argued below, the expulsion of

Ghanaians from Nigeria may have indirectly encouraged further diasporisation by removing one of the principal regional destinations for would-be migrants.

In several of the cases there was re-emigration or return of migrants to the country they were obliged to leave during the migration crisis. This varied in scale and in timing, but marked to different degrees a reaffirmation of transnationalism or a resumption of the prior migration order. As is shown below, this occurred almost immediately after the exodus in the case of the Haitians from the Dominican Republic; soon after the exodus in the case of some of the Ghanaians from Nigeria, the Mexicans from the US, and some of the ethnic Turks from Bulgaria; within a number of years in the case of the Rohingyas; and long after the exodus in the case of some of the Ugandan Asians. Most of these movements involved some choice on the part of migrants. The Haitian and Rohingya episodes were exceptions. Haitian re-emigration to the Dominican Republic followed a military coup in Haiti and an outflow of refugees, including those just expelled from the Dominican Republic. In the Rohingya case, migrants' choice in the decision to return to Myanmar has been hotly disputed. Whether by force or choice, all of these movements might be described as the reaffirmation of the transnational community, and as a reassertion of the prior migration order.

The processes of re-diasporization, regrouping and re-affirmation of the transnational community involved in each of the 10 episodes examined are summarized in Table 6.1 and considered in greater detail below. As is already evident, while I consider each case within the rubric of diaspora enhanced, diminished and reaffirmed, the complexity of most of the episodes means that few fit exclusively or completely comfortably within these categories.

Diaspora enhanced

As Table 6.1 shows, several of the migration crises led to dispersal of migrant communities or enhanced existing diasporas. This diasporization varied in strength and was often

Table 6.1 Diasporas enhanced, diminished and reaffirmed

		Diaspora remade	Diaspora unmade	Transnationalism reaffirmed
Uganda	Asians	+		+
Nigeria	Ghanaians	+	+	+
Kuwait	Palestinians	+	+	
Saudi Arabia	Yemenis		+	
Bulgaria	ethnic Turks		+	+
Greece	Albanians		+	+
Myanmar	Rohingyas	+	+	+
Bhutan	ethnic Nepalis	+	+	
US	Mexicans		+	+
Dom. Rep.	Haitians		+	+

somewhat ambivalent. Here the contribution of migration crisis to the diasporization of South Asians, Palestinians, the Rohingyas and Ghanaians is examined. In the first three cases, dispersal occurred at the time of the migration crisis or soon after it, while in the Ghanaian case diasporization was a delayed response to the migration crisis and took longer to get under way.

The Ugandan Asians: diaspora reinvigorated
In the later 1980s there were estimated to be nearly 8.7 million South Asians living outside South Asia; 66 countries in Asia, Africa, the Pacific, Europe, North America and the Caribbean hosted South Asian populations of more than 2,000 (Clarke et al 1990). The expulsion of Ugandan Asians in 1972 had contributed modestly to this worldwide South Asian diaspora, but invigorated in particular its component of East African provenance.

Diasporization has been a long-standing South Asian household strategy, and this population has thus accumulated substantial migratory cultural capital. This partly explains the success often reported of Ugandan Asians as they have remade their lives in new societies. Before the expulsion from Uganda, as Asians generally had grown less secure in East Africa, they had developed a form of transnational insurance: "The most highly skilled would try to go to North America; the other working family members would head for Britain; while the old, the retired and the wealthy would probably decide to return to India or Pakistan" (Tinker 1977: 134). Many of the Uganda Asians holding British passports straddled three allegiances – to Uganda, to India and to the UK. As Twaddle put it, paraphrasing a Gujarati proverb, this yielded "the paradoxical situation whereby many a Ugandan Asian kept his *man* (heart) in India and his *dhan* (wealth) in Britain while still managing to retain his *tan* (body) in East Africa" (Twaddle 1975: 13). This divided loyalty was prominent among the grievances exasperating Amin and many black Ugandans, as his speech to the Asian community showed (see pp. 68–69).

The Ugandan Asians both reaped the negative consequences of multifarious allegiances and cashed in the insurance policy these diverse allegiances endowed. While the largest proportion of the Asians expelled from Uganda ended up in a single country – the UK, the former colonial power – substantial numbers were spread among other destinations, augmenting the South Asian diaspora. The Ugandan Asians who settled in Britain were British citizens, or at least British protected persons, but for many actual links with Britain were limited. There was some regrouping, of an unknown scale, in the place of origin several generations before – India, and to a lesser extent Pakistan and Bangladesh. As well as moving to the UK or the South Asian region, Uganda Asians were resettled in other parts of Europe and North America, augmenting South Asian populations there. As these additions to the South Asian diaspora remade their homes in their new host societies, they reinvigorated already established South Asian diaspora populations but also established new communities in new locations in North America and Europe.

The Kuwait Palestinians: a kind of homecoming
The mass exodus of Palestinians from Kuwait and other states in the region as the Gulf crisis unfolded added to the already far-flung Palestinian diaspora, radiating from Israel and the Occupied Territories to Jordan, Lebanon, Syria, the Gulf states, Libya and countries outside the Middle East. Around 1992, the

population of Palestinians worldwide was thought to total 5.4 million (Adelman 1995). The Palestinians in Kuwait had constituted a significant proportion of this population, and a still greater proportion – about 12 per cent – of the Palestinian population of 3 million living outside what had been the British Mandate of Palestine in 1948. For most of the Kuwait Palestinians though, the exodus of 1990–92 resulted in a kind of homecoming – to Jordan, the country of citizenship (or, at least, the country of which they were passport-holders) – and to a lesser extent to the Occupied Territories, for many of them the place of origin.

As I indicated in Chapter 5, the gross total of Palestinian arrivals in Jordan in 1990–92 was about 360,000 (including those already in the country on holiday or visits). Some 30–40,000 are thought to have moved on to the West Bank. This option was officially possible only for those who held Israeli-issued identity cards or their immediate relatives, and for most of the latter stays were limited. This greatly restricted the possibility of family reunion and hampered the prospect of reintegration in the Occupied Territories (Nour 1993). Another 21,000 Gulf Palestinians – mainly those with wealth, family already abroad or other connections – are thought to have emigrated to the US, Canada, Latin America, Europe and Australia. A further 4,000 are thought to have gone subsequently to Saudi Arabia and Gulf states other than Kuwait. As was indicated above, this meant a net gain in Jordan's population of about 300,000 "returnees" (Van Hear 1995). This episode thus significantly reinforced the Palestinian diaspora, but was principally a kind of homecoming, or near homecoming, for those who remade their lives in Jordan, as was described in Chapter 5. Further progress on the resolution of the conflict between Israel and the Palestinians notwithstanding, it is likely that the majority of those who were forced to move from Kuwait to Jordan will stay put in the Hashemite Kingdom.

Like the Ugandan Asians, many of the Palestinians maintained a complex triple allegiance – to the lives they had built in Kuwait, to the adoptive home of Jordan of which they were nationals, and to the Palestinian homeland from which they or their forebears were dispossessed. Palestinians elsewhere in the diaspora have also developed enduring transnational networks. One way such links were and are expressed was through associations based on communities in the homeland (see Ghabra 1987); while the focus binding the diaspora remained the homeland community, the networks generated by such allegiance transcended it.

While many Palestinians in the diaspora have built successful lives in exile, their presence is based on fragile foundations, as the events in Kuwait, other Gulf states, and recently Libya have shown. In 1995, several thousand of Libya's Palestinian long-settled community of about 30,000 were ordered out of the country, to show Muammar Qadaffi's ire at the peace agreement between Israel and the Palestine Liberation Organisation. The expulsion was coupled with another threat to expel more than a million foreigners said to be illegally resident in Libya, partly to press the international community to lift sanctions imposed since 1992 over alleged Libyan involvement in terrorism, and partly to attempt to reduce economic pressures wrought by the sanctions. Some of the Palestinians expelled managed to travel overland through Egypt to Gaza or the West Bank. After tortuous voyages by sea, others eventually reached Syria or Jordan. However, up to a thousand others – mainly those originating from Gaza whom other states would not admit – remained stranded in desperate conditions on the border between Libya and Egypt for nearly two years until Qadaffi relented and most were readmitted. Of the other foreign workers, at least 20,000 of the Sudanese community of up to 450,000 were expelled, along with thousands of Egyptians, Chadians, Malians and others from West Africa (Reuter, Associated Press October 1995; *Guardian* 19 October 1995; *Independent* 19 October 1995; Shiblak 1996; US Committee for Refugees 1996). For Palestinians this upheaval represented yet another forced onward movement.

In 1996, the Palestinian population worldwide numbered perhaps 6.4 million, of whom 60 per cent lived outside historic Palestine. Of the total, less than half, perhaps 2.7 million, had citizenship of some kind (Arzt 1997: 60–1). The standing of the remainder was ambivalent: in particular the residency status of many Palestinians in much of the Middle East has been undermined in recent years as Palestinian nationalism has come into conflict with Arab host states (Shiblak 1996). Notwithstanding developments in the mid-1990s – the faltering peace process, the issue of passports by the nascent Palestinan authority and the drafting of a Palestinian citizenship law – the uncertain status of most diaspora Palestinians persists, as their experience in Kuwait and Libya in the 1990s shows.

The Rohingya diaspora: Asia's new Palestinians?

As is shown later in this chapter, a majority of the Rohingyas who fled Myanmar in 1992 eventually returned under repatriation programmes. However, some joined and augmented the Rohingya diaspora in the Middle East, Pakistan and elsewhere. Early in 1993 there were reported to be more than 200,000 Rohingyas in Pakistan, about that number in Saudi Arabia, 20,000 in the United Arab Emirates, between 3,000 and 5,000 in Jordan and 1,500–2,000 in Qatar (Lintner 1993). Most of this population were established prior to the events of 1992: they arrived in the wake of the 1978–79 expulsion or had settled before.

As well as a kind of re-diasporization, in a sense this was a regrouping or in-gathering many generations and centuries on. As Lintner (1993: 23) put it, "The diaspora of Burma's Rohingya Muslims to the Middle East ... completes a journey that began more than a millennium ago when their Moorish and Persian ancestors settled in the country's Arakan region." Deprived of citizenship by successive Burmese governments, many had arrived in the Middle East on fake Pakistani or Bangladeshi passports. A few still held Burmese travel documents, now expired, issued by Burma's first post-independence government. Some of this diaspora had become wealthy. Linter (1993) sketches the migratory biography of one such early exile who left Arakan in 1955 for Pakistan and arrived in Dubai five years later. A Dubai resident for more than 30 years, he arrived before the discovery of oil and concomitant prosperity, but managed to build up a thriving garment business.

A trickle of expatriates from the 1960s was supplemented by Muslim militants and separatists who fled after failed insurgency in the 1950s and 1960s, first to what was then East

Pakistan and then to the Middle East. They were joined by some of those who did not return to Burma after the 1978 exodus, when many continued "to go into exile in countries as far apart as Pakistan, Egypt, and across the Arab world where they have often been dubbed Asia's 'new Palestinians' " (Smith 1991: 241). Seeing no prospects in Bangladesh, many moved to Pakistan or on to Saudi Arabia and other Gulf states, where they formed new Rohingya settlements (Lintner 1993; US Committee for Refugees 1993, 1994).

Saudi Arabia appears to have been the principal Middle Eastern destination (US Committee for Refugees 1993, 1994). The Saudi Arabian towns of Nakasa and Jarwal near Mecca accommodate the largest concentration of Rohingyas in the Middle East; tens of thousands are said to have lived here in poor conditions since the 1960s. Those in the United Arab Emirates are said to be better off, living mainly in Dubai, Sharjah and Ajman. The flow to Pakistan and the Middle East continued modestly in the 1980s (Lintner 1993).

It is unclear how many made their way to these destinations after the 1991–92 mass exodus. A survey in November 1993 found that up to 20,000 refugees had disappeared from the camps in Bangladesh; these had either integrated into the local community or had left Bangladesh on false travel documents for the Middle East and elsewhere (Reuter 19 and 21 April 1994; US Committee for Refugees 1996). The diaspora already present elsewhere in Asia and in the Middle East provided support for the newcomers. Diaspora connections between Rohingyas resident in the Middle East and those in camps in Bangladesh were substantial. Rohingyas in Saudi Arabia have sent clothing and other supplies to assist refugees in camps in Bangladesh (Lambrecht 1995). In addition to humanitarian assistance, wealthy Rohingya residents in the Middle East were alleged to give financial backing to militant Rohingya groups operating in the camps and on the Burma–Bangladesh border (Lintner 1993; Weiner 1993a). Indeed, concern about the prospect of increased Islamist militancy supported by Rohingyas in the Middle East may well have prompted the Bangladeshi authorities to take a firmer line over repatriation (Lintner 1993 and see below).

Some of the Rohingyas in the mass exodus of 1992 made their

way less far afield to southeast Asian countries, particularly
those with substantial populations of Muslims. Between 6,000
and 7,000 Rohingyas were reported to have fled from Burma to
Malaysia, for example (*Burma Briefing* 15 July 1992). A substantial number also moved to southern Thailand, where much
of the population is Muslim, and where they felt safer than in
Bangladesh. Overall, the evidence for substantial movement of
Rohingyas to destinations other than Bangladesh or Burma after
the exodus of 1991–92 is not strong, but they do appear to have
modestly supplemented the Rohingya diaspora in the Middle
East, Pakistan and parts of Southeast Asia.

The Ghanaians: delayed diasporization

The three cases just considered featured diasporization either
accompanying migration crisis, or occurring soon after it. This
section examines in more detail the case of the Ghanaians,
whose diaspora was strongly enhanced some years after the
migration crisis.

Initially at least, the migrants expelled to Ghana in 1983
stayed put in their country of nationality. Many did return to
Nigeria after the expulsion, only to have their presence
challenged again subsequently: in this sense the prior migration
order was at least partly restored. But a plausible argument can
be made that the expulsion accelerated the diasporization of
Ghanaians in the longer term. By cutting off a principal
destination for Ghanaian migrants, the expulsion, and its
aftermath of economic decline and reduced opportunities in
Nigeria, encouraged Ghanaians to seek opportunities further
afield. The scale of expulsions and deportations after 1983 –
particularly those in 1984 and 1985 (Van Hear 1985) – suggest
that considerable numbers of migrants returned to Nigeria. But
many others sought alternative destinations in Africa and
increasingly outside the continent.

The pattern of Ghanaian diasporization can be pieced
together from local level studies of emigration in Ghana, from
Ghana government figures, and from statistics covering their
countries of destination, principally Europe. As might be
expected, diasporization accelerated at first within Africa,
extending already existing migratory networks beyond the

western part of the continent. Ghanaians' migratory impulse was not thwarted by the expulsions from Nigeria. A study of a small Ghanaian town of about 5,800 people found just under 300 returnees from Nigeria in 1983. By 1989, 38 had left again for Nigeria, Libya or other destinations (Dei 1992). Another study looked at a sample of emigrants from a suburb of Ghana's capital Accra in 1993, and found wide dispersal among them in the 1990s (Peil 1995).

West African destinations were still the most important numerically in the 1990s. Ghanaians were to be found mainly in Côte d'Ivoire, where one estimate was that they numbered a million, although this seems high; in Nigeria, where they may have numbered half a million, despite the expulsions of the 1980s; and in Togo, where many have kin connections (Peil 1995). But smaller numbers were to be found in most African countries, from Libya to South Africa.

Increasing numbers of Ghanaians sought destinations outside the continent, again building on already existing networks. Military service has been one long-standing source of dispersal. Ghanaian troops served in East Africa, India and Burma during the Second World War, and more recently in UN peace-keeping forces in Africa, the Middle East and former Yugoslavia. There have also been long-standing movements abroad of Ghanaian professionals and students. Ghana may have lost 14,000 qualified teachers, among them 3,000 university graduates, in the period 1975–81. Doctors and other professionals joined the exodus – perhaps half to two-thirds of the country's high-level manpower. Many of them entered UN or other international organizations, went to oil-rich countries of the Middle East, or made for English-speaking countries anywhere (Peil 1995; Rado 1986).

In the later 1980s diasporization appears to have accelerated, so that by the 1990s the global reach of the Ghanaian diaspora was considerable. The presence of Ghanaians in large numbers was noted in London, Amsterdam, Hamburg, New York and other world cities: Toronto was said to have a Ghanaian population of 20,000 in 1995 (Peil 1995). Returnees to Ghana from Germany and indeed from other destinations were popularly known as "Hamburgers" in the 1980s. Emigrants from

Peil's 1993 sample were found in the UK, Belgium, France, Germany, Italy, the Netherlands, Russia and Switzerland in Europe, as well as further afield in Australia, Burma, Canada, India, Israel, Japan, Saudi Arabia and the US. The sample yielded factory workers in Britain, Italy, Japan and Senegal, a film actor in Italy, a lecturer in Australia and an accountant in Israel, and Ghanaians running businesses in Belgium, Britain, Burkina Faso, Italy and the US (Peil 1995).

Macro-level evidence confirms the growth of Ghanaian diasporization. While the most common destinations for Ghanaian migrants or would-be migrants were in Africa, Europe or North America, the dispersal was in fact much wider, as evidenced by Table 6.2, which reproduces Ghana Immigration Service figures for deportees to Ghana in 1993. What is significant is not so much the total of deportees arriving in Ghana, as the number of countries from which they were deported – no less than 58 in 1993, indicating the wide spread of destinations, or would-be destinations, and hence the diasporization of Ghanaians. On the evidence of deportations, the trend towards diasporization is increasing. In the first five months of 1994, 2,000 Ghanaians were deported, compared with 2,194 in the whole of 1993 and 1,882 in 1992; Germany accounted for nearly a quarter of the

Table 6.2   Countries deporting Ghanaians, 1993

	Deportees and stowaways
Germany	885
UK	312
Netherlands	184
Italy	142
Switzerland	89
Côte d'Ivoire	83
France	66
USA	49
Canada	43
Spain	39
South Africa	31
Belgium	27
Japan	22
Bulgaria	18
Senegal	16
Zimbabwe	15

Table 6.2 continued

	Deportees and stowaways
Egypt	14
Libya	11
Gambia	13
Saudi Arabia	13
Sweden	13
Russia	12
Sierra Leone	10
Austria	6
Brazil	6
Malaysia	6
Portugal	6
Hong Kong	5
Korea	5
Cameroon	4
Greece	4
Guinea	4
Liberia	4
Denmark	3
Malta	3
Benin	2
Czech Republic	2
Finland	2
Israel	2
Jordan	2
Mexico	2
Nigeria	2
Taiwan	2
Algeria	1
Angola	1
Australia	1
Bermuda	1
China	1
Gabon	1
Ireland	1
Jamaica	1
Morocco	1
Norway	1
Philippines	1
Poland	1
Romania	1
Singapore	1
Turkey	1
	2194

Source: Ghana Immigration Service, *Annual Report on Deportees and Stowaways*, Accra, 1993.

Table 6.3 Immigration by Ghanaians to countries of the European Union, 1985–93

	1985	1986	1987	1988	1989	1990	1991	1992	1993
Germany	–	–	–	2351	4483	5404	4652	6848	3793
UK	1600	600	300	600	300	800	900	500	400
Netherlands	342	682	2567	1238	1331	1638	1930	1329	1306
Other	126	120	148	139	124	79	93	125	89
Total	2068	1402	2715	4228	5938	7921	7675	8171	5123

Source: Eurostat, Migration statistics database, 20 January 1997
Note: Immigration is taken to involve the intention to settle for more than one year.

deportations, the UK for 7 per cent, while other would-be destinations for substantial numbers of failed migrants included the Netherlands, the US, Italy and Switzerland (*West Africa* 27 June 1994).

Diasporization trends are also indicated by statistics for migration to Europe, which show how destinations for Ghanaian immigrants within Europe have shifted. Table 6.3 illustrates immigration of Ghanaians to countries of the European Union in 1985–1993; immigration is taken to mean the intention to settle for more than one year.

Some caveats are in order over the table's figures, which like much statistical data on migration, are imperfect. First, they record official migration only, and much Ghanaian migration has been unauthorized. Second, the statistics for the UK appear to be rounded estimates. Third, not all countries appear to have filed returns; Italy for example was reported in 1995 to have a Ghanaian population of 14,000 (*West Africa* 20 March 1995), suggesting substantial immigration in the 1990s. Nevertheless the table gives some idea of trends and magnitudes.

The figures show that overall, Ghanaian entries into Europe steadily increased until 1992, and then sharply declined. Their principal destination, Germany, shows this pattern most clearly, with entries peaking in 1990–92, followed by a marked decline in 1993, when new asylum legislation came into force. After a peak in 1987, there has been a steady flow of Ghanaians into the Netherlands since the later 1980s. The figures for the UK do not present any discernible pattern.

Table 6.4   Ghanaian asylum applications in Europe, 1985–1994 (in thousands)

	1985	1986	1987	1988	1989	1990	1991	1992	1993	1994
Germany	4.0	5.8	0.8	1.3	3.2	3.8	4.5	7.0	2.0	...
France	2.6	1.8	1.1	1.2	1.4	1.1	0.7	...	0.4	0.3
UK	0.1	0.2	0.1	0.2	0.3	1.0	2.4	1.6	1.8	2.0
Netherlands	...	0.1	2.5	0.9	0.8	0.7	0.5	0.1	0.7	0.7
Belgium	...	...	...	...	...	...	1.4	0.9	1.0	0.3

Sources: Eurostat 1994a, 1994b; Migration statistics database, 20 January 1997.

Much of the movement of Ghanaians outside Africa, and particularly to Europe, has been by the asylum route. Table 6.4 shows the principal destinations in Europe for Ghanaian asylum seekers from the mid-1980s to the early 1990s. The figures for Germany show a peak in the mid-1980s, after the expulsion from Nigeria, then a sharp fall, followed by a rise from 1989, the year of unification, to another peak in 1992; applications fell again following the reform of German asylum law in 1993. Asylum applications to France show a similar peak in the mid-1980s, but a decline thereafter. Applications to the UK and the Netherlands do not really replicate this pattern, although applications to the latter peaked in 1987.

It is widely recognized (not least by many Ghanaians) that the asylum route has been used or attempted by people whose emigration has little basis in persecution. Stricter application of asylum procedures has diversified the means of entry used, so that, like other migrants, they may enter illegally, or arrive on visitors' or students' visas and stay on; others are helped by relatives legally resident, by "fixers" in the migration industry, or marry nationals in order to stay (Peil 1995).

The evidence seems to suggest then first that substantial Ghanaian emigration was sustained in the 1980s and 1990s. Peil (1995) cites estimates that between 10 and 20 per cent of Ghanaians may have been abroad in this period, the upper figure probably including Ghanaian children born abroad who may have different nationality. Second, the evidence shows that the destinations sought in the 1980s and 1990s had diversified considerably from West Africa. A culture of migratory entrepreneurship with a worldwide reach, transcending earlier, traditional destinations like the UK, has emerged over the last decade. Destinations are eclectic: there is "a wide dispersion of individuals and small colonies in such diverse places as the Virgin Islands and Papua New Guinea" (Peil 1995: 346). Peil remarks that "there seems to be no major emigration stream for moves outside Africa; individuals take whatever opportunities they find, according to their education, training and contacts" (1995: 357). However, movement is not as random and arbitrary as this perhaps suggests, for Peil's sample also revealed the common household strategy of spreading family members widely – in the US, Europe, the Middle East and Africa.

Ghana's migration history shows, once again, the complex relationship between migration and the economic and political arenas. In earlier periods, immigration into Ghana and emigration from it more or less matched respectively periods of relative prosperity and stability, and of economic decline and concomitant political and social insecurity. Thus the period of relative prosperity from the Second World War to the latter half of the 1960s was broadly a period of immigration, while the period of economic decline and social insecurity from the late 1960s to the first half of the 1980s was one of emigration. During these periods, migration appeared to conform to the usual expectations of economic and political "push" and "pull" factors. But the period of emigration in the later 1980s occurred when Ghana's economy was picking up as economic reforms began to have their effect and when democratization began to take some tentative steps forward. Of course, both of these developments were relative. Structural adjustment was painful, particularly in terms of employment, with heavy redundancies in the state sector; consumers were hit by the removal of subsidies, as were the users of health, education and other services. The Rawlings regime also still targeted political opponents, at times ruthlessly. But there was relative prosperity and the repression and violence was nothing on the scale of Zaire, Liberia or Rwanda. Yet emigration continued despite improvements in Ghana's economic and political prospects.

If this current phase of emigration is not explicable, at least in a direct way, by economic and political push factors, or the structural and proximate domains outlined in Chapter 2, the explanation may well lie in the intervening domain, the factors consolidating and accelerating migratory flows – and in particular to the accumulation of the migratory culture mentioned above, including bridgeheads and networks already established. The emergence of such a culture is not difficult to account for. Its roots lie in pre-colonial trading diasporas in West Africa. More recently, during the post-war period of immigration, Ghanaians as a host, accommodating community made connections and created networks with Nigerians and other West African migrants in Ghana in the 1950s and 1960s (Eades 1987b). These connections and networks were later put to use when the regional migration order began to reverse in the 1970s, a turnaround ironically marked by the expulsion of aliens from Ghana in 1969, another expulsion watershed. Subsequently the migratory net spread further afield to other parts of the African continent and beyond, building on connections established earlier through military service, through students abroad, and through trade and professional links.

Despite the setbacks of deportation for individuals as revealed in the statistics contained in Table 6.2, the Ghanaian diaspora is now well established. There is an increasing population of second generation Ghanaians abroad, often settling there, while maintaining links with home. One measure of the extent of this diasporization is in the scale of remittances. Peil (1995) cites an estimate of Ghanaians remittances from the US of $250–350 million a year. Much of Ghana's housing industry depends on remittances, house building being a focus of many migrants abroad.

The partial demise of Nigeria as a principal destination for Ghanaian migrants in the early 1980s was among the factors that contributed to the diasporization of the later 1980s and 1990s. If the expulsions of the early 1980s did mark the partial closure of Nigeria as a migratory destination, stimulating the subsequent wider dispersal of Ghanaian would-be migrants, this shows that close attention should be paid to such developments; for although seemingly of little consequence outside the region at the time, they can later work through to have much wider impacts.

Diaspora diminished

As Table 6.1 indicates, in almost all the cases reviewed, migration crisis led to an unmaking or diminution of a migrant or diaspora community by the forced movement of part of it to an original homeland – however notional or putative that homeland might be, particularly for those long-settled abroad. For some this undoing was partial and ephemeral, for others it was more substantial and enduring. Here I consider three cases of diaspora unmaking that endured – the ethnic Nepalis from Bhutan, the Yemenis from Saudi Arabia and the ethnic Turks from Bulgaria – together with the case of the Albanians, whose ousting was short-lived.

The exodus of southern Bhutanese: "greater Nepal" deflated?

Despite lengthy and tortuous negotiations, there has been no significant repatriation of ethnic Nepalis expelled from Bhutan. The prospect of an ethnic Nepali return to Bhutan appears increasingly remote and an absorption of the refugees in camps into Nepal increasingly likely. At the time of writing, the ethnic Nepalis in camps in Nepal were in a condition of involuntary immobility, notwithstanding an attempted protest march by the exiles through India to the borders of Bhutan. The migration crisis of 1991–92 can therefore be seen as a forced repatriation to the original homeland, notwithstanding the fact that most of the returnees had never lived there. The Nepali authorities may have to accept this view, and may already tacitly do so. In terms of the framework employed in this chapter, this was a manifestation of de-diasporization, or the partial unmaking of a diaspora.

Nepalis are widely spread in the northern part of South Asia, particularly in Sikkim, in Darjeeling and other northern parts of West Bengal, in Assam, and also in northern Uttar Pradesh and Himachal Pradesh to the northwest of Nepal towards Kashmir (Baral 1996; Martensen 1995). Indeed, Nepalis are in the majority in several of these areas, so much so as to feed fears among some neighbours of a Nepali ambition for "a greater Nepal"; as was shown in Chapter 3, this was among the factors that generated Bhutanese moves against the ethnic Nepalis.

Nepalis are also spread widely further afield, not least through their involvement in the British military, notably the Gurkha regiments. The ethnic Nepali presence in several Indian states can be traced to their service in the British army in the nineteenth century (Martensen 1995). More than 50,000 Nepalis were recruited into Gurkha regiments in the First World War, and many did not return on discharge. Recruitment continued in the 1920s and 1930s, and then, after partition, into the Indian army. Dispersal through military service has combined with economic migration in search of land or employment in northern India, and gravitation to Indian cities to make for a substantial Nepali population in India (Seddon 1995).

By the 1930s one in 20 Nepali–born persons was living in India; in 1961 more than a million Nepalese speakers were said to live there. In the 1960s the number of Nepalis officially resident abroad stood at about 361,000, but this was an underestimate, since it did not include temporary migrants. Most temporary migrants staying more than six months still go to Indian cities where they work as watchmen, or in Assam and the border regions where they work in construction, forestry or porterage. In the later 1980s and 1990s, female emigration increased significantly as the employment opportunities for men declined. Nepali women are casually employed, often in the sex industry in India and Thailand. Seddon (1995) offers an estimate of between 500,000 and 1 million for the total of short and long-term migrants abroad.

While the exodus of 1991–92 constituted principally a forced regrouping of the Bhutanese component of the Nepali diaspora, the migration crisis also modestly augmented the Indian element of this transnational community. According to one estimate, of the 132,000 habitual residents of Bhutan living in exile in 1994, 30,000 ethnic Nepali former residents of Bhutan were living in India (US Committee for Refugees 1995), many fleeing there from the beginning of the migration crisis in 1991. It is not clear if this figure for the exiled population in India includes Nepali migrant workers deported before the mass exodus of 1991–92. India was a destination for substantial numbers, not just because it was an immediate neighbour, nor only because there were already substantial numbers of Nepalis settled in India from earlier migrations, but also because a 60-mile strip of West Bengal had to be traversed to reach refuge in southeast Nepal and some are likely to have dispersed en route (Baral 1996).

Although the mass exodus modestly reinforced the "near diaspora" of Nepalis within the region, the bulk of the ethnic Nepalis obliged to leave Bhutan look likely to stay put in Nepal. In 1996 several thousand ethnic Nepali exiles crossed the Nepali border into India with the intention of marching to Bhutan to press their case, but they were arrested and turned back by the Indian authorities (Jesuit Refugee Service 1996). Eventual incorporation of this community into Nepal looks the most likely prospect, confirming that a partial unmaking of the Nepali diaspora appears to be the enduring outcome of the mass exodus of 1991–92.

The Yemenis: diaspora undone

As with the ethnic Nepalis from Bhutan, in the case of the Yemenis there appeared little prospect of return to the previous host countries of Saudi Arabia or Kuwait, or of movement to some other destination, despite the existence of a long-established and far-flung Yemeni diaspora. The people of the Hadramawt in particular have a centuries-old tradition of residence abroad, constituting a diaspora of merchants, traders and bankers, not only in Saudi Arabia and elsewhere in the Arab world, but also in eastern Africa, and in south and southeast Asia. There were large out-migrations of Muslim scholars and traders from the Hadramawt to Africa in the fourteenth and fifteenth centuries, and in the seventeenth century to India and what is now Indonesia where they dealt in batik and other textiles (Serjeant 1988). Some attribute the spread of Islam to these territories to this diaspora. There are also more recent, though nonetheless well-established Yemeni communities in Britain and in North America. Much of the Yemeni population in Britain is descended from seafarers who settled in Cardiff and South Shields, later moving to industrial cities like Birmingham, Manchester and Sheffield; at its peak this population may have numbered about 15,000 (Halliday 1992).

The returnees of 1990 were not in a position to take

advantage of this well-established diaspora to seek new destinations abroad, probably for want of links with its members. The Hadrami diaspora differed significantly from most of the returnees in terms of class, wealth, social standing and place of origin. There were likewise few links with other components of the Yemeni diaspora. The population of Yemeni origin in Britain were largely drawn from the hinterland of Aden, and were most unlikely to be able to accommodate newcomers, even in the unlikely event of entry into the UK being allowed.

The expulsion from Saudi Arabia and from other parts of the Middle East does not appear then to have contributed to Yemenis' further diasporization, but was rather an episode contributing to de-diasporization from several of their major long-standing places of residence in the Middle East. The mass exodus of 1990 thus diminished the Yemeni diaspora; it was a partial, though substantial undoing of this transnational community. However, late in 1997, there were reports that some Yemenis were returning to Saudi Arabia to replace Asian and other migrants who were being expelled as illegals; the cycle of re-diasporization continued.

Bulgaria's ethnic Turks: post-Ottoman in-gathering

As was indicated in Chapter 5, between half and two-thirds of the ethnic Turks expelled from Bulgaria in 1989 appear to have opted to stay put in Turkey, assisted by substantial subsidies from the Turkish authorities and the Council of Europe. In terms of the framework used in this chapter, the episode could be seen as an in-gathering or de-diasporization. However, unlike other episodes considered, this was an acute manifestation of a long-standing process: the migration crisis of 1989 in Bulgaria was a magnification of an emigration trend lasting more than a century. Its outcome was to accelerate rather than to initiate an in-gathering of the ethnic Turks dispersed over the centuries at the instigation of the Ottoman imperial authorities. Brubaker (1996) has described how "the protracted disintegration of the Ottoman Empire" took from the late eighteenth century until after the First World War. "Throughout this period, and even earlier, the shrinkage of Ottoman political space was accompanied by centripetal migration of Muslims from the lost territories to remaining Ottoman territories" (Brubaker 1996: 152). Forced displacements, featuring what Lord Curzon described as the "unmixing of peoples" as multinational empires were transformed into nation-states, were concentrated in the latter half of this period. If the expulsions of the early 1950s and the late 1980s were of the same lineage, the return of a large number of the expellees to Bulgaria shortly after the 1989 exodus, considered below, can be seen as a reaffirmation of the Bulgarian component of the Turkish diaspora.

The regrouping or in-gathering continued after the 1989 mass exodus, alongside waves of general Bulgarian emigration which gathered momentum in 1990–91 to Western Europe and North America (OECD SOPEMI 1994). Emigration of ethnic Turks took off again from 1992, prompted largely by the effects of economic liberalization in Bulgaria – notably unemployment following privatization, reform of landholding and the removal of subsidies – and by Turkey's contrasting economic buoyancy. By mid-1992, 80,000 ethnic Turks had emigrated and many thousands more had applied to leave for Turkey; the outflow accelerated from 1993 (OECD SOPEMI 1994; Poulton 1994). In contrast to other migration crises considered in this book, the mass exodus of 1989 was congruent with the long-established flow of emigrants and the existing migration order – the in-gathering of the descendants of the Ottoman dispersal.

The Albanians: diasporization thwarted?
The recent movements between Albania, Greece and Italy are just one dimension of Albanian diasporization, for substantial populations of ethnic Albanians live in Kosovo and Macedonia in former Yugoslavia. This near diaspora comprises nearly nine-tenths of the 2 million inhabitants of Kosovo, formerly an autonomous province of Yugoslavia, and a quarter of the population of Macedonia, which also totals about 2 million. Against the background of repression and of attempts to resettle Serbs in Kosovo, large numbers of Albanians have left for parts of the European Union, notably Germany. There are also

significant numbers of long-settled people of Albanian origin in the US.

Against this wider background of dispersal, the migration crises involving Albanians in Greece and Italy might be seen as attempts to roll back further diasporization of Albanians. However, the effort to turn back or expel would-be migrants has not been very successful, for the movement of Albanians into Greece, Italy and elsewhere in Europe has continued. A brisk traffic in migrants by speedboat between Albania and southern Italy has assisted Albanians from Kosovo as well as migrants from Albania itself. The repeated expulsions of Albanians from Greece and Italy in the first part of the 1990s indicate the scale of re-emigration by these migrants. Moreover, the migration crises since 1990 have transformed Albania not just from a country of immobility to one of out-migration, but more recently into a country of transit for a variety of nationalities – notably Chinese migrants and people from the Middle East – seeking entry into the European Union through Italy.

After nearly three years of mass emigration and forced return, Albania's economy was buoyant by 1993. The economy reached its nadir in 1992, but turned around in the following year, registering substantial growth (Economist Intelligence Unit 1994). Remittances from the Albanian diaspora in Greece and elsewhere – thought to total $400 million by 1995 (*Guardian* 13 March 1995) – helped to sustain this recovery, indicating that far from being thwarted, Albanian diasporization appeared to be continuing apace. However, the recovery, if such it was, was short-lived. Emigration was given new impetus by the collapse of pyramid investment schemes involving huge losses in Albanians' savings in 1996. The unrest and violence that followed prompted the departure of yet another wave of Albanians to Italy and Greece. While the Italian authorities were anxious that they should return, many of the new arrivals will augment Albanian diasporization under way since the early 1990s. By the later 1990s, 500,000 Albanians, or one in seven of the population were thought to be outside the country in Greece, Italy, Germany and other parts of Europe (*Migration News* March 1997).

Transnationalism reaffirmed

Previous sections have shown how the episodes reviewed in this book contributed to the making, remaking and unmaking of diaspora populations. As Table 6.1 suggests, there is another outcome to consider, for in several of the cases there was a mass return of expelled populations to their erstwhile places of residence. These movements involved a reaffirmation of the transnational community, a reassertion of the prior migration order.

Reference has already been made to the return to Nigeria of substantial numbers of Ghanaian migrants after the expulsion of 1983 and the return of Albanian migrants to Greece after successive operations to remove them. The very fact of subsequent expulsions attests to the resurgence and persistence of the prior migration order. In each of these cases this order was reasserted almost immediately after the migration crisis, and although the re-migration was, as before, determined largely by economic disparities between the places of origin and destination, the return movement was largely a matter of choice. The remainder of this section looks at other reassertions of the prior migration order. These movements occurred on different scales, after the elapse of different periods of time, and involved varying degrees of force and choice. The return of a portion of the ethnic Turks to Bulgaria, of Mexicans to the US, and of a small number of Ugandan Asians to Uganda are considered. In these cases return was largely a matter of choice; a difference is that while return of the ethnic Turks and of the Mexicans was almost immediate, the return of Ugandan Asians occurred decades after expulsion. Two other cases exemplify forced returns of different kinds, again occurring over different periods: the return of Haitian migrants to the Dominican Republic took place almost immediately after their mass exodus from that country, while the repatriation of Rohingyas to Myanmar was more protracted.

The return of ethnic Turks to Bulgaria
While up to two-thirds of the ethnic Turks expelled from Bulgaria remade their lives in Turkey, the return to Bulgaria of at

least a third of the ethnic Turks who fled marked a partial reaffirmation of this community as a component of the Turkish diaspora. As the account in Chapter 4 showed, the mass return was predicated on the continued unravelling of the communist regime, ensuing liberalization and the dropping of the assimilation policy directed against Turks. It was also prompted by the realization that while Turkey's free market economy was more buoyant than Bulgaria's, the social benefits that went with a planned economy were lacking in Turkey. The return marked not just a spatial reassertion of the ethnic Turks' transnational community, but also a cultural restoration, as manifested in the restitution of Turkish language and schooling in Bulgaria.

Nevertheless, even though their absence was brief, the reintegration of returning Turks did not proceed smoothly in Bulgaria. The demise of the assimilation campaign was unpopular among some of the majority Slav population who continued to agitate against the Turks. Restitution of property for those returning was difficult; some found that their homes had been destroyed, others that their property had been occupied. Lack of housing and employment made many consider leaving once again (Poulton 1994). Homelessness persisted; a year after the mass return, more than 1,000 families were reported to be still without housing, and a decree requiring all government bodies to return property was not yet in effect (US Department of State 1991; Vasileva 1992). As unemployment rose, Turks claimed discrimination in employment, and exclusion from responsible positions, despite reform measures designed to combat discrimination. On the other hand Slav Bulgarians claimed discrimination in employment in areas where Turks formed a majority (US Department of State 1991). Provision of schooling in Turkish, while a welcome turnaround, was also the pretext for protest among ethnic Bulgarians. Anti-Turkish nationalism was among the most disturbing and enduring of the social consequences of the whole debacle. The scepticism of the 200,000 expellees who remained in Turkey over improved social and political conditions in Bulgaria had at least some foundation. While these were offered permanent residence and citizenship, the status of subsequent Turkish arrivals from Bulgaria was uncertain. In 1996, the Turkish government was considering inducing some 200,000 arrivals since the beginning of 1993 to go back to Bulgaria.

Mexicans in the US: migration unabated

Chapter 4 indicated that although Operation Wetback temporarily retarded the flow of Mexican migration, it did not end large-scale illegal movement from Mexico, as subsequent history shows. The prior migration order was strongly reasserted almost immediately. The long-established transnational community spanning Mexico and the US proved enduring, as the history of Mexican migration has demonstrated in the four decades that have elapsed since Operation Wetback.

A fall in the number of illegals apprehended and increases in the number of braceros contracted after Operation Wetback appeared to lend support to those who argued for the bracero programme, and the farm lobby successfully pressed for its renewal until 1964. However bracero contracts began to decline after 1960 and the number of illegals apprehended rose again. Claims for even a temporary stemming of illegal migration may have been unfounded, since many apprehended wetbacks simply legalized their status by becoming braceros. Moreover, employers began to hire undocumented workers in large numbers, even before the end of the bracero programme in 1964 (Garcia 1980).

New legislation in 1965 and 1968 made it more difficult to enter the US legally, and increased the incentive for illegal entry. Meanwhile, pressures encouraging emigration from Mexico continued to increase. Mexico's population more than doubled between 1940 and 1963, from 22 million to 45 million. Given lack of economic opportunity, rates of underemployment and unemployment remained high. Encouraged by expansion in the US economy, illegal immigration increased significantly in the late 1960s, but as involvement in Vietnam came to an end and Americans began to feel the impact of economic problems, the illegal immigration issue again rose up the public and government agenda, and debate reminiscent of the 1950s reappeared on the political scene (Garcia 1980).

Restrictive measures were again proposed in the 1970s amid fears that a large presence of undocumented workers was exacerbating unemployment and creating serious social, economic and political problems. The measures proposed were similar to those of the 1950s: increases in border patrol personnel, penalization of employers using illegal labour, and closer cooperation with the source countries of illegal entrants. The regularization of migrants' status was discussed, including an amnesty for illegals already in the country (Garcia 1980).

Meanwhile apprehensions of undocumented migrants continued to rise, passing a million in 1978 and reaching this figure again several times in the first half of the 1980s. By this time concern was again spreading that the US was losing control of its borders and there was a widespread perception that millions of illegal immigrants were sinking roots in the US. Pressure for legislative changes grew, resulting eventually in the Immigration Reform and Control Act of 1986, a complex piece of legislation that tried to accommodate the conflicting interests of those favouring tighter control, employers and civil libertarians. The Act introduced long-debated employer sanctions against engaging illegal workers, while at the same time making provision for amnesties for illegal migrants already in the country (Calavita 1992, 1995).

While the Immigration Reform and Control Act allayed some fears about US loss of control over its borders, there was little abatement of migration into the country. A further round of restrictionism gathered momentum in the 1990s, seen in the passage of Proposition 187 in California, which gave rise to similar initiatives in other states, amid great debate about the costs and benefits to the US of both legal and illegal immigration (Calavita 1995). The number of apprehensions of illegal immigrants both at the border and within the US regularly topped one million in the 1990s; while the number of apprehensions did not accurately reflect the numbers of illegal immigrants – since a single migrant might be caught several times – it provided some indication of the scale of the illicit movement. In 1994–95 the INS launched a further series of campaigns against illegal immigrants in the southern states of the US, notably "Operation Gatekeeper" in the San Diego area, a principal crossing point for Mexican undocumented migrants. Some 512,000 apprehensions were recorded in the San Diego area alone in 1994–95 (*Migration News* October 1995). The Illegal Immigration Reform and Immigrant Responsibility Act of 1996 introduced further measures to strengthen border control and to combat alien smuggling (Immigration and Naturalisation Service *Press Release* 26 March 1996). The proliferation of Operation Wetback's descendants attests to the enduring character of the migration order and the transnational community spanning the border between Mexico and the US. As if to underline that resilience, apprehensions and removals of illegal immigrants were estimated to total 1.6 million in 1996, of whom 97 per cent were Mexicans (*Migration News* May 1997).

Uganda's Asians: tentative return

If scrutiny of Operation Wetback allows a 40-year historical perspective on the impact of a crisis in the US–Mexico migration order, the protracted history of the Ugandan Asian case provides another long-term perspective on the making and unmaking of diasporas, for a return of Asians to Uganda has been under way in recent years. Although small scale, this was a limited reaffirmation of the South Asian presence in East Africa.

In part this was the story of the pursuit of compensation and restitution, itself in a way evidence of enduring transnational links with the erstwhile country of residence. The pursuit of redress by Uganda Asians has been long and tortuous (Patel 1992). They sought assistance first through the British government with no success, and there was no movement for the best part of a decade. Then, under pressure from western donors whose assistance was needed to rebuild Uganda's economy, the Ugandan government introduced the Expropriated Properties Act in 1982, which though hedged with ambiguities, appeared to bring the prospect of compensation or restitution slightly closer on the horizon. The fitful application of the 1982 Act led to the restitution of some assets to their Asian former owners. Modest recovery from the late 1980s was accompanied by the trickle back of Asians to Uganda, including some prominent business families. In 1991, partly due to pressure from the World

Bank, President Museveni formally invited expelled Asians to return, with a view to boosting investment. About 1,900 properties and enterprises had been returned to Asian owners by early 1993, against a background of resistance by their current occupants, many of whom were politicians or army officers. However, this did not necessarily indicate a renewed commitment to Uganda as home, for while some Asians – mainly the well-to-do – refurbished property recovered and relaunched businesses, others sold the assets they retrieved and returned with the proceeds to their countries of resettlement (*The Courier* 1993). The majority of Asians remained committed to the countries of resettlement in which they had remade home, most focusing their claims on compensation for assets lost rather than on restitution of them.

The return of Asians to reclaim their assets and restart businesses coincided with accelerated economic recovery in Uganda. By 1993, Uganda was being feted as a World Bank success story, with growth in GDP of 5 per cent anticipated, attributed to the country's adherence to World Bank-directed economic reform (*Financial Times* 25 May 1993). The return of Asians – either temporarily or on a more enduring basis – gathered momentum, so that early in 1996 it was reported that 7,000 had come back (although some of these may have been Asian "newcomers" from Kenya and India, indicating that a new wave of diasporization was under way). Asians were said to have contributed perhaps $500 million to the $2 billion of foreign investment over a 5-year period (*Migration News* March 1996). While it is impossible precisely to quantify the impact on Uganda's economy of either the Asians' departure or their gradual return 20 years later, it is not unreasonable to conclude that the former contributed to Uganda's decline and the latter to the country's recovery.

*

In the three cases just reviewed, the return of forced emigrants to their place of residence prior to the migration crisis was largely a matter of choice, although they were driven to different extents by economic necessity. In the following two cases of return, compulsion was more nakedly in evidence as the prior migration order reasserted itself.

Haitian expellees: out of the frying pan and into the fire
As the account in Chapter 4 showed, the expulsion of people of Haitian origin from the Dominican Republic was short-lived. It was prominent among the factors precipitating the coup of September 1991 that overthrew the government led by Jean-Bertrand Aristide. The repatriation was discontinued immediately after the coup, which precipitated a counter-flow of refugees to the Dominican Republic from the new military regime in Haiti. Perhaps two-thirds of those who left in the expulsion returned, together with many first time migrants seeking work in the sugar industry and new refugees escaping from the regime in Haiti. Human rights groups reported that many of the new arrivals were in severe straits. They had lost or had had to sell their possessions during the expulsion, and now returned to the Dominican Republic with nothing. Few applied formally for refugee status (Ferguson 1992; Kirk 1992; *Refugee Reports* 31 May 1994; US Department of State 1993).

The influx of people fleeing the coup meant that there was no need for forced recruitment for the sugar industry as in the past. Nevertheless some human rights groups claimed those who crossed the borders were detained by the military and then bussed to the plantations, where they were confined for the 7-month harvest of 1991–92. There were modest improvements in conditions for sugar workers subsequently. Housing conditions improved, sugar cane cutter unions were legalized, wages were raised (although from a very low base), and forced child labour diminished (Americas Watch 1992). A small number of workers were issued with one-year renewable work permits, affording them some protection, but abusive treatment continued. Human rights groups visiting in 1994 found that labour and living conditions for sugar workers had got better, but about four-fifths still had no documents, making them vulnerable to exploitation and abuse (*Refugee Reports* 31 May 1994).

Haitian migrants were often reminded of their insecurity by

smaller scale round-ups and deportations in subsequent years. A few thousand were forcibly repatriated in a military campaign in 1993, and more were expelled in 1996 (US Committee for Refugees 1994, 1996; US Department of State 1993). The presence of Haitians in the Dominican Republic was a prominent issue in the presidential elections of 1994 and 1996, when incumbent Balaguer accused his main challenger, who was black, of really being a Haitian and intent on merging the two countries (*Refugee Reports* 31 May 1994). However, Balagner's successor, President Fernandez, continued the policy of periodically deporting Haitian migrants en masse: early in 1997 some 15,000 people of Haitian origin were repatriated in a move very reminiscent of the 1991 expulsion (National Coalition for Haitian Refugees 1997).

The events of 1991 constituted a very short-lived repatriation to Haiti of part of the population of Haitian origin in the Dominican Republic, followed by a rapid reassertion of the prior migration order. In broader perspective, the crisis of Haitian-origin migrants in the Dominican Republic should be seen against the background of wider movements of Haitians. By 1990, more than a million Haitians – about one-sixth of the country's population – were thought to live in exile. As well as the estimated 500,000 in the Dominican Republic, perhaps 450,000 lived in the US, 45,000 in Canada, 15,000–30,000 in France, 30,000 in the Bahamas, 6,000 in Venezuela, and 30,000 in other Caribbean countries (Forced Migration Projects 1997; US Committee for Refugees 1991). Movement of boat people making for the US has been under way since the early 1970s, when Haitians fled the repressive Duvalier regime. The exodus by sea ebbed and flowed in the 1980s but was given extra momentum by the coup of September 1991 and subsequent events (Costello 1996; US Committee for Refugees 1994, 1995, 1996). Interdiction of Haitians at sea by the US Coast Guard has encouraged them to seek other destinations in the region and beyond. The wider migration order also featured what has been called a "double diaspora" (Ferguson 1992): the presence of about 500,000 Haitians in Dominican Republic had its counterpart in the absence of about a million Dominicans in Puerto Rico and the US mainland, once again demonstrating the potency of economic disparities in shaping migration orders.

The repatriation of the Rohingyas

The final episode considered in this chapter examines another reaffirmation of a prior order that involved force. As the account above showed, modest enhancement of the Rohingya diaspora was an outcome of the crises of 1978–79 and 1991–92, as exiles joined co-ethnics in the Middle East, Pakistan and Southeast Asia. But most of the expelled community in both episodes returned to their erstwhile territory of residence, Burma/Myanmar. At best, given their circumstances in Bangladesh, most had little choice but to return; at worst, this was a forced repatriation. It was a reassertion under duress of the prior order; the ambiguous membership of the Rohingyas in Burmese society remained unresolved, and indeed their status was if anything weaker.

The similarities between the repatriations after the exoduses of both 1978 and the 1991–92 are striking. In each case, Burma and Bangladesh reached an agreement on repatriation within months of the mass exodus, despite the strain between the two countries caused by the forced movement. The Burmese government may have been swayed by concern that the refugee crisis might rebound on it internationally; it feared that supporters of the Rohingyas in the Muslim world might bankroll insurgency, and that international finance for the opening up of the Burmese economy might be jeopardized. For their part, the Bangladesh authorities were convinced, under pressure from local residents and with some justification, that the country could not sustain a protracted presence of refugees.

Under the agreement reached in July 1978, refugees who could provide evidence of lawful residence in Burma were to be allowed to return in stages. At first, the repatriation had few takers among the refugees since there was little to assure them of their safety on return. Towards the end of the year however, repatriation suddenly took off, so that by early 1979 nearly 61,000 of the 200,000 refugees had returned. This turnaround was partly prompted by news from the first returnees that the security situation had improved and that their land had not been taken over. But almost certainly more significant were the appalling conditions in the camps in Bangladesh. Epidemics precipitated largely by malnutrition led to a rapid rise in mortality, which coincided with the increasing pace of repatriation. By the end of 1978, 10,000 refugees had died, more than two-thirds of them children. There is evidence that restriction of food rations by the authorities contributed to the high death rates, and thus to pressure for refugees to leave the camps and return to Burma. The voluntary nature of the repatriation was thus called into question. By the end of 1979, just over 187,000 refugees had repatriated (Aall 1979; Reid 1994).

The repatriation agreement between the governments of Bangladesh and Myanmar in April and May 1992, again within months of the mass exodus, claimed to provide for "safe and voluntary" return, but was widely and heavily criticized for the lack of mechanisms to ensure either the voluntary nature of repatriation or safety after it. Human rights organizations alleged that food supplies were reduced, provision of shelter and sanitation was slowed down, the operations of relief organizations were circumscribed, and refugees were restricted from access to local markets or to paid work (US Committee for Refugees 1992a); all of these allegations were strongly reminiscent of the 1978–79 episode. International outcry and protest by refugees stalled the repatriation efforts; batches of refugees were nevertheless repatriated under duress. Suppression of refugees' protests led to several hundred deaths, arrests and detentions; beatings and other intimidation increased towards the end of 1992 (Asia Watch 1993; Piper 1994; Reid 1992).

Given these circumstances, and perhaps mindful of criticism of its record in the events of 1978–79, the UNHCR was wary of involvement. However in 1993 the UNHCR reached agreement with both the Bangladesh and Myanmar governments to assure "safe and voluntary" repatriation of the Rohingyas; the agreements allowed UNHCR access to potential returnees in Bangladesh and a presence in Arakan state to monitor the return. Towards the end of the year repatriation started to pick up, so that by May 1994 55,000 Rohingyas had returned (Piper 1994).

Allegations nevertheless continued that great pressure was being put on the refugees to return: verbal, physical and sexual abuse of refugees by the Bangladeshi military and paramilitary forces in charge of the camps continued, according to human rights visitors. Moreover, many remained sceptical about the refugees' safety in Arakan should they return. Refugees and human rights groups reported continuing abuses of Rohingyas by the Burmese military; repatriates were not allowed to return to their villages, but were relocated by the government; and forced recruitment for portering and other labour continued (Asia Watch 1993; Piper 1994; Refugees International 1994; US Committee for Refugees 1994).

Nevertheless, in August 1994 the Bangladesh government and the UNHCR started to accelerate repatriation. This was claimed to be justified by three developments: indications among the refugees of a desire to return; improvement of the human rights situation in Arakan; and establishment of a UNHCR presence in Arakan (UNHCR 1995a). Human rights groups and non-government organizations disputed these claims of improvement. Doubts were raised about the validity of the campaign to register refugees for repatriation, which many were said not to understand; abuses in camps in Bangladesh were still alleged to be creating pressure to repatriate; forced labour and other human rights abuses were still said to be prevalent in Arakan; and the efficacy of the UNHCR's monitoring capacity in Arakan was called into question (Lambrecht 1995; Médecins Sans Frontières 1995a, 1995b).

The repatriation nevertheless continued. The UNHCR reported in mid-1995 that only 55,000 remained in camps in Bangladesh, and that 11 of the 20 refugee camps had been closed (UNHCR 1995a). The organization estimated that 125,000 Rohingyas had repatriated since late 1993, in addition to 55,000 prior to UNHCR involvement; this implied that up to 20,000 may have absconded for fear of repatriation. Despite criticism of the repatriation, the UNHCR continued to maintain that the return was voluntary, and that conditions in Myanmar were conducive to return; it claimed to have free access to the returnees in Myanmar, that most of the returnees had been able to return to their homes and land, that physical abuse and extortion was minimal, and that the burden of compulsory labour – although still a nation-wide practice – had diminished. The UNHCR, the World Food Programme and two non-governmental organizations were implementing small-scale projects to assist the reintegration of returnees by improving services for them and local communities (UNHCR 1995a, 1995b).

While the nature of the repatriation remained a matter of dispute, one issue seemed to be resolved unambiguously to the disadvantage of the Rohingyas, with potentially serious implications for the future. The UNHCR appeared to accept that most of the Muslims of Arakan state were not entitled to citizenship under Myanmar's citizenship laws (UNHCR 1995a, 1995b, and above, Chapter 3). As non-nationals, Rohingya returnees therefore lived as resident foreigners, with freedom of movement restricted and with the burden of proving that they were lawfully resident. This view appeared to endorse the Myanmar government's perspective of the Rohingyas as foreign immigrants rather than citizens long-established in Burma, diminishing their security and laying the foundations for the prospect of further expulsions in future: they were effectively stateless (Human Rights Watch Asia 1996). It was indeed a reaffirmation of the prior order. While the repatriation appeared to remove the grounds for the metaphor of the Rohingyas as "Asia's Palestinians" alluded to above, the reaffirmation of the Rohingyas' ambivalent status in Myanmar may yet uphold the validity of the analogy.

Conclusion

All of the populations reviewed constituted transnational communities in the sense outlined in Chapter 1. Most, but not all of these transnational communities were part of wider diasporas, also as defined in the opening chapter. Some of these diasporas were more widely scattered than others – a distinction might be drawn between "near diasporas" (a term echoing Russia's "near abroad") spread among a number of contiguous territories and those scattered further afield. To give some examples of these distinctions, Mexican migrants to the US constituted not a diaspora, but a transnational community which endured across the border over several decades; the ethnic Nepalis formed a near diaspora spread mainly among contiguous nation-states in the northern part of South Asia, as did the Albanians in Greece and former Yugoslavia; and the Ugandan Asians and the Kuwait Palestinians formed part of a diaspora with a global reach.

Almost all of the episodes reviewed involved at least a partial unmaking or a temporary diminution of these trans-national communities or diasporas, in the shape of reluctant home-comings; some consequences of these movements were described in Chapter 5. As was shown in this chapter, some cases involved the making, remaking or enhancement of diasporas, as some or all of the populations concerned moved on to disparate destinations. Still others, over varying periods of time, involved the reassertion of the old migration order, a reaffirmation of transnationalism, as populations forced to leave returned to their erstwhile places of residence. Many cases featured a combination of these developments, and they involved differing degrees of force and choice.

Outcomes were also mixed over time. The episodes involving Bulgaria and Turkey featured the involuntary "return" of ethnic Turks to Turkey, a reassertion of the prior dispensation through a later return to Bulgaria, and then a further reassertion of the out-migration from Bulgaria under way for more than a century. The case of the Ugandan Asians featured enhancement of the South Asian diaspora and much later a reassertion of their presence by a limited return to Uganda. The Ghanaian episode featured all three outcomes: forcible homecoming, reassertion of the prior order, and later diasporization. These and other cases indicate that the outcomes of migration crises were often diverse and rarely conclusive. Forced return to a putative or notional homeland may have diminished the transnational or diaspora community, but did not spell its end, any more than did the "return" of Jews, ethnic Greeks and Germans from the former eastern bloc respectively to Israel, Greece and Germany has meant the demise of their respective diasporas on a worldwide scale. As the cases reviewed and the concluding chapter show, this dispersal and regrouping of transnational communities is set to accelerate as globalization gathers momentum.

SEVEN

Migrants and hosts, transnationals and stayers

Since the research on which this book is based was begun, episodes of mass exodus, regrouping and counter-movements involving migrant communities have proliferated. Volatility in the CIS region, former Yugoslavia and Central Africa were the background to three clusters of such movements in the mid-1990s.[1]

The migratory flux set in motion by the disintegration of the USSR continued in the mid and later 1990s. While fears of a large east–west exodus had faded, the international community was sufficiently concerned to organize a major conference to attempt to address the issues thrown up by the vortex of movement in the region. Held jointly by the International Organisation for Migration, UNHCR and the Organisation for Security and Cooperation in Europe, the CIS conference on refugees and migrants identified no less than eight categories of displaced people: refugees, people in "refugee-like circumstances", internally displaced people, "involuntarily relocating people", "repatriants", formerly deported peoples, illegal migrants and ecological migrants (UNHCR 1996b). While most of these categories had implications for the formation of

---

[1]Even as this book was going to press, mass expulsions of migrant workers were being carried out by Saudi Arabia and other oil-rich states in the Middle East, and by Malaysia, South Korea and Thailand among the Asian "tiger" economies, bearing out some of the predictions made earlier in this volume.

233

transnational communities, the two categories involuntarily relocating people and repatriants – representing respectively forced and voluntary returnees to their countries of origin or citizenship – were among the most significant for the making, and more particularly the unmaking of diasporas. As elsewhere, the degree of choice and force involved in these movements was a matter of dispute.

Identification of the two categories recognized that ethnic unmixing and in-gathering continued to gather momentum in the mid-1990s, particularly as people of Slav origin made for the successor states representing their historic territories of origin: Russia, Ukraine and Belorus. The largest movements continued to be of Russians, driven from the Central Asian republics of Kazakhstan, Uzbekistan and Tajikistan, and from the Caucasus by conflict, discrimination, insecurity, economic disparities, or simply the feeling that life might be better at "home". Many remained with insecure status in the restored Baltic states, particularly in Estonia and Latvia, where they fell foul of citizenship laws which insisted on local language proficiency and other complex naturalization procedures for people – mainly the Russians – who moved to the territories after their incorporation into the Soviet Union in 1940. In Estonia, for example, only 90,000 out of some 500,000 Russian residents have managed to naturalize since 1992. About 100,000 have opted for Russian citizenship, while others have had to accept aliens' passports and 2- or 5-year residence permits (*Guardian* 11 January 1997). Even so, unlike their co-ethnics in Central Asia, Russians showed little inclination to leave the Baltic states in substantial numbers given the greater prosperity of their economies relative to that of the homeland (*Forced Migration Monitor* January 1997).

Even after coming "home", many returnees have not had a comfortable time, running into problems acquiring residence permits needed to access employment, housing, education, health care and other services: the Soviet *propiska* system had nominally been abolished but was still applied by local authorities, in part to control internal migration. In some cases, these difficulties, coupled with depressed employment opportunities and lack of familiarity with the "homeland", have prompted counter-movements back to the territories only recently left (Human Rights Watch, Helsinki 1996; UNHCR 1996a). These movements and counter-movements of Russians and others within the CIS region show some of the same patterns of diaspora regrouping and diaspora reaffirmation that feature in some of the cases covered earlier in this book.

Diasporization of former Yugoslavs – particularly people from Bosnia Herzegovina – was the continuing legacy in the mid-1990s of the disintegration of the Socialist Federal Republic of Yugoslavia, subsequent armed conflicts in and among its successor states, and the ethnic cleansing and displacement that resulted within and beyond former Yugoslavia. As well as among the successor states of the SFRY, Bosnians were scattered in large numbers throughout Europe in the mid-1990s. In 1996, 10 European states hosted Bosnian populations of more than 10,000 – in descending order of magnitude, Germany, Austria, Sweden, the Netherlands, Switzerland, Denmark, the UK, France, Norway and Italy – with smaller numbers scattered among other European states and North America (US Committee for Refugees 1997). With the conflict over, but with serious tensions remaining, the future of this nascent diaspora was uncertain. Would it endure, enhancing its precursor created by Yugoslav labour migration in Europe? Or would Europe witness another in-gathering of a recently formed, or recently enhanced diaspora? While there was strong pressure among host countries to repatriate the Bosnians, questions remained: first, did the refugees wish to return and could they be made to; and second, where would they return to, particularly if their places of origin had changed profoundly in their absence, as many had by ethnic cleansing? Only a minority of refugees were willing to leave their host countries, in which over time they were increasingly becoming integrated, for an unsure future in their territories of origin sometimes now so different that return and reconstruction of lives was all but impossible. There were signs that many European countries tacitly accepted that the "temporary protection" accorded to Bosnians was likely in fact to mean permanent settlement: even Germany, which with by far the largest population of Bosnian refugees had the greatest interest in repatriation, has been unwilling or unable to repatriate them on a very large scale, despite resolving to do so in 1996 (US Committee for Refugees 1997). At the time of writing then, a substantial in-gathering of this recently formed diaspora from Europe hung in the balance.

The conflict in the Great Lakes region of Central Africa has been one of the most graphic recent examples of how diasporization coupled with disputed nationality can lead to violent conflict and mass displacement. The Banyarwanda, as they are known, are scattered throughout east-central Africa, and trace their origins in three main ways. The ancestors of some, particularly those in Uganda and Zaire, as well as in Rwanda itself, lived in pre-colonial kingdoms in what are now these countries. Others are descendants of labour migrants and settlers who moved, or were induced to migrate, during the colonial period. Still others were refugees, or their descendants: mainly Tutsi refugees who fled Rwanda in 1959–63, and mainly Hutu refugees who fled following the genocide in 1994 and the victory of the Rwandese Patriotic Front. The treatment of the Banyarwanda has varied from country to country: at times they have been welcomed, well-integrated and offered citizenship; at others they have been deprived of citizenship and expelled (Prunier 1995; US Committee for Refugees 1991a).

This ambivalent treatment was at root of the conflict that engulfed Central Africa in the mid-1990s. Like the invasion of Rwanda by the RPF from Uganda in 1990, the insurgency in eastern Zaire in 1996 instigated by ethnic Tutsis long resident in Zaire had at its core elements of a diaspora with unsettled nationality or disputed citizenship. In both cases the insurgents were drawn from populations with long and complex histories of migration, which had a strong bearing on their uncertain citizenship status.

Like others long-settled in the region, many of the ethnic Rwandese of eastern Zaire had a strong claim for citizenship of Zaire on grounds of birth, descent and residence. However, their citizenship has been disputed since the 1970s. Moves against the Banyarwanda intensified in the early 1990s, leading to serious conflict, killings and displacement. Tensions and violence increased further following the influx of mainly Hutu refugees from Rwanda in 1994, after which there was more pressure by the Zairean authorities on the ethnic Rwandese.

The climax came early in October 1996, when the regional administration threatened ethnic Tutsis with expulsion. To many this appeared a call to another genocide. In response they launched a well-organized and concerted military campaign, sweeping disorganized Zairean armed forces before them. Tutsis in the north of the region meanwhile attacked and removed Hutu militias and ex-Rwanda government forces from the refugee camps on the Zaire–Rwanda border. This prompted further involuntary movement: the repatriation of Hutu refugees to Rwanda, and the flight of other refugees and Zaireans within Zaire where many thousands were forced into desperate conditions without assistance in remote forest (Amnesty International 1997; Prunier 1997; US Committee for Refugees 1997).

Unlike other cases examined in this book, and in contrast to the earlier fate of their co-ethnics in Rwanda, this is a rare case of a portion of a diaspora successfully resisting expulsion – although admittedly at the expense of other sections of the population. Eventually this led to the downfall of the regime that attempted to engineer the expulsion. The rebellion in eastern Zaire instigated by denationalized Tutsis transmuted into a coalition of opponents of the Mobutu regime which swept westwards in a 7-month military campaign that led to the fall of Mobutu in May 1997.

In the remainder of this section I recapitulate the ideas that have been developed in this book to analyse such complex movements. As I set out in the introduction, one of my chief concerns has been to locate mass exodus of migrant communities in a wider, unfolding migratory dispensation, and to assess whether such episodes are merely ephemeral events or signal significant change in what I have called "migration orders". Drawing on and refining the hitherto largely separate discourses on economic and forced migration, I outlined the notion of migration order, and explored the way such orders change. As I suggested in Chapter 2, migration orders encompass individual and household decision-making, economic and political disparities between places of migrant origin and destination, the state of migrant networks and institutions, and the migration regime, defined as the body of law, institutions and policy dealing with the movement of people. All of these are shaped by the wider macro-political economy, the distribution of power and resources worldwide, which is manifested in the current era by global economic restructuring and by the disintegration and reconstitution of nation-states.

I suggested a scheme of four domains to integrate these features. In the first domain are located what are often described as root causes, or structural factors which predispose a population to migrate. The second domain includes proximate factors that bear more immediately on migration and derive from the working out of structural features. In the third domain are precipitating factors, or those actually triggering departure. The fourth domain includes intervening factors, or those that enable, facilitate, constrain, accelerate or consolidate migration. While the structural and proximate domains generate the necessary conditions for the initiation of migration, the precipitating factors trigger the actual decision to move, and the domain of intervening factors in turn shapes the decisions how and when to depart, who should leave, and where to go.

I then turned to the place of force and choice in shaping migration orders, suggesting that migration may be disaggregated into five elements – movement outward, inward, back, onward and staying put – and that these may involve varying degrees of choice and compulsion. Migrants' experience of diverse permutations of movement by choice or compulsion leads to the development of complex migration biographies. I suggested that looking at migration in this way might help reconcile the disparate discourses on economic and forced migration.

Migration orders are dynamic and change. Changes in migration orders come about because of shifts in the configuration of factors located in the four domains outlined above. The more far-reaching of these changes I called migration transitions. Some of these changes, while profound, are gradual and were termed cumulative transitions. Other changes to migration orders may be more acute and result in ruptures or upheavals; these I termed migration crises, involving sudden, massive disorderly population movements of the kind investigated in Chapters 3 to 6. This book has focused on acute changes, for it is at such moments of crisis that the dynamics of migration orders are thrown into relief.

The working out of migration orders and of cumulative and acute changes in them generate or transform transnational communities. In almost all the cases I have reviewed migration crisis led to the unmaking of transnational communities or the diminution of diasporas by forced movement to an original or historic homeland – a form of repatriation often notional in the case of those long-settled abroad. For some, like the Mexicans and the Albanians, this undoing was partial and ephemeral. For others, like the ethnic Nepalis from Bhutan, the Yemenis from Saudi Arabia and the ethnic Turks from Bulgaria it was more substantial and enduring.

Several of the cases featured the dispersal of migrant communities or the enhancement of existing diasporas as a result of migration crises. This dispersal varied in strength and over time. Migration crises contributed to the diasporization of South Asians, Palestinians, the Rohingyas and Ghanaians. In the first three cases, dispersal accompanied the migration crisis or occurred soon after it, while in the Ghanaian case diasporization took longer to get under way.

A third outcome was a return, often partial, of expelled populations to the territories they had been forced to leave. These movements involved a reaffirmation of the transnational community, a reassertion of the prior migration order. This was the case with return to Nigeria of substantial numbers of Ghanaian migrants after expulsion in 1983, and with the return of Albanian migrants to Greece after successive deportations in 1990–94. Indeed, subsequent expulsions demonstrate the resilience of the prior migration order. The return of some of the ethnic Turks to Bulgaria, of Mexicans to the US and of a small number of Ugandan Asians to Uganda are other examples. Again, the timing of these return movements varied: while return of the ethnic Turks and of the Mexicans occurred almost immediately after expulsion, the return of Ugandan Asians took place decades later. Two other such movements – the return of Haitian migrants to the Dominican Republic and the re-

239

patriation of Rohingyas to Myanmar – involved more force than these episodes: the former took place almost immediately after their mass exodus, while the latter was more protracted.

Migration crises could have three outcomes then for transnational communities. The expelled population might remain in the country to which they were obliged to move – usually their territory of origin, historic or otherwise. There might be movement on to another destination. Or there might be a return of some or all of the population to the territory from which they had been forced to move. As was suggested in Chapter 6, these outcomes represented respectively the unmaking, the remaking and the reassertion of transnational communities.

The crises also marked changes of varying depth in each migration order. For some, notably the African and Middle East cases, the crisis did mark a profound, enduring transformation in the migration order. For others, the shift may have been fundamental but only partial, the prior migration order resuming more weakly than before. In still other cases, the crisis marked only a temporary shift in the migration order, which soon reasserted its prior shape. For still others, the crisis marked an accentuation of a process already in motion. For some, the migration crisis was the culmination of what had been long under way; for others it was a marked upheaval in the migration order. Many of these features and outcomes have been reproduced elsewhere, as the examples drawn from the CIS region, former Yugoslavia and Central Africa at the beginning of this chapter show.

Is it possible to predict migration crises, and to suggest what their outcomes might be for migration orders and for migrant communities? It is notoriously difficult to make predictions in the migration field – early warning has yet to convince – and perhaps foolhardy to attempt to do so. However, I have offered some indications – which are largely common sense – along the way in this book. In Chapter 2, I suggested that profound cumulative change in the economic arena tended to precipitate migration crisis when coupled with contingent upheaval in the political domain; this was certainly borne out in many of the crises considered. What then about the depth of migration crises? What determines whether they are enduring or merely ephemeral? What determines the outcomes of such crises for the migrant communities involved: diasporization, regrouping or reaffirmation of the transnational community? In seeking answers to these questions three dimensions stand out. First, the outcome of a crisis for the migration order, and for the migrant community involved, depends on the persistence or diminution of economic, political and security disparities between the territories the migration order encompasses. We might call this the differential in human security between the territories involved: this "human security differential" can of course vary greatly over time. Second, the outcome will be shaped by the creation or enhancement of migrant networks prior to and in the course of the migration crisis; the existence or maintenance of links in other territories will facilitate accommodation or integration, while the absence or neglect of such connections will make restarting life difficult following a migration crisis. Finally, the outcome will depend a great deal on the migration antecedents. As the cases I have examined demonstrate, a look at history shows that migration crises are rarely single events coming from nowhere – even though they are regrettably often perceived as such by organizations charged with dealing with them; rather they have antecedents which should inform our investigation of them and the ways they are to be handled and resolved.

Giving content to transnationalism

Having summarized some of the ideas used in this book to explore migration crises, in this section I offer some further remarks on the notions of transnationalism and diaspora. As Chapter 1 indicated, these notions have become part of the currency of debate about migration. But while much has been made of the emergence of new forms of transnational population, the literature is short on specification of what kinds of population are transnational or what makes them trans-national. Much of the literature – such as that carried in the journal *Diaspora*, for example – has been concerned with issues of identity surrounding diaspora or transnational communities.

This book has been concerned not so much with identity as such, as with the material basis or socio-economic dimensions of such identity. Recapitulating the definition offered in Chapter 1, transnational communities are spread across borders, have an enduring presence abroad, and take part in some kind of exchange between or among spatially separated component groups. Diasporas are one kind of transnational community, distinguished by dispersal among several, usually separated territories.

What then might be measures of "transnationalism"? What tells us that a population is transnational? The material and the analysis in this book have indicated some ways of giving these terms content by suggesting a number of measures or indicators. One method is to assess the strength or weakness of commitment of a given population to its place of origin, to its current place of residence and to others in the diaspora. Among the measures of such commitment considered in earlier chapters have been the length of stay abroad, nationality, socio-economic status and the level of transactions with the place of origin.

The episodes examined in Chapters 3 and 4 featured long-settled minority populations, short-term migrants and intermediate categories; in other words they included people with varying commitment to the countries in which they were living and working. The ethnic Turks in Bulgaria, the Asians in Uganda, the Rohingyas in Burma and the ethnic Nepalis in Bhutan were nationals or habitual residents of these countries for generations. Some of the Palestinians in Kuwait, some of the Yemenis in Saudi Arabia and some of the people of Haitian origin in the Dominican Republic were resident for decades. The Mexicans deported from the US, the Ghanaians expelled from Nigeria and the Albanians removed from Greece were largely temporary migrants, as were many of the Yemeni and Haitian expatriates.

While the period away from the place of origin provides some indication of the level of commitment, it is not a sure guide. As was noted in Chapter 6, some populations held or exhibited multiple or elastic allegiances or affinities, used or given emphasis at different times and in different contexts. Thus the three allegiances straddled by the Uganda Asians – to

Uganda, to South Asia and to the UK – and by the Palestinians – to their lives in Kuwait, to Jordan, and to their Palestinian homeland – were maintained uncomfortably at best and impossibly when it came to crisis.

Nationality or citizenship are limited as measures of commitment since migrant communities generally have little say in determining them. Of the cases considered, only the Ugandan Asians were able to exercise some choice in determining their citizenship, and where they could they hedged their bets by encouraging household members to acquire diverse nationalities as a means of insurance. Otherwise, only the ethnic Turks in Bulgaria were unambiguously nationals. For the ethnic Nepalis in Bhutan, the Rohingyas in Myanmar and some of the people of Haitian origin in the Dominican Republic, citizenship was disputed. None of the other migrant communities considered had a claim on the nationality of their host country, notwithstanding moral claims to membership based on their social and economic contributions.

Turning to socio-economic status, types of occupation, ownership of businesses, investment patterns, financial transfers and social exchanges may indicate allegiance to community and place. On these criteria, the evidence for commitment is mixed, for the populations reviewed each featured diversity in socio-economic status. Some of the populations contained a substantial proportion whose occupations, business interests and investments indicated an enduring commitment to the country of residence, as well as others whose economic attachment was less lasting.

The wealthier Ugandan Asians, for example, had a long history of investment in Uganda, as well as of stewarding their capital in and out of the country. It was the latter concern that came to the fore from the late 1960s, for among the accusations against Uganda's Asian population were that they were damaging the economy by exporting capital. As was pointed out in Chapter 3, there was some foundation to this charge and a circularity about it: as they witnessed antagonism rising against them in the region, Asians who were able transferred their assets to safety, bringing more accusations of capital flight and exacerbating their insecurity. Measured by financial transactions then, Asian commitment to Uganda was ambivalent.

Remittances to relatives and maintenance of property implied commitment among many Palestinians to the place of origin (Palestine) or to the adoptive homeland (Jordan), despite long residence abroad. Most remitted funds to relatives in the Occupied Territories or in Jordan or in some cases both. Many also spent their holidays in Jordan, or in the Occupied Territories. Many maintained some kind of claim to property in the Occupied Territories or in Jordan. However for a significant minority, such connections with the original or adoptive home-land were diminishing. These sent no remittances – usually because all of their family was in Kuwait or because no close relatives still lived in Jordan or the Occupied Territories. More than half of those who moved from Kuwait to Jordan in 1990–92 had no fixed assets in Jordan and 15 per cent had no claim to property in the Occupied Territories. This reinforced the con-clusion that the Palestinians increasingly constituted a semi-permanent community in Kuwait (Van Hear 1995).

Among Yemenis, frequency of visits and remittances home varied according to the length of residence abroad, with, as might be expected, both visits and remittances tailing off among those who had effectively settled abroad (Van Hear 1994). As was noted in Chapter 3, a long-term decline in remittances in part reflected the increased proportion of long-term Yemeni migrants who had settled with their families and therefore no longer remitted part of their income to support them. Among those who were more clearly temporary migrants, such as the Mexicans, Ghanaians, some of the Yemenis and the Albanians, the level of remittances and their use, particularly in house-building, indicated commitment to the place of origin. As Peil (1995: 362) noted of Ghanaians abroad, "A house proclaims both their attachment to home and their success abroad."

To summarize, measured by length of stay abroad, nationality, socio-economic status and the level of transactions with the place of origin, substantial variation in allegiance is revealed. Moreover allegiance was not fixed, but was commonly elastic. The ambiguous position of migrant communities was often compounded by the variety of statuses held by them, for historical reasons which included the complex routes by which they had arrived and settled. This mix of statuses was made still more complex by the fact that members of the same household might have maintained different citizenship claims, sometimes as a matter of strategy, since dispersal of household members in different countries was seen as a form of insurance against misfortune – such as mass expulsion. The very ambivalence of these communities' membership status played a part in their forced departure. In particular the multiple affinities referred to above were almost bound to generate among host populations suspicion, hostility and accusations of divided loyalties under conditions of strain. Ambivalence towards "home" in the country of residence or "home" in the country of origin was also expressed in economic terms. Among the long-established communities of migrant origin, enduring material conditions of home were made in the country of settlement. Allegiances to the homeland were nevertheless maintained to varying degrees through social and economic transactions. All the same, as expatriates made their homes abroad, over time some lost their links with the homeland in the process.

If these were among the measures of the migrant populations' commitment to their homes in their countries of origin and their countries of residence abroad, what of their commitment to their new homes following migration crisis? Migration crises demanded the remaking of the material conditions of home. What then were the socio-economic indicators of commitment to the new place of residence or home?

For the temporary migrants, like the Mexicans, the Ghanaians, the Albanians, the majority of the Yemenis and many of the Haitians, repatriation was to a home they knew. For others, like the Asians from Uganda, the ethnic Turks, the Palestinians obliged to leave Kuwait, some of the Yemenis, some of the Haitians, the Rohingyas in Myanmar and the ethnic Nepalis in Bhutan, the forced movement was to countries of which they were at best only nominally or notionally members. The Ugandan Asians settling in Britain had claims to British citizenship, but for many their social and material connections with Britain were modest. Similarly, the Palestinians who settled in Jordan may have been Jordanian citizens, but many had never lived in or known that country. The term "return" was also a misnomer for many of the Yemenis, since a large minority had been away for decades, or had been born and brought up abroad, and had lost or never had meaningful social and economic links with the country of notional nationality. Most of the Rohingyas and the ethnic Nepalis, and some of the people of Haitian descent had likewise never known their putative place of origin.

Seen from a macro- or national point of view, the absorption of these populations was an issue of integration. From the point of view of the new arrivals, the question was how quickly their lives could be rebuilt and their homes re-established. Among the factors influencing the ease and speed with which lives were remade were the nature and state of the society into which displaced populations were received; the links which were maintained while abroad, which were considered above; the presence of extended families, kin or co-ethnics in the countries accommodating them; the provision of assistance, both immediate and long term; and the availability of assets and capital, either recovered or mobilized anew. Patterns of accom- modation, employment and investment provide indicators of the extent of reintegration, of how solidly and enduringly the material conditions of home were re-established, and of com- mitment to the new place of residence.

As was shown in Chapter 5, the Ugandan Asians arriving in the UK and elsewhere in 1972 rapidly constructed the material conditions of home. For the most part, Asians expelled from Uganda embraced the UK and other developed countries in which they settled as home. Without diminishing the difficulties involved, the conditions for such integration – particularly the economic climate – were more favourable than they were for the other displaced populations reviewed. However, while most remained materially committed to their new homelands, some, with greater assets at stake, returned to Uganda to retrieve them when the conditions allowed, as Chapter 6 showed. The return of Asians to Uganda under way in recent years again raises the question of allegiance. This return did not necessarily indicate a renewed commitment to Uganda as home, for while some reinvested in Uganda the assets they recovered, others returned with the proceeds to their countries of resettlement. The majority of Asians remained committed to the countries in which they had remade home.

Despite the dire economic straits of Ghana's economy, the returnees in 1983 were reintegrated relatively rapidly and easily, credit for which is generally agreed to lie partly with their own efforts and partly with the absorptive capacity of their extended families and communities. At the same time, opportunities for re-emigration were open to Ghanaian migrants, if not on the same scale as before; they made for Côte d'Ivoire and Nigeria once again, as evidenced by the repeat expulsions from Nigeria in 1984 and 1985. This suggests that the embrace of "home" was not wholehearted, but contingent on access to land or other assets. The subsequent diasporization of Ghanaians described in Chapter 6 supports this view.

As might be expected, the more recent cases of Yemen and Jordan both display more ambivalence on the part of returnees towards their relocation in its early years (Van Hear 1994, 1995). In Yemen the essential division was between those returnees who had sent home remittances, made visits and kept up links with their home communities, and former long-term Yemeni residents abroad who had all but lost their connections with the place of origin. Since the prospects for re-emigration were modest or non-existent, Yemeni returnees had little option but to try to remake their homes in their country of nationality. As with the Jordanian case, much depended on the assets they were able to bring back from abroad, or the resources they were able to mobilize after return; in contrast to some of the Palestinians, these assets and resources were often meagre.

As I noted in Chapter 5, Jordanian returnees' kin networks provided substantial assistance while they attempted to re-establish themselves, but such support had limits. Resettlement was eased for some returnees to Jordan by the ownership of housing or access to family homes, a result of the maintenance of links while abroad. Returnees' circumstances also much depended on the recovery of assets from the countries they were obliged to leave. The uses to which these assets were put provide a further indication of the level of commitment to the new homeland. Much was spent on buying houses, building new ones or extending what was formerly vacation accommodation. Otherwise, returnees tended to keep their capital liquid. For understandable reasons – among them insecurity resulting from the recent trauma of uprooting and the prospect of a settlement in the Occupied Territories – after investing in building, returnees with capital generally avoided committing their assets in the long term. Perhaps a test of deeper allegiance will come if and when return to a re-emergent Palestine becomes feasible; commitment may then be partly gauged by the volume of returnee capital that is retained in Jordan or moved to the new polity.

Other migrant communities showed similar ambivalence towards the new home. For the Bulgarian ethnic Turks arriving in Turkey, state and international subsidy played a large part in integrating them and eliciting their allegiance. However, a large minority – at least one-third of those who departed in 1989 – did not feel committed enough to stay in their new home in Turkey, and returned to Bulgaria. As if to emphasize their transience, some of these subsequently re-emigrated to Turkey. As might be expected, the temporary migrants – notably the Mexicans and the Albanians – were highly footloose, moving across borders as the opportunity or necessity arose. The same was true of the Haitians, though much more by force than choice. Since they were confined to camps, the commitment to their host country of the Bhutanese ethnic Nepalis in Nepal and the Rohingyas in Bangladesh was not put to the test: both aspired to return to the territories they regarded as home – Bhutan and Arakan state in Myanmar.

In summary, there was considerable variation in the degree to which the 10 migrant communities embraced the places in which they found themselves after their migration crisis as home, ranging from commitment to ambivalence and uncertainty. Much depended on the time spent abroad, connections with the new home country, the options for return or onward movement, and the past experience of displacement. Many of the migrants away for a relatively short time sought employment abroad again, indicating continuing ambivalence towards their country of origin. Those with restricted prospects for re-emigration had little choice but to accommodate themselves in their country of origin as best they could. Those that had maintained links with their home communities fared much better than those who had let such links lapse. Some migrant communities with a long collective history of displacement were understandably cautious in committing themselves whole-heartedly to their new homes.

While dual allegiance to place of origin and the place of current residence is a mark of a transnational community, the notion of diaspora involves a still wider spread of allegiances. People experiencing migration crises of the kind reviewed in this book may develop allegiances transcending the homes to which they have hitherto been attached, a process itself part of the emergence or consolidation of diasporas. Such communities develop networks which materially substitute for territorial homes; not least, they may assist for example with re-emigration after an episode of mass exodus.

Such networks may be based on the household or on wider connections. Stark (1991a, 1991b) contemplates what he calls the "portfolio" strategy of migrant households: "migration decisions are ordered by family needs for stable income levels, provided by a diversified portfolio of laborers, both male and female, and the need to insure the family's well-being" (1991a: 39). This perspective may be overly economistic, overstating the notion of "family as firm", but it may enhance understanding of the formation of some transnational populations and of decision-making among them. It certainly strikes a chord with Tinker's (1977) depiction of the dispersal strategy of East African Asians (see Chapter 6, pages 198–9), and the Ugandan Asians illustrate this very clearly. While Ugandan Asians consolidated their material presence in their new European or North American homes, the material basis of a transnational community was also established or extended, by building on an already-established strategy of spreading household members around the globe. Palestinians exhibited such networks, often based on the town or village of origin, as was indicated in Chapter 6. Ghanaian diasporization from the late 1980s was also facilitated and sustained by existing Ghanaian networks, and the same is true of other African diasporization. As Ellis has put it,

Africans who are finding it difficult to earn a living at home in straitened circumstances may use the international networks emanating from the African metropolitan areas to seek work in the big cities of Europe and North America, keeping entire families back home solvent with remittances. Citizens of some African countries, such as Ghana, Nigeria and Senegal, are spreading out as fast as international immigration officials will allow them, forming international diasporas which also function as trading networks (1996: 13).

As I argue later in this chapter, links with others in the diaspora are not straightforward, but are often ambivalent. Like relations with the established and home communities mentioned in Chapter 2, relations with the wider transnational community of other migrants may be actively maintained, dormant, latent, or avoided. Paraphrasing Marx, it might be suggested that where diasporas are dormant, latent or avoided, diaspora exists "in itself", and where diasporas are actively maintained and where migrants actively engage in them, diaspora exists "for itself". Political impacts of active diaspora have been explored more fully elsewhere (see for example, the contributions to Sheffer 1986), but some of the social implications of such activity are explored further in the section on migrant networks, below.

In this section I have offered some measures of transnationalism in terms of commitment to place and community. Ambivalent allegiance and questioned commitment are among the defining features of transnational populations; they are also among the features that make them vulnerable to the crises that have been described in this book. To state a simple couplet of propositions, the greater the ambivalence, the weaker the roots in a single territory, the stronger is the claim to the transnational or diaspora condition; and the stronger the transnational condition, the more likely is mass exodus at times of crisis.

Transnationals, globalization, cosmopolitans and parochials

If the content of transnationalism and diaspora have been hard to pin down, these concepts form part of a wider discussion surrounding an even more nebulous idea – globalization – most accounts of which feature an eclectic collection of symptoms and manifestations. In the opening chapter I outlined some of the features of globalization which bear particularly on migration. I have also obliquely referred to it as the twin processes of global economic restructuring and the disintegration and reconstitution of nation states.

To offer a more explicit formulation, I re-render briefly here a useful summary of the shape and processes of globalization by UNRISD (1995). The notion encompasses a configuration of economic, technological, geo-political, cultural and ideological changes, some more recent than others. Central to the notion of globalization is accelerated integration and interdependence of the world economy, seen most dramatically in the mobility of capital, but also in the liberalization of world trade in goods and services. The main proponents and beneficiaries of this integration are transnational corporations which control much of the world's trade in goods and services. Economic integration has been facilitated by the transformation of production and labour markets, in which more advanced technology, higher levels of skill, and smaller, more mobile units of production than conventional plant are key features. From the point of view of the labour force, the new features of flexibility and mobility mean greatly reduced security of employment.

These developments have been made possible by rapid technological advance, particularly in electronics, communications and transport, to which I referred in the introduction. Facilitated by leaps in computer technology, the speed and volume of telecommunications have increased exponentially. These technological developments have also given new impetus to the development of global media – particularly television, video and the internet. The new scope and speed of information flows has helped to diffuse cultural and consumption patterns, of the West in general and the US in particular, making for an increasingly uniform cosmopolitan culture and patterns of consumerism. These trends feature particularly in what are called "global cities", whose emergence is itself another manifestation of globalization.

Accompanying these economic and technological changes have been profound political and ideological transformations. These include the spread of liberal democracy following the demise of communism and a concomitant acceleration of the spread of economic liberalism in the shape of the growing dominance of market forces and private enterprise, which the collapse of the communist bloc has made possible (UNRISD 1995).

Characterized in these terms, globalization seems such a spectacular and heady process that it is possible to over-state its reach. It may sound a contradiction in terms, but globalization is partial, incomplete; it has not reached everywhere. In fact it is uneven spatially and sectorally (Dahrendorf 1995). Migration is a case in point. While the movement of people has increased greatly in volume and scope, it is way outstripped by the furious pace of the circulation of money, goods and services. In many ways, migration is paradoxically the exception to the rule of intensified mobility that is held to be characteristic of globalization.

Moreover, globalization may experience reverses. In small ways, the episodes reviewed in this book have contributed to both the enhancement and diminution of globalization. As has been shown, in different measures, migration crises resulted in the unmaking, the remaking and the reaffirmation of transnational communities, and by extension marked reversals in migration orders, their redirection or their reassertion. Since migration is both a manifestation and a consequence of globalization, and since transnational communities and migration orders may be regarded as constituents or manifestations of globalization, it follows that migration crises have at times enhanced and at others diminished globalization.

Some caution is also in order in relation to the social dimensions of globalization. One such dimension is held to be the emergence of a world middle class or elite which shares tastes and values, mostly modelled on the US, and which is sharply distinct in terms of wealth, resources and culture from the lower classes of the society in which it is located. This class is assertively cosmopolitan and is characterized by widely spreading transnational connections. Its members are increasingly influential and powerful in the world economy and world affairs. Despite ethnic, nationality and other differences, members of this class have far more in common with each other than with their fellow, poorer co-nationals or co-ethnics: as Lasch (1995: 46) has acidly observed, "The privileged classes in Los Angeles feel more kinship with their counterparts in Japan, Singapore and Korea than with most of their own countrymen."

Diasporas are held by some to be the bearers of this cosmopolitanism. Writing of "globally dispersed ethnic groups", Kotkin (1992: 3–4) declares, "These global tribes are today's quintessential cosmopolitans, in sharp contrast to narrow provincials. As the conventional barriers of nation-states and regions become less meaningful under the weight of global economic forces, it is likely such dispersed peoples – and their worldwide business and cultural networks – will increasingly shape the economic destiny of mankind." Coming from a completely different, less celebratory perspective, Harris (1995: 217) asserts, "... for the new cosmopolitan worker, nationality is a garment to be donned or shed according to convenience. Income and class, as well as mobility, divide the cosmopolitan and the local."

For many such commentators, there is an equation implicit in this discussion; migrants and transnationals are cosmopolitans, while those who stay behind are parochials. This perspective is at least partly shaped by the predilections of those who comment on these matters. Transnational populations are seen as thrusting, energetic entrepreneurs or cultural innovators, breathing life into the societies that accommodate them. A stimulating heterogeneity is held to be produced by migration and mixing. Transnationalism is redolent of multiplicity, pluralism and fertile hybridity.

While there is indeed much truth in this characterization, some reservations need to be made, not least about the character of cosmopolitanism itself. As Lasch (1995) has argued in a withering critique, cosmopolitanism has a "darker side".

Writing of US elites, but in terms applicable to footloose cosmopolitans worldwide, he observes,

> The new elites, which include not only corporate managers, but all those professions that produce and manipulate information – the lifeblood of the global market – are far more cosmopolitan, or at least more restless and migratory, than their predecessors. Advancement in business and the professions, these days, requires a willingness to follow the siren call of opportunity wherever it leads. Those who stay at home forfeit the chance of upward mobility. Success has never been so closely associated with mobility ... (Lasch 1995: 5).

Getting ahead means turning one's back on the parochialism and dowdiness of home, which the elites willingly do. Lasch continues venomously,

> "Multiculturalism", on the other hand, suits them to perfection, conjuring up the agreeable image of a global bazaar in which exotic cuisines, exotic styles of dress, exotic music, exotic tribal customs can be savored indiscriminately, with no questions asked and no commitments required. The new elites are at home only in transit ... theirs is essentially a tourist's view of the world ... (Lasch 1995: 6).

Lacking commitment to a shared history, a shared culture, the new elites are out of touch with the "common life", he continues (1995: 46–7). Ultimately, Lasch argues, "the cosmopolitanism of the favored few, because it is uninformed by the practice of citizenship, turns out to be a higher form of parochialism" in which "their acknowledgement of civic obligations does not extend beyond their own immediate neighborhoods" (1995: 47).

Lasch's remarks about the "secession" of the new US elites from commitment to place and community have resonances with some diasporas and some of the migrant communities discussed in this book, although the latter's lack of commitment to or ambivalence about place is much more a matter of compulsion than choice. Other reservations about the notion of cosmopolitanism relate specifically to the nature of transnational communities.

First, the presence of transnational populations peaks in certain pivotal sites or locations, such as "global cities" (Sassen 1991) like Hong Kong, Singapore, Sydney, Toronto, New York, Los Angeles and London. As Ellis (1996: 13) has observed of current diasporization of Ghanaians, Nigerians, Senegalese and other Africans, the dispersal is predicated on the emergence of "nodal points, great metropolitan areas which suck in wealth, irrespective of formal national frontiers". In these sites "cosmopolitanism" and its images are generated and transmitted to less mixed, less cosmopolitan hinterlands, for just as culture and populations are not homogeneous, so cosmopolitanism is not evenly spread. Bombarded by cosmopolitan images from electronic media, the populations of these hinterlands are coupled at a distance with the global village or global capitalism – and also with the impact of transnational populations. In other words, to reiterate, globalization has a differential reach.

Second, by no means all, or even most, transnational populations are thrusting cosmopolitans. On the contrary, many are rather parochial transnationals – people with transnational networks and links, but with a parochial outlook or world-view. At the other end of the spectrum from Lasch's US elite, examples that could be drawn from Britain include Chinese restaurant workers in London portrayed in Mo's *Sour sweet* (1982), or the Yemenis in UK described by Halliday (1992), each of whom reproduce the home village in Soho or South Shields. Similar examples can be found in most countries of immigration. The parochialism, provincialism and particularism so tellingly – and sympathetically – delineated by Lasch in an earlier work (Lasch 1991) may be as strong among migrant communities as among those who do not move. Moreover, there may well be diversity of outlook within particular transnational communities; just as membership of migrant communities is often diverse in socio-economic, religious, ethnic and other terms, as this book has shown, so may be the embrace by members of that community of cosmopolitan or parochial outlooks.

Third, while much is made of the embrace of transnational networks, not all members of transnational populations see such networks as wholly beneficial. Indeed, there are many who wish to have as little to do with their co-ethnics as possible, not least because engagement with co-ethnics can involve enormous burdens of hospitality and assistance that it may be impossible to sustain, given the limited resources particularly of recently arrived migrants. Similarly, while transnational communities can be the source of useful sustaining networks and solidarity, there may also be profound divisions within them. Global village there may be, but villages are often rife with suspicion, bickering and backbiting. Such divisions in transnational communities may reproduce cleavages at home – and may indeed be one of the reasons for people to leave. Gold (1992: 19) draws attention to such differences among Soviet Jewish and Vietnamese refugee communities in the US, based on region, class, religion, generation and period of migration. Similarly, McDowell (1996) points to divisions of class, caste and place of origin among the Sri Lankan Tamil "asylum diaspora" in Switzerland. Divisions may also arise between the established populations of migrant origin and newcomers – including between different cohorts of the same ethnic or national group. There may be relations of exploitation that may only be overcome by minimizing contact with co-ethnics in the diaspora. By no means all the putative members of a given transnational or migrant community necessarily embrace that community. Some of these and other dimensions of transnational networks are revisited below.

Between departure and arrival: migrant networks revisited

The proliferation of migrant networks and the burgeoning of migrant trafficking are further manifestations of transnationalism. Networks of varying degrees of sophistication have been significant for most of the migrant populations considered in this book. Drawing on personal, family, kin, friendship, community and ethnic links, networks provide potential migrants with information about destinations, contacts with gatekeepers, and sometimes funds for travel and brokers' charges. They may provide migrants with support en route. In destination countries, they may provide help with accommodation and finding employment. Later they may form channels of communication with the community of origin (Goss & Lindquist 1995).

Attracting increasing attention in recent years, migrant networks have indeed been suggested as the elusive integrating element sought for migration studies (see Chapter 2): since they lie somewhere between the individual and society, such networks might be seen as arenas where both individual activity and the wider political economy are manifested. While recognition of the importance of migrant networks is an important advance, there are shortcomings in this approach, not least in its idealization of "community"; as noted in the previous section, like other social phenomena, migrant networks are socially dynamic and include exploitative social relations (Goss & Lindquist 1995).

As I noted in Chapter 2, migrants' networks commingle with a proliferating array of recruiters, organizers, fixers, brokers and other intermediaries – some of whom may be returned migrants attempting to capitalize on their experience. As this arena has become increasingly commercialized and professionalized, a burgeoning "migration industry" has emerged, which includes travel and shipping agents, consultants and advisors, lawyers, marriage and adoption agencies, smugglers, and purveyors of false documents (Hugo 1995; Lim 1987; Spaan 1994). These agents, acting both legally and illegally, have played an important, if ambivalent role in sustaining migration. From the migrants' point of view these intermediaries range in decreasing benevolence from relatives, friends and acquaintances in the migrants' own networks, through casual smugglers and border guides and more sophisticated organizations spanning maybe two or three countries, to sophisticated, transnational, criminal syndicates. Migration networks thus embrace a continuum from the migrant-benign to the migrant-abusive.

Scholars of migration in Southeast Asia have been among the first to give convincing empirical and analytical accounts of the operation of these networks. In a description of the Indonesian recruitment system, Spaan writes, "Brokers and middlemen have facilitated migration by increasing the awareness of employment possibilities overseas, providing loans and organising the actual migration" (1994: 109). The negative aspects of the relationship are the dependence and exploitation it may engender. Nevertheless, "many migrants still opt for informal recruitment channels, either because they are unaware of the safer and legal agencies or because they consider migration via local brokers faster and more efficient". Even if brokers are known to make large profits at migrants' expense, "they still are considered more trustworthy than far-off, anonymous agencies as they generally form part of the migrant's social environment or personal network, as patrons or otherwise" (Spaan 1994: 109). Migrants often prefer clandestine migration to avoid the bureaucracy and costs – official fees and unofficial charges and bribes – incurred in official migration programmes. Spaan notes of the official Indonesian system of recruitment that up to 20 different documents are required before a migrant can leave for overseas (Spaan 1994: 105). Goss and Lindquist (1995) also point to the ambivalence of networks of intermediaries in the operation of what they call the "migrant institution". They identify three kinds of brokers or gatekeepers operating in the Philippines: the local patron, the returned migrant and the private recruiter. "These individuals are critical to the functioning of the migrant institution – they exploit the institution for their individual benefits but in doing so play roles as institutional agents by enforcing rules and distributing its resources" (Goss & Lindquist 1995: 341).

Despite this ambivalence, networks fall in the domain of facilitating and enabling migration outlined in Chapter 2. The intermediaries and brokers within them shape migratory flows by influencing the selection of migrants, destinations and types of employment (Goss & Lindquist 1995). They may also provide the link between different migration orders: Spaan (1994) shows how brokers and migrant networks interlink migratory flows within Southeast Asia and between that region and the Middle East. In a sense, brokers and traffickers, like migrant networks as a whole, are agents of dispersal and diasporization.

Networks can sustain migration when the initial impetus to migrate is gone. As was observed in Chapter 2, migrant networks may become self-sustaining, superseding the factors which may have initiated migration. As Lim (1987), Massey (1990) and others have pointed out, the development of social networks among migrants explains why migration flows continue when the forces initiating them no longer exist. To borrow a metaphor from quantum physics, migration networks may reach a critical mass after which migration is self-sustaining: "once the number of network connections in an origin area reaches a critical level, migration becomes self-perpetuating because migration itself creates the social structure to sustain it" (Massey 1990: 8).

This critical mass may facilitate the transformation of a migration order. Conversely, migration crises can precipitate this state of critical mass, predisposing a migration order to further transitions. A migration upheaval can lead to experience gained, new opportunities perceived, new resources accumulated, new infrastructure developed and people mobilized. In other words a migration upheaval can lay the groundwork for further transition, of which one consequence may be diasporization. The case of Albania seems to exemplify this. As was recounted in Chapter 4, an explosion of emigration from Albania precipitated expulsion from Greece and Italy. Thereafter Albania changed from being a country of emigration to one of transit – a conduit for would-be migrants, mainly using the asylum seeker route, and among them not just Albanians, but Chinese, Vietnamese, Kurds and Chechens, trying to get into Europe via Italy's heel. The networks and trafficking system developed to handle Albanian emigration were thus also lucratively deployed for would-be migrants of diverse other nationalities. As this and other examples presented in this book show, networks can then be enhanced by migration transitions, as well as helping to bring about such changes in migration orders.

The significance and insignificance of migration

It has become a commonplace view that migration is an inexorably expanding phenomenon on the world stage, leading some to speak of a "global migration crisis" (Weiner 1995). But while the perceived crisis is much vaunted, it is by no means self-evident that there is one. Rather there has been a series of migration crises around the world – some of which I have examined in some detail in this book.

To recast globalization in a currently unfashionable discourse, the ubiquity of migration is a result of the success of capitalism in fostering the penetration of commoditization into far-flung peripheral societies and undermining the capacity of these societies to sustain themselves. Insofar as this "success" will continue, so too will migrants continue to wash up on the shores of capitalism's core.

Or will they? In the mid-1980s, Stephen Castles wrote a valediction for the guest worker in Europe (Castles 1986). From the early 1990s, as the flow of asylum seekers to the affluent world appeared to be waning, others began to sound the last post for asylum, at least in its current form (Shacknove 1993). Repatriation to and containment in countries or regions of origin have become the order of the day. Are we then perhaps nearing the end of what some have called the "age of migration" (Castles and Miller 1993)? Or will migrants, driven by necessity and force, find other routes, other means of entry? Bald statistics – 5 million illegal immigrants in the US, and 460,000 asylum cases pending there – perhaps suggest the latter, as does the raft of recent legislation designed to control migration to North America and Europe, and not least the increasing volume of migration among developing countries and recently industrialized states.

All the same, while anxiety about international migration has risen, particularly among the richer nations that are the destination of many migrants, the number of migrants crossing borders is actually quite small relative to the total world population. In the early 1990s total international migration (both labour migration and refugee movements) was estimated at 100 million, somewhat less than 2 per cent of the world's population, and roughly equivalent to the annual increase in that population (Castles & Miller 1993; Russell & Teitelbaum 1992; Weiner 1995). A later estimate suggested that the total population outside their countries of origin had reached 125 million (World Bank 1995). Whichever figure is nearer the mark, the proportion relative to the world total suggests that most people live in their countries of birth and citizenship, and that those who take up residence abroad are exceptional.

This in turn implies that attention may have been overly focused on people who leave. As Hammar (1995: 184) has put it, concentration on migrants and why people migrate has led to neglect of "the much more common case, namely that people do not migrate but remain where they are". The question to be asked

> ... is not "why migration?", but rather, "why not much more migration?", or, "why is there no migration although most conditions for large out-migration seem to be at hand?" ... Reformulating the question, the group of people studied might be enlarged, including those who remain immobile, instead of concentrating all efforts in those who are mobile (Hammar 1995: 176).

As I indicated in Chapter 2, people who stay put – by choice or necessity – need to be taken account of in any complete account of migration. Attention might be shifted from factors generating migration to those constraining it.

Host or established populations also tend to be neglected in considerations of migration. It is often forgotten that not only the newcomers or incoming population have to adapt to new circumstances, but so too does the host or established population in the society receiving them. Choice in this respect can be almost as limited for hosts as for newcomers. The situation is similar with the reintegration of homecoming migrants or returnees, for both the returnees and the accommodating population change during the absence of the migrants, necessitating a renewal of relations on their return. The question then arises how much established communities can reasonably be expected to change in the face of migration.

Diversity may be a virtue in a tolerant and pluralistic society, but there is a tension between diversity, such as is fostered by migration and the presence of transnational populations, and social cohesion. Some of the bases of social cohesion – such as shared values and attachment to place – cannot but be eroded by newcomers, since the prior community must adapt to their presence. Migration may then be socially, culturally, morally and economically desirable, but it may affect the capacity of host or established populations to determine the character of their community. The aspiration should surely be for the greatest possible *choice* of movement – people should be able to move, or stay put, if they wish to, not because they have to. The proviso is that this movement is compatible with the rights of others – notably the right of a community to determine its own composition, values and character. How to strike this balance is *the* challenge.

Most commentators on this issue fall into two camps, which can be caricatured as follows. What might be termed the "migration paranoiacs" – those who take the perspective of the state and see migration largely as a threat – have elevated to pre-eminence the rights of host, prior or established communities and have sometimes exploited their fears. On the other hand, what might be termed the "migrant romantics" – liberal commentators and the advocates of migrants' and refugees' rights – have focused attention on the rights of newcomers and migrants and how they are wronged.

The latter position is understandable since in many cases migrants have unjustly been denied their rights. But the perspective of the established population should also be given greater consideration among those who aspire to a tolerant and pluralistic society. Among the "migrant romantics", the established population tends to be seen implicitly as a body to be badgered or cajoled from its at best stubbornly inert position into accepting newcomers, or at worst its overtly racist, hostile and violent stance against accommodating them. This does injustice to the fund of good will that most established communities hold, and which, provided that principles of justice and equity are upheld, they will usually extend. A perspective which is more sympathetic to the legitimate concerns of the host population may help countervail those in power, and aspirants to it, who play upon the fears of established communities.

The right of the greatest free movement possible, or the greatest possible *choice* as to whether to move or stay put, has to be balanced against the right of a community to determine its own composition and values. In the current world of transient populations, either notions of membership will have to be reformed or the very notion of the nation-state will have to be re-thought. Perhaps some kind of universally recognized resident status can be developed, secure but short of full citizenship, and which takes account of the concerns of established communities. Perhaps rights of membership can be disassociated from attachment to a particular nation-state. Perhaps regional mechanisms for membership can be developed. Whatever the means of resolution, erosion of the sovereignty of the nation-state is likely, since one of the primary prerogatives deriving from national sovereignty would be diminished, namely the power to determine membership. Resolution of this question is nonetheless the key to stemming the forced mass exodus that appears to be increasing alarmingly in the current era, and amelioration of the human insecurity which such upheaval creates.

Migration raises issues of social, political and economic participation that have a profound bearing on social integration and cohesion. Not least are the issues of equity raised by the outcome of migration. While migration may have increased the life-chances and fostered the integration of some, economic and political restructuring have resulted in the social, political and economic marginalization of many other migrants, deepening the gulf between those included and those excluded in both affluent and less developed societies. Most migrants' social and political integration in their host society is not commensurate with their economic participation. Ostensibly, democracies are founded on the principle that all members of society should belong to the political community. Migration is challenging this principle in two ways, one negative, the other creative. Migrants form a significant proportion of the politically, socially and economically excluded underclass in the affluent or post-industrial countries, and increasingly in newly-industrializing societies. At the same time, more and more migrants hold multiple identities, affiliation, membership or citizenship, so that such affiliation itself may change in the direction of some form of "transnational" citizenship (Baubock 1994). Such developments may well suit transnational communities, but will again raise serious concerns about the erosion of common values lamented by Lasch and others.

Nevertheless, footloose populations with multifarious links, such as some of the migrant communities reviewed in this book, ultimately may well be better placed than people with more conventional roots in the face of world economic restructuring and of nation-state disintegration and reconstitution. In other words, such populations might be well advised to maintain or extend their diaspora or transnational character than to diminish it by commitment to a single homeland, however appealing the notion of such a home may seem. Such people may well find themselves to be advantaged over those with a single affiliation as globalization accelerates. In the current dispensation of flux and uncertainty however, the proposition articulated above still holds: the stronger the transnational condition, the greater the vulnerability to forced mass exodus.

Bibliography

Aall, C. 1979. Disastrous international relief failure: a report on Burmese refugees in Bangladesh from May to December 1978. *Disasters* **3**(4), 429–34.

Abdalla, N. 1991. *Impact of the Gulf crisis on developing countries*. Report prepared for the United Nations Development Programme Gulf Task Force. New York: UNDP, June.

Abella, M. (ed.) 1994. Turning points in labour migration. Special issue, *Asian and Pacific Migration Journal* **3**(1).

Adelman, H. 1995. The Palestinian diaspora. In *The Cambridge Survey of World Migration*. R. Cohen (ed.), 414–17. Cambridge: Cambridge University Press.

Addleton, J. 1991. The impact of the Gulf war on migration and remittances in Asia and the Middle East. *International Migration* **29**(4), 509–21.

Adepoju, A. 1984. Illegals and expulsion in Africa: the Nigerian experience. *International Migration Review* **18**(3).

Adepoju, A. 1986. Expulsion of illegals from Nigeria: round two. *Migration World* **14**(5), 21–4.

Adomako-Sarfoh, J. 1974. The effects of the expulsion of migrant workers on Ghana's economy, with particular reference to the cocoa industry. In *Modern migrations in West Africa*. S. Amin (ed.), 138–52. London: Oxford University Press.

Ahmed, I. 1996. Refugees and security: the experience of Bangladesh. In *Refugees and regional security in South Asia*. S. Muni & L. Baral (eds), 121–51. Delhi: Konark.

Amato, T. 1991. *A childhood abducted: children cutting sugar cane in the Dominican Republic*. New York: Lawyers Committee for Human Rights.

Amerah, M., M. Khasawneh, N. Nabhani, F. Sadeq 1993. *Unemployment in Jordan: dimensions and prospects*. Amman, Jordan: Royal Scientific Society.

Americas Watch 1991. *Half measures: reform, forced labour and the Dominican sugar industry*. New York: Human Rights Watch.

Americas Watch 1992. *A troubled year: Haitians in the Dominican Republic*. New York: Human Rights Watch.

Americas Watch/National Coalition for Haitian Refugees 1990. *Harvesting oppression: forced Haitian labour in the Dominican sugar industry*. New York: Americas Watch/National Coalition for Haitian Refugees.

Amin, S. 1974. *Modern migrations in West Africa*. London: Oxford University Press.

Amjad, R. (ed.) 1989. *To the Gulf and back: studies on the economic impact of Asian labour migration*. New Delhi: UN Development Programme/ International Labour Organisation.

Amman Financial Market 1993. *Monthly Statistical Bulletin*. Amman Financial Market, Research and Studies Department, Amman, 3, March.

Amnesty International 1990. *Saudi Arabia: torture, detention and arbitrary arrest*. London: Amnesty International.

Amnesty International 1992a. *Bhutan: Human rights violations against the Nepali-speaking population in the south*. London: Amnesty International, ASA 14/04/92.

Amnesty International 1992b. *Union of Myanmar (Burma): human rights violations against Muslims in the Rakhine (Arakan) state*. London: Amnesty International, ASA 16/06/92.

Amnesty International 1994. *Bhutan: forcible exile*. London: Amnesty International, ASA 14/04/94.

Amnesty International 1997. *Great Lakes region. Still in need of protection: repatriation, refoulement and the safety of refugees and the internally displaced*. London: Amnesty International, AFR 02/07/97.

Appleyard, R. 1991. *International migration: challenge for the nineties*. Geneva: International Organisation for Migration.

Argent, T. 1992. *Croatia's crucible: providing asylum for refugees from Bosnia and Herzegovina*. Washington DC: US Committee for Refugees.

Arhin, K. 1994. The re-accommodation of Ghanaian returnees from Nigeria in 1983 and 1985. In *When refugees go home*. T. Allen & H. Morsink (eds), 268–75. London: UNRISD/James Currey.

Arzt, D. 1997. *Refugees into citizens: Palestinians and the end of the Arab-Israeli conflict*. New York: Council on Foreign Relations.

Asia Watch 1993. *Bangladesh: abuse of Burmese refugees from Arakan* 5(17), 9 October.

Asian Regional Programme on International Labour Migration 1993. *Newspaper clippings and reprints of periodicals.* Bangkok: International Labour Organisation, Regional Office for Asia and the Pacific. RAS/88/029.

Asian Regional Programme on International Labour Migration 1994. *Migration clippings.* Quezon City, Philippines: Scalabrini Migration Center. RAS/88/029.

Bach, R. 1993. *Changing relations: newcomers and established residents in US communities.* New York: Ford Foundation.

Balderrama, F. & R. Rodriguez 1995. *Decade of betrayal: Mexican repatriation in the 1930s.* Albuquerque, New Mexico: University of New Mexico Press.

Baral, L. 1996. Bhutanese refugees in Nepal: insecurity for whom? In *Refugees and regional security in South Asia.* S. Muni & L. Baral (eds), 152–77, Delhi: Konark.

Batchelor, C. 1995. UNHCR and issues related to nationality. *Refugee Survey Quarterly* **14**(3), 91–112.

Baubock, R. 1991. Migration and citizenship. *New Community* **18**(1), 27–48.

Baubock, R. 1994. *Transnational citizenship: membership and rights in international migration.* Aldershot: Edward Elgar.

Berry, J. 1992. Acculturation and adaptation in a new society. *International Migration* **30**, 69–85.

Bilsborrow, R. & H. Zlotnik 1995. The systems approach and the measurement of the determinants of international migration. In *Causes of international migration.* R. van der Erf & L. Heering (eds), 61–76. Luxembourg: Office for Official Publications of the European Communities.

Birks, J., I. Seccombe, C. Sinclair 1988. Labour migration in the Arab Gulf states: patterns, trends and prospects. *International Migration* **26**(3), 267–86.

Birks Sinclair and Associates. 1990. The crisis in Yemeni return migration from Saudi Arabia in 1990: background, nature and consequences. Draft working paper. Durham: Birks Sinclair and Associates, December.

Black, R. 1994a. Asylum policy and the marginalisation of refugees in Greece. In *Population migration and the changing world order.* W. Gould & A. Findlay (eds), 145–60. Chichester: Wiley.

Black, R. 1994b. Livelihood under stress: a case study of refugee vulnerability in Greece. *Journal of Refugee Studies* **7**(4), 360–77.

Bonacich, E. 1973. A theory of middleman minorities. *American Sociological Review* **38**, 583–94.

Boutang, Y. & D. Papademetriou 1994. Typology, evolution and performance of main migration systems. In *Migration and development:*

new partnerships for cooperation, 19–35. Paris: Organisation for Economic Cooperation and Development.

Boyd, M. 1989. Family and personal networks in international migration: recent developments and new agendas. *International Migration Review* **23**(3), 638–70.

Brand, L. 1988. *Palestinians in the Arab world: institution building and the search for state*. New York: Columbia University Press.

Bremmer, I. & R. Taras (eds) 1993. *Nation and politics in the Soviet successor states*. Cambridge: Cambridge University Press.

Brown, M. 1989. Nigeria and the ECOWAS protocol on free movement and residence. *Journal of Modern African Studies* **27**(2), 251–73.

Brubaker, W. 1996. *Nationalism reframed: nationhood and the national question in the New Europe*. Cambridge: Cambridge University Press.

Brydon, L. 1985. Ghanaian responses to the Nigerian expulsions of 1983. *African Affairs* **84**(337), 561–86.

Byrne, R. & A. Shacknove 1996. The safe country notion in European asylum law. *Harvard Human Rights Journal* **9**, Spring, 185–228.

Calavita, K. 1992. *Inside the state: the Bracero programme, immigration and the INS*. New York: Routledge.

Calavita, K. 1995. Mexican migration to the US: the contradictions of border control. In *The Cambridge Survey of World Migration*. R. Cohen (ed.), 236–44. Cambridge: Cambridge University Press.

Castles, S. 1986. The guest-worker in Europe: an obituary. *International Migration Review* **20**(4).

Castles, S. & G. Kosack 1973. *Immigrant workers and class structure in western Europe*. London: Oxford University Press.

Castles, S. & M. Miller 1993. *The age of migration: international population movements in the modern world*. Macmillan: London.

Central Bank of Jordan 1990, 1991. *Annual Report 1990, 1991*. Amman: Central Bank of Jordan.

Central Bank of Jordan 1992, 1993. *Monthly Statistical Bulletin*. Amman: Central Bank of Jordan.

Chaliand, G. & J-P. Rageau 1995. *The Penguin atlas of diasporas*. New York: Viking Penguin.

Chesnais, J-C. 1992. Introduction. In *People on the move: new migration flows in Europe*. J-C. Chesnais (ed.), 13–40. Strasbourg: Council of Europe.

Chesnais, J-C. 1993. Soviet emigration: past, present and future. In *The changing course of international migration*, 105–12. Paris: Organisation for Economic Cooperation and Development.

Clark, L. 1989. *Early warning of refugee flows*. Washington D.C.: Refugee Policy Group.

Clarke, C., C. Peach, S. Vertovec 1990. Introduction: themes in the study of the South Asian diaspora. In *South Asians overseas: migration and ethnicity.* C. Clarke, C. Peach, S. Vertovec (eds), 1–29. Cambridge: Cambridge University Press.

Clay, J. 1984. *The eviction of Banyaruanda: the story behind the refugee crisis in southwest Uganda.* Cambridge, MA: Cultural Survival.

Cohen, R. 1989. Citizens, denizens and helots: the politics of international migration flows in the post-war world. *Hitotsubashi Journal of Social Studies* **21**(1), 153–65.

Cohen, R. 1995. Rethinking Babylon: iconoclastic conceptions of the diasporic experience. *New Community* **21**(1), 5–18. ✳

Coleman, D. 1992. The world on the move? International migration in 1992. Presented to the European Population Conference, Geneva, March 1993, UN Economic Commission for Europe/Council of Europe/UN Population Fund, E.Conf.84 RM.EUR/wp.1.

Coles, G. 1983. The problem of mass expulsion. A background paper prepared for the working group of experts on the problem of mass expulsion convened by the International Institute of Humanitarian Law, San Remo, Italy, April.

Conquest, R. 1960. *The Soviet deportation of nationalities.* Macmillan: London.

Cordell, D., J. Gregory, V. Piche, 1996. *Hoe and wage: a social history of a circular migration system in West Africa.* Boulder, Colorado: Westview.

Costello, P. 1996. Haiti: prospects for democracy. *Refugee Survey Quarterly* **15**(1), 1–34.

Council of Europe 1991. Parliamentary Assembly, *Report on the reception and settlement of refugees in Turkey.* Doc 6267, 18 January.

Council of Europe, 1993. *Council of Europe Resettlement Fund, Report of the governor 1993.* Strasbourg: Council of Europe.

Council of Europe 1994. *Social development fund: Fact sheets.* Strasbourg: Council of Europe, 26 September.

The Courier 1993. Uganda: winning over foreign investors. *The Courier* 141, September–October.

Dahrendorf, R. 1995. *Economic opportunity, civil society and political liberty.* UNRISD Discussion Paper 58. Geneva: UN Research Institute for Social Development.

Davies, N. 1995. Blood and water. *The Guardian.* 11 December.

Dei, G. 1992. A Ghanaian town revisited: changes and continuities in local adaptive strategies. *African Affairs* **91**(362), 95–120.

Eades, J. 1987a (ed.). *Migrants, workers and the social order.* London: Tavistock.

Eades, J. 1987b. Prelude to an exodus: chain migration, trade and the Yoruba in Ghana. In *Migrants, workers and the social order.* J. Eades (ed.), 199–212. London: Tavistock.

Economist Intelligence Unit. 1994. *Country report: Romania, Bulgaria, Albania, 3rd quarter.* London: Economist Intelligence Unit.

Edge, S. 1992. *Yemen: Arabian Enigma*. Middle East Economic Digest Profile Number 7. London: East Midlands Allied Press Business Information.

Edge, S. 1993. Special report: Jordan. *Middle East Economic Digest*. 28 May.

Edge, S. & P. Dougherty 1992. Jordan returns to the fold. *Middle East Economic Digest*. 2 October.

Elahi, K. 1987. Rohingya refugees in Bangladesh: historical perspectives and consequences. In *Refugees: a Third World dilemma*. J. Rogge (ed.), 227–32. New Jersey: Rowman and Littlefield.

Ellis, S. 1996. Africa after the Cold War: new patterns of government and politics. *Development and Change* **27**(1), 1–28.

Eurostat 1994a. *Asylum-seekers and refugees: a statistical report*. Volume 1: EC member states. Luxembourg: European Communities.

Eurostat 1994b. *Migration statistics*. Luxembourg: European Communities.

Fawcett, J. 1989. Networks, linkages, and migration systems. *International Migration Review* **23**(3), 671–80.

Ferguson, J. 1992. *The Dominican Republic: beyond the lighthouse*. London: Latin America Bureau.

Findlay, A. 1987a. *The Jordanian migration system in transition*. International Migration for Employment Working paper. Geneva: International Labour Organisation.

Findlay, A. 1987b. *The role of international labour migration in the transformation of an economy: the case of the Yemen Arab Republic*. International Migration for Employment Working paper. Geneva: International Labour Organisation.

Findlay, A. 1994. Return to Yemen: the end of the old migration order in the Arab world. In *Population migration and the changing world order*. W. Gould & A. Findlay (eds), 205–23, Chichester: John Wiley.

Forced Migration Monitor 1995. Former Soviet Union: citizenship and statelessness. *Forced Migration Monitor*. 3, January.

Forced Migration Monitor 1997. Civil society challenges in the Baltics. *Forced Migration Monitor*. 15, January.

The Forced Migration Projects of the Open Society Institute 1996. *Crimean Tatars: repatriation and conflict prevention*. New York: Open Society Institute.

The Forced Migration Projects of the Open Society Institute 1997. *Haitian boat people: causes and methods of migration*. Special Report April 1997. New York: Open Society Institute.

Garcia, J. 1980. *Operation Wetback: the mass deportation of Mexican undocumented workers in 1954*. Westport, Connecticut and London: Greenwood Press.

Ghabra, S. 1987. *Palestinians in Kuwait: the family and politics of survival*. Boulder, Colorado: Westview Press.

Glick Schiller, N., L. Basch, C. Blanc-Szanton. 1992. Towards a transnational perspective on migration: race, class, ethnicity and nationalism reconsidered. *Annals of the New York Academy of Sciences* 645. New York: New York Academy of Sciences.

Glytzos, N. 1995. Problems and policies regarding the socio-economic integration of returnees and foreign workers in Greece. *International Migration* 33(2), 155–73.

Gold, S. 1992. *Refugee communities: a comparative field study*. London: Sage.

Goss, J. & B. Lindquist 1995. Conceptualising international labour migration: a structuration perspective. *International Migration Review*, 29(2), 317–51.

Graham-Brown, S. 1994. Palestinians in Kuwait after the 1991 war. Gulf Information Project. London: British Refugee Council.

Gravil, R. 1985. The Nigerian expulsions order of 1983. *African Affairs* 84(337), 523–38.

Halliday, F. 1992. *Arabs in exile: Yemeni migrants in urban Britain*. London: I B Tauris.

Hamilton, G. 1978. Pariah capitalism: a paradox of power and dependence. *Ethnic Groups* 2.

Hammar, T. 1990. *Democracy and the nation state: Aliens, denizens and citizens in a world of international migration*. Aldershot: Avebury.

Hammar, T. 1995. Development and immobility: why have not many more emigrants left the south? In *Causes of international migration*. R. van der Erf & L. Heering (eds), 173–86. Luxembourg: Office for Official Publications of the European Communities.

Hansen, H. & M. Twaddle (eds) 1988. *Uganda now: between decay and development*. London: James Currey.

Hansen, H. & M. Twaddle (eds) 1991. *Changing Uganda: the dilemmas of structural adjustment and revolutionary change*. London: James Currey.

Harris, J. & M. Todaro 1970. Migration, unemployment and development: a two-sector analysis. *American Economic Review* 60, 126–42.

Harris, N. 1995. *The new untouchables: immigration and the new world worker*. London: I. B. Tauris.

Henckaerts, J-M. 1995. *Mass expulsion in modern international law and practice*. The Hague: Martinus Nijhoff.

Hood, M. 1994. The Taiwan connection. *Los Angeles Times Magazine*. 9 October.

Hugo, G. 1994. Migration as a survival strategy: the family dimension of migration. *Population distribution and migration, proceedings of the UN expert meeting*. Santa Cruz, Bolivia, January 1993. ST/ESA/SER.R/133.

Hugo, G. 1995. Illegal international migration in Asia. In *The Cambridge Survey of World Migration*. R. Cohen (ed.), 397–402. Cambridge: Cambridge University Press.

Human Rights Watch/Asia 1996. *Burma: The Rohingya Muslims: ending a cycle of exodus?* New York: Human Rights Watch.

Human Rights Watch/Helsinki 1996. *The Commonwealth of Independent States: Refugees and internally displaced persons in Armenia, Azerbaijan, Georgia, the Russian Federation and Tajikistan.* New York: Human Rights Watch.

Hutt, M. 1994. Introduction. In *Bhutan: perspectives on conflict and dissent.* M. Hutt (ed.), 5–19. Gartmore, Scotland: Kiscadale.

Hutt, M. 1996. Ethnic nationalism and refugees: the case of Bhutan. *Journal of Refugee Studies* 9(4), 397–420.

Hyman, A. 1993. Russians outside Russia. *The World Today* November, 205–8.

International Labour Office 1991. *Migrant workers affected by the Gulf crisis, Report of the Director-General, Third Supplementary Report,* GB.249/15/7. Geneva: International Labour Office, January.

International Labour Office 1992. *World Labour Survey.* Geneva: International Labour Office.

International Labour Organisation 1990. *Yearbook of labour statistics: Retrospective 1945-89.* Geneva: International Labour Office.

International Law Association 1986. *Declaration of principles of international law on mass expulsion,* adopted at the 62nd conference. Seoul, August 1986.

International Monetary Fund 1990. *Balance of payments statistics: Yearbook 1990.* Washington DC: International Monetary Fund.

International Organisation for Migration 1993. *Profiles and motives of potential migrants: Albania, Bulgaria, Russia, Ukraine.* Geneva: International Organisation for Migration.

International Organisation for Migration 1994. *Transit migration in Bulgaria.* Geneva: International Organisation for Migration.

International Organisation for Migration 1995. *Profiles and motives of potential migrants from Albania.* Geneva: International Organisation for Migration.

International Organisation for Migration 1997. *The Baltic Route: the trafficking of migrants through Lithuania.* Geneva: International Organisation for Migration.

Jesuit Refugee Service 1996. Bhutanese Demonstration Update. Jesuit Refugee Service, Asia-Pacific, 17 January.

Jordan, Hashemite Kingdom of, Department of Statistics 1992. *Returnees: August 10 1991 to December 31 1992.* Amman: Hashemite Kingdom of Jordan, Department of Statistics.

Jordan, Hashemite Kingdom of, Ministry of Labour 1991. *Annual Report 1991.* Amman: Hashemite Kingdom of Jordan, Ministry of Labour.

Jordan, Hashemite Kingdom of, National Centre for Educational

Research and Development (NCERD) 1991. *The socio-economic characteristics of Jordanian returnees.* Amman: Hashemite Kingdom of Jordan.

Kapur, I., M. Hadjimichael, P. Hilbers, J. Schiff & P. Szymczak, 1991. *Ghana: adjustment and growth, 1983–91.* IMF Occasional Paper 86. Washington DC: International Monetary Fund, September.

Katzman, K. 1993. *Iraq: compensation issues.* Washington DC: Congressional Research Report Service, Report for Congress, 93-964 F.

Kirisci, K. 1996. Refugees of Turkish origin: 'coerced immigrants' to Turkey since 1945. *International Migration* **34**(3), 385–410.

Kirk, R. 1992. *Stone of refuge: Haitian refugees in the Dominican Republic.* Issue Paper. Washington DC: US Committee for Refugees.

Kostanick, H. 1957. *Turkish resettlement of Bulgarian Turks, 1950–1953.* Berkeley, California: University of California Press.

Kotkin, J. 1992. *Tribes: how race, religion, and identity determine success in the new global economy.* New York: Random House.

Kreindler, I. 1986. The Soviet deported nationalities: a summary and an update. *Soviet Studies* **38**(3), 387–405.

Kritz, M., L. Lim, H. Zlotnik (eds) 1992. *International migration systems: a global approach.* Oxford: Clarendon Press.

Kunz, E. 1973. The refugee in flight: kinetic models and forms of displacement. *International Migration Review* **7**(2), 125–46.

Lambrecht, C. 1995. *The return of the Rohingya refugees to Burma: voluntary repatriation or refoulement?* Issue Paper. Washington DC: US Committee for Refugees.

Lasch, C. 1991. *The true and only heaven: progress and its critics.* London: Norton.

Lasch, C. 1995. *The revolt of the elites and the betrayal of democracy.* New York: Norton.

Lawyers' Committee for Human Rights 1991 *Expulsions of Haitians and Dominico-Haitians from the Dominican Republic.* New York: Lawyers' Committee for Human Rights.

Lawyers' Committee for Human Rights 1992 *Kuwait: building the rule of law: human rights in Kuwait after occupation.* New York: Lawyers' Committee for Human Rights.

Lawyers' Committee for Human Rights 1993. *Laying the foundations: human rights in Kuwait: obstacles and opportunities.* New York: Lawyers' Committee for Human Rights.

Lesch, A. 1991. Palestinians in Kuwait. *Journal of Palestine Studies* **20**(4), 42–54.

Lim, L. 1987. IUSSP committee on international migration: workshop on international migration systems and networks. *International Migration Review* **21**(2), 416–23.

273

Lim, L. & Abella, M. 1994. The movement of people in Asia: internal, intra-regional and international migration. *Asian and Pacific Migration Journal* 3(2–3), 209–50.

Lintner, B. 1993. Distant exile: Rohingyas seek new life in Middle East. *Far Eastern Economic Review* 28(1), 23–4.

Loescher, G. 1993. *Beyond charity: international cooperation and the global refugee crisis*. Oxford: Oxford University Press.

Mamdani, M. 1973. *From citizen to refugee: Uganda Asians come to Britain*. London: Frances Pinter.

Mamdani, M. 1993. The Ugandan Asian expulsion: twenty years after. *Journal of Refugee Studies* 6(3), 274–85.

Marett, V. 1988. *Immigrants settling in the city*. London: Leicester University Press/Pinter.

Marett, V. 1993. Resettlement of Ugandan Asians in Leicester. *Journal of Refugee Studies* 6(3), 248–59.

Marie, C-V. 1994. The European Union confronted with population movements: reasons of states and rights of individuals. Discussion paper presented to the International Organisation Migration seminar on The international response to trafficking in migrants and the safeguarding of migrant rights, Geneva, October 1994.

*Marienstras, R. 1989. On the notion of diaspora. *Minority peoples in the age of nation states*. G. Chaliand (ed.). London: Pluto Press.

Martensen, R. 1995. *From bona fide citizens to unwanted clandestines: Nepali refugees from Bhutan*. Itineraires, Notes et Travaux 43. Geneva: Institut Universitaire d'Etudes du Developpement.

Martin, P. & J. Taylor, 1996. *Managing migration: the role of economic policy*. Migration policy in global perspective series, Occasional Paper No 2. New York: International Center for Migration, Ethnicity and Citizenship.

Massey, D. 1990. Social structure, household strategies, and the cumulative causation of migration. *Population Index* 56(1), 3–26.

Massey, D., J. Arango, G. Hugo, A. Kouaouci, A. Pellegrino, J. Taylor
* 1993. Theories of international migration: a review and appraisal. *Population and Development Review* 19(3), 431–66.

McDowell, C. 1996. *A Tamil asylum diaspora: Sri Lankan migration, settlement and politics in Switzerland*. Oxford: Berghahn.

Médecins Sans Frontières (MSF) 1995a. *Awareness survey: Rohingya refugee camps, Cox's Bazar district, Bangladesh, 15 March 1995*. Amsterdam: MSF France and Holland.

Médecins Sans Frontières (MSF) 1995b. *MSF's concerns on the repatriation of Rohingya refugees from Bangladesh to Burma*. Amsterdam and Paris: MSF Holland and France, May.

Messina, C. 1996. Refugees, forced migrants or involuntarily relocating persons: refugee definitions in the countries of the CIS. Paper presented at the conference on Refugee rights and realities, University of Nottingham, November 1996.

Meznaric, S. 1985. Explaining migration: internal, external and return migration: the case of Yugoslavia. Paper presented at the conference on International migration in the contemporary economic crisis, Dubrovnik, June 1985.

Meznaric, S. & J. Caci-Kumpes 1993. Yugoslavia: emigration out of necessity. In *The politics of migration policies: settlement and integration. The first world into the 1990s.* D. Kubat (ed.), 337–45. New York: Center for Migration Studies.

Miège, J. 1993. Migration and decolonisation. *European Review* 1(1), 81–86.

Mo, T. 1982. *Sour sweet.* Harmondsworth: Penguin.

Morland, M. 1993. *Emerging markets: Egypt, Jordan, Morocco, Syria, Tunisia: The stock markets of Mediterranean Arabia.* London: Lehman Brothers.

Nagayama, T. 1992. Clandestine migrant workers in Japan. *Asian and Pacific Migration Journal* 1(3–4), 623–36.

National Coalition for Haitian Rights 1996. *Beyond the Bateyes: Haitian populations in the Dominican Republic.* New York: NCHR.

National Coalition for Haitian Rights 1997. Dominican Republic launches massive deportation. NCHR statement before the Inter-American Commission on Human Rights, 12 February 1997.

National Foundation for the Reception and Resettlement of Repatriated Greeks, nd. The situation in Albania today and NFRRRG activities. Athens: NFRRRG.

Nazi, F. 1994. The Greek–Albanian conflict. *Balkan War Report*, No. 29. October/November, 3–5.

Nour, A. 1993. *Coming home: a survey of the socio-economic conditions of West Bank and Gaza Strip returnees after the 1991 Gulf War.* Jerusalem: Palestine Human Rights Information Center, August.

OECD SOPEMI 1994. *Trends in international migration: Annual Report 1993.* Paris: Organisation for Economic Cooperation and Development.

Okolo, J. 1984. Free movement of persons in ECOWAS and Nigeria's expulsion of illegal aliens. *The World Today*, 428–36.

Onwuka, R. 1982. The ECOWAS protocol on the free movement of persons. *African Affairs* 81(323), 193–206.

Overseas Development Institute 1991. *The impact of the Gulf crisis on developing countries.* ODI briefing paper. London: Overseas Development Institute.

Owen, R. 1985. *Migrant workers in the Gulf.* London: Minority Rights Group.

Pang, E. 1992. Absorbing temporary foreign workers: the experience of Singapore. *Asian and Pacific Migration Journal* 1(3/4), 495–509.

275

Patel, P. 1992. The Uganda Evacuees Association. Mimeo. London.

Peil, M. 1971. The expulsion of West African aliens. *Journal of Modern African Studies* **9**(2), 205–29.

Peil, M. 1995. Ghanaians abroad. *African Affairs* **94**(376), 345–67.

Peretz, D. 1993. *Palestinians, refugees and the Middle East peace process.* Washington DC: US Institute of Peace Press.

Petras, E. 1981. The global labour market in the modern world economy. In *Global trends in migration: theory and research on international population movements*, M. Kritz, C. Keely & S. Tomasi (eds) 44–63. New York: Center for Migration Studies.

Pettifer, J. 1992. Albania: a challenge for Europe. *The World Today*, June.

Pillai, P. 1992. *People on the move: an overview of recent immigration and emigration in Malaysia.* Kuala Lumpur: Institute of Strategic and International Studies.

Piore, M. 1979. *Birds of passage: migrant labor in industrial societies.* Cambridge: Cambridge University Press.

Piper, T. 1994. Myanmar: exodus and return of Muslims from Rakhine state. *Refugee Survey Quarterly* **13**(1), 11–29.

Portes, A. & J. Walton 1981. *Labor, class and the international system.* New York: Academic Press.

Poulton, H. 1994. *The Balkans: minorities and states in conflict* 2nd edn. London: Minority Rights Publications.

Prados, A. 1994. *Yemen: civil strife.* Washington DC: Congressional Research Report Service, Report for Congress, 94-297 F.

Prunier, G. 1995. *The Rwanda crisis 1959–1994: history of a genocide.* London: Hurst.

Prunier, G. 1997. The Great Lakes crisis. *Current History* **96**(610), 193–99.

Rado, E. 1986. Notes on a political economy of Ghana today. *African Affairs* **85**(341), 563–72.

Read, J. 1975. Some legal aspects of the expulsion. In *Expulsion of a minority: essays on Ugandan Asians*. M. Twaddle (ed.), 193–209. London: Athlone Press.

Refugee Reports 1994. Haitians in the Dominican Republic. Washington DC: US Committee for Refugees, 31 May.

Refugees International 1994. *Rohingya refugees in Bangladesh.* Report by Y. Pierpaoli, June.

Reid, A. 1992. Political studies in the voluntary repatriation of refugees. Unpublished PhD thesis, Deakin University.

Reid, A. 1994. Repatriation of Arakanese Muslims from Bangladesh to Burma, 1978–79: "arranged" reversal of the flow of an ethnic minority. Paper presented to the International Research and Advisory Panel on Refugees Conference, Oxford, January 1994.

Reilly, R. 1994. Life and work in the refugee camps of southeast Nepal.

In *Bhutan: perspectives on conflict and dissent*. M. Hutt (ed.), 129–40. Gartmore, Scotland: Kiscadale.

Republic of Yemen 1991. *Expatriates: final statistics of the returnees since 2 August 1990*. Sanaa, Yemen: Central Statistical Organisation, Ministry of Planning and Economic Development.

Republic of Yemen 1992. *Statistical yearbook 1991*. Sanaa, Yemen: Central Statistical Organisation, Ministry of Planning and Economic Development.

Ricca, S. 1989. *International migration in Africa: legal and administrative aspects*. Geneva: International Labour Office.

Richmond, A. 1993. Reactive migration: sociological perspectives on refugee movements. *Journal of Refugee Studies* **6**(1), 7–25.

Richmond, A. 1994. *Global apartheid: refugees, racism and the new world order*. Oxford: Oxford University Press.

Rimmer, D. 1993. *Staying poor: Ghana's political economy 1950–1990*. Oxford: Pergamon.

Roberts, K. 1997. China's "tidal wave" of migrant labor: what can we learn from Mexican undocumented migration to the United States? *International Migration Review* **31**(2), 249–93.

Robinson, V. 1986. *Transients, settlers and refugees: Asians in Britain*. Oxford: Clarendon Press.

Robinson, V. 1990. Boom and gloom: the success and failure of South Asians in Britain. In *South Asians overseas: migration and ethnicity*. C. Clarke, C. Peach, S. Vertovec (eds), 269–96, Cambridge: Cambridge University Press.

Robinson, V. 1993. Marching into the middle classes? The long-term resettlement of East African Asians in the UK. *Journal of Refugee Studies* **6**(3), 230–47.

Rocha-Trindade, M. 1995. The repatriation of Portuguese from Africa. In *The Cambridge Survey of World Migration*. R. Cohen (ed.), 337–41. Cambridge: Cambridge University Press.

Ruiz, H. 1992. Bhutanese and Tibetan refugees in Nepal. *Refugee Reports* **13**(4), 30 April.

Russell, S. & M. Al-Ramadhan. 1994. Kuwait's migration policy since the Gulf crisis. *International Journal of Middle East Studies* **26**, 569–87.

Russell, S. & M. Teitelbaum. 1992. *International migration and international trade*. World Bank discussion paper 160. Washington DC: World Bank.

Safran, W. 1991. Diasporas in modern societies: myths of homeland and return. *Diaspora: a journal of transnational studies* **1**(1), 83–99.

Sassen, S. 1988. *The mobility of capital and labor: a study in international investment and labor flow*. Cambridge: Cambridge University Press.

Sassen, S. 1991. *The global city: New York, London, Tokyo*. Princeton, New Jersey: Princeton University Press.

Scott, W. 1991. *Ethnic Turks from Bulgaria: an assessment of their employment and living conditions in Turkey.* World Employment Programme working paper. Geneva: International Labour Organisation.

Seddon, D. 1995. Migration: India and Nepal. In *The Cambridge Survey of World Migration.* R. Cohen (ed.), 367–70. Cambridge: Cambridge University Press.

Serjeant, R., 1988. The Hadrami network. *Marchands et hommes d'affaires asiatiques dans l'ocean Indien et la mer de Chine, 13e–20e siècles.* D. Lombard & J. Aubin (eds). Paris: Editions de l'Ecole des Hautes Etudes en Sciences Sociales.

Shacknove, A. 1985. Who is a refugee? *Ethics* **95**, 274–84.

Shacknove, A. 1993. From asylum to containment. *International Journal of Refugee Law* **5**(4), 516–33.

Shaw, B. 1994. Aspects of the "southern problem" and nation-building in Bhutan. In *Bhutan: perspectives on conflict and dissent.* M. Hutt (ed.), 141–64. Gartmore, Scotland: Kiscadale.

Sheffer, G. 1986 (ed.) *Modern diasporas in international politics.* London: Croom Helm.

Sheffer, G. 1993. Ethnic diasporas: a threat to their hosts? In *International migration and security.* M. Weiner (ed.), 263–85. Boulder, Colorado: Westview.

Shiblak, A. 1996. Residency status and civil rights of Palestinian refugees in Arab countries. *Journal of Palestine Studies* **25**(2), 36–45.

Simsir, B. 1986. Migrations from Bulgaria to Turkey: 1950–51 exodus. *Foreign Policy: a quarterly review of the Foreign Policy Institute* (Ankara) **12**(3–4).

Sinha, A. 1994. Bhutan: political culture and national dilemma. In *Bhutan: perspectives on conflict and dissent.* M. Hutt (ed.), 203–16. Gartmore, Scotland: Kiscadale.

Smith, M. 1991. *Burma: insurgency and the politics of ethnicity.* London and New Jersey: Zed Books.

Smith, M. 1994. *Ethnic groups in Burma: development, democracy and human rights.* London: Anti-Slavery International.

Spaan, E. 1994. Taikongs and calos: the role of middlemen and brokers in Javanese international migration. *International Migration Review* **28**(1), 93–113.

Stark, O. 1991a. Migration in LDCs: risk, remittances and the family. *Finance and Development* December, 39–41.

Stark, O. 1991b. *The migration of labour.* Oxford: Basil Blackwell.

Strawn, C. 1994. The dissidents. In *Bhutan: perspectives on conflict and dissent.* M. Hutt (ed.), 97–128. Gartmore, Scotland: Kiscadale.

Strizhak, E. 1993. The Ugandan Asian expulsion: resettlement in the USA. *Journal of Refugee Studies* **6**(3), 260–64.

Suhrke, A. 1997. Towards a better international refugee regime. Unpublished paper, Chr. Michelsen Institute, Norway.

Swindell, K. 1990. International labour migration in Nigeria 1976–86: employment, nationality and ethnicity. *Migration* **8**, 8–27.

Tabatabai, H. 1988. Agricultural decline and access to food in Ghana. *International Labour Review* **127**(6), 703–34.

Tandon, Y. 1984. *The new position of East Africa's Asians: problems of a displaced minority*. London: Minority Rights Group.

Tinker, H. 1977. *The banyan tree: overseas emigrants from India, Pakistan and Bangladesh*. Oxford: Oxford University Press.

Tinker, H. 1990. Indians in southeast Asia: imperial auxiliaries. In *South Asians overseas: migration and ethnicity*. C. Clarke, C. Peach, S. Vertovec (eds), 39–56. Cambridge: Cambridge University Press.

Todaro, M. 1989. *Economic development in the Third World*. New York: Longman.

Tölölyan, K. 1991. The nation-state and its others: in lieu of a preface. *Diaspora: a Journal of Transnational Studies* **1**(1), 3–7.

Toye, J. 1992. World Bank policy-conditioned loans: how did they work in Ghana in the 1980s? In *Policy adjustment in Africa: Case studies in economic development*. C. Milner & A. Rayner (eds). London: Macmillan.

Tribe, M. 1975. Economic aspects of the expulsion of Asians from Uganda. In *Expulsion of a minority: essays on Ugandan Asians*. M. Twaddle (ed.), 140–76. London: Athlone Press.

Twaddle, M. 1975. Was the expulsion inevitable? In *Expulsion of a minority: essays on Ugandan Asians*. M. Twaddle (ed.), 1–14. London: Athlone Press.

Twaddle, M. 1990. East African Asians through a hundred years. In *South Asians overseas: migration and ethnicity*. C. Clarke, C. Peach, S. Vertovec (eds), 149–63. Cambridge: Cambridge University Press.

UN 1979. *Demographic yearbook 1979*. UN Department of International Economic and Social Affairs, Statistical Office. New York: United Nations.

UN Development Programme (UNDP), 1992, 1993, 1994. *Human development report 1992, 1993, 1994*. Oxford: Oxford University Press.

UN Development Programme (UNDP) 1993a. *Vocational training and job placement of Bulgarian ethnic Turks: Project final report*. TUR/90/R51. Ankara: UNDP, April.

UN ECOSOC 1994. *Report on the situation of human rights in Myanmar, prepared by Mr. Yozo Yokota*. Commission on Human Rights, UN ECOSOC, E/CN.4/1994/57, 16 February.

UN General Assembly 1993. *UNHCR activities financed by voluntary funds: report for 1992–1993 and proposed programmes and budget for*

1994. Part II Asia and Oceania. Executive Committee of the High Commissioner's Programme. Forty-fourth session. A/AC.96/808. 9 August.

UN High Commissioner for Refugees, Office of the (UNHCR) 1991. Massive expulsion of Haitians from the Dominican Republic. Geneva: UNHCR, 15 July.

UNHCR 1993. *UNHCR Factsheet: Nepal.* Geneva: UNHCR, 15 October.

UNHCR 1994. *UNHCR Factsheet: Bangladesh.* Geneva: UNHCR, 1 March.

UNHCR 1995a. *Return to Myanmar: repatriating refugees from Bangladesh.* UNHCR Information Bulletin. Geneva: UNHCR, June.

UNHCR 1995b. *The state of the world's refugees: in search of solutions.* Oxford: Oxford University Press.

UNHCR 1996a. *The CIS conference on refugees and migrants.* Geneva: UNHCR.

UNHCR 1996b. *Report of the regional conference to address the problems of refugees, displaced persons, other forms of involuntary displacement and returnees in the countries of the Commonwealth of Independent States and relevant neighbouring states. 30–31 May 1996.* CISCONF/1996/6. Geneva: UNHCR.

UNHCR 1997. *The state of the world's refugees: a humanitarian agenda.* Oxford: Oxford University Press.

United Nations Children's Fund (UNICEF) 1992. *The Hashemite Kingdom of Jordan: Unicef Annual Report 1992.* Amman: UNICEF, October.

UNRISD 1995. *States of disarray: the social effects of globalization.* An UNRISD report for the World Summit for Social Development. Geneva: United Nations Research Institute for Social Development.

US Committee for Refugees 1989, 1990, 1991, 1992, 1993, 1994, 1995, 1996, 1997. *World Refugee Survey 1989, 1990, 1991, 1992, 1993, 1994, 1995, 1996, 1997.* Washington DC: US Committee for Refugees.

US Committee for Refugees 1983. *Refugees in Uganda and Rwanda: the Banyarwandan tragedy.* Washington DC: US Committee for Refugees.

US Committee for Refugees 1991a. *Exile from Uganda: background to an invasion.* Washington DC: US Committee for Refugees.

US Committee for Refugees 1992a. Bangladesh's about-face puts Burmese refugees at risk. *News from the US Committee for Refugees,* 2 July.

US Department of Commerce, Bureau of the Census 1956. *Statistical Abstracts of the United States, 1956.* Washington DC.

US Department of Justice 1955. *Annual Report of the Immigration and Naturalisation Service 1955.* Washington DC. See Garcia 1980.

US Department of State 1991. *Reports on Human Rights practices, 1991: Bulgaria.* Washington DC: US Department of State.

US Department of State 1993. *Reports on Human Rights practices, 1993: Dominican Republic*. Washington DC: US Department of State.

US General Accounting Office (USGAO) 1991. *Refugees: US assistance to Bulgarian ethnic Turks in Turkey*. NSAID-92-59. Washington DC: US General Accounting Office, December.

Van Hear, N. 1982. Northern labour and the development of capitalist agriculture in Ghana. Unpublished PhD thesis, University of Birmingham.

Van Hear, N. 1983. Expulsions promise labour problems in both countries, and Expulsions dislocate Nigerian labour market. *African Business*. March and April.

Van Hear, N. 1985. Nigeria expels aliens again. *African Business*. June.

Van Hear, N. 1987. Mass expulsions: causes and consequences. Report for the Independent Commission on International Humanitarian Issues. Geneva: Independent Commission on International Humanitarian Issues.

Van Hear, N. 1992. *Consequences of the forced mass repatriation of migrant communities: recent cases from West Africa and the Middle East*. Geneva: United Nations Research Institute for Social Development (UNRISD), Discussion paper 38.

Van Hear, N. 1993. Mass flight in the Middle East: involuntary migration and the Gulf conflict, 1990–91. In *Geography and refugees: patterns and processes of change*. R. Black & V. Robinson (eds), 64–83. London: Belhaven.

Van Hear, N. 1994. The socio-economic impact of the involuntary mass return to Yemen in 1990. *Journal of Refugee Studies* 7(1), 18–38.

Van Hear, N. 1995. The impact of involuntary mass "return" to Jordan in the wake of the Gulf crisis. *International Migration Review* 29(2), 352–74.

Vasileva, D. 1992. Bulgarian Turkish emigration and return. *International Migration Review* 26(2), 342–52.

Verona, S. 1993. Bulgaria: recent political crisis and new prospects. Washington DC: Congressional Research Report Service, Report for Congress, 93-362 F.

Voutira, E. 1991. Pontic Greeks today: migrants or refugees? *Journal of Refugee Studies* 4(4), 400–20.

de Waal, C. 1995. Decollectivisation and total scarcity in High Albania. *Cambridge Anthropology* 18(1), 1–22.

Wang, G. 1991. *China and the Chinese overseas*. Singapore: Times Academic Press.

Weiner, M. 1986. Labour migrations as incipient diasporas. In *Modern diasporas in international politics*. G. Sheffer (ed.), 47–74. London: Croom Helm.

Weiner, M. 1993a. Rejected peoples and unwanted migrants in south Asia. In *International migration and security*. M. Weiner (ed.), 149–78. Boulder: Westview.

Weiner, M. 1993b. Security, stability and international migration. In *International migration and security*. M. Weiner (ed.), 1–35. Boulder: Westview.

Weiner, M. 1995. *The global migration crisis: challenge to states and to human rights*. New York: HarperCollins.

Widgren, J. 1990. International migration and regional stability. *International Affairs* 66(4), 749–66.

Widgren, J. 1995. Global arrangements to combat trafficking in migrants. *Migration World* 23(3), 19–23.

Wolfrum, R. 1993. The emergence of "new minorities" as a result of migration. In *Peoples and minorities in international law*. C. Brolmann, R. Lefeber, & M. Zieck (eds), 153–66. Dordrecht: Martinus Nijhoff/Kluwer.

Wolpe, H. 1972. Capitalism and cheap labour-power in South Africa: from segregation to apartheid. *Economy and Society* 1(4).

World Bank 1983, 1984, 1985, 1990, 1991, 1992, 1993, 1994, 1995. *World Development Report 1983, 1984, 1985, 1990, 1991, 1992, 1993, 1994, 1995*. Washington DC: Oxford University Press.

World Bank 1984a. *Ghana: Policies and program for adjustment*. A World Bank Country Study. Washington DC: World Bank.

Yeboah, Y. 1987. *Migrant workers in West Africa, with special reference to Nigeria and Ghana*. International Migration for Employment working paper. Geneva: International Labour Office.

Zang, T. 1989. *Destroying ethnic identity: the expulsion of the Bulgarian Turks*. A Helsinki Watch report. New York: Helsinki Watch, October.

de Zayas, A-M. 1988. A historical survey of twentieth century expulsions. In *Refugees in the age of total war*. A. Bramwell (ed.), 15–37. London: Unwin Hyman.

Zimmerman, W. 1993. Migration and security in Yugoslavia. In *International migration and security*. M. Weiner (ed.), 65–81. Boulder, Colorado: Westview.

Zlotnik, H. 1992. Empirical identification of international migration systems. In *International migration systems: a global approach*. M. Kritz, L. Lim, H. Zlotnik (eds), 19–40. Oxford: Clarendon Press.

Zolberg, A. 1989. The next waves: migration theory for a changing world. *International Migration Review* 23(3), 403–30.

Zolberg, A., A. Suhrke, S. Aguayo, 1989. *Escape from violence: conflict and the refugee crisis in the developing world*. New York: Oxford University Press.

[BIBLIOGRAPHY]

Press sources and periodicals

Associated Press
Burma Briefing, London
Burma Update, London
The Courier, Brussels
Diaspora: a Journal of Transnational Studies, New York
The Economist, London
Financial Times, London
Forced Migration Monitor, New York: Open Society Institute.
Guardian, London
International Herald Tribune
Independent, London
INS Press Release
Jesuit Refugee Service Bulletin, Rome
Liberation, Paris
Middle East Economic Digest, London
Migration News, Davis, California
Refugee Reports, US Committee for Refugees, Washington DC
Reuter
Voice of America
Washington Post, Washington DC
West Africa, London

Index